# SHORT

The journey of

Francis de Witt Bell

A Biography by

# Jennifer Anne Bell

*For Peter, Sally and Judy*

'The truth is rarely pure, and never simple.'
Oscar Wilde - *The Importance of Being Ernest (1895)*

**Larks Press**

Published by the Larks Press
Ordnance Farmhouse, Guist Bottom,
Dereham, NR20 5PF
01328 829207
larks.press@xlnmail.com
Website: www.booksatlarkspress.co.uk

September 2013

British Library Cataloguing-in-Publication Data
A catalogue record for this book is available
from the British Library

No part of this book or its illustrations may be
reproduced in any way without permission
from the publisher and the author.

Printed by
Short Run Press, Exeter

**Front cover**: Francis de Witt Bell, aged 18
**Back cover**: Photograph by kind permission of Ashill Fruit Farm

© Jennifer Anne Bell 2013

Jennifer Anne Bell has asserted her right under the Copyright, Designs
and Patents Act 1988 to be identified as the author of this work.

ISBN 978 1 904006 68 8

# Acknowledgements

I owe thanks to the following members of Francis Bell's family for the support they have given me by sharing their memories, providing letters and photographs, and encouraging my efforts

**Judy Altarmirano (née Bell)** for reading and checking the manuscript, for memories of her father and mother, Francis and Barbara, and of family life.
**Anthea Bell** for permission to quote from her father, Adrian Bell's books, for memories of Barbara Rowe and the Hanbury family, and for reading, advising and checking the manuscript.
**Barbara Bell** for many hours of conversation, memories of Francis, the Kingston family and details of family life.
**Martin Bell** for encouraging me to write, memories of his Uncle Farncis, reading the manuscript and for his most excellent Introduction.
**Peter Bell** for many hours of conversation, reading and checking the manuscript, memories of his father and mother, Francis and Barbara, and for giving me space to write.
**Geraldine Brown (née Thorpe)** for details about her mother and father, Stephanie (née Bell) and Jack Thorpe, for memories of Francis and details of the Home Guard.
**Sally Carr (née Bell)** for details of family life and memories of her father and mother, Francis and Barbara, of her time in California and for access to family letters.
**Cynthia Peacock,** wife of the late Carlos Peacock, for memories of Fanny and Kate and for access to Carlos' unpublished manuscript, *'Notes and Impressions – Fragments from a Life'*. Also for artistic information about Aunt Ada and the Hanbury family.
**Sylvia Proudman (née Bell)** for memories of Barbara Rowe and the Hanbury family and of her Uncle Francis, for reading the manuscript and for information regarding the Indian Police.

I am also deeply indebted to:

**Susan Yaxley,** publisher of the Larks Press, for all her support and encouragement and for her excellent work in preparing this book for publication.
**Michael Berry** for details about the Berry family and memories of Francis.
**Justin Brooke Junior** for support to the Bell family and letters to Barbara and Peter between 1964 and 1986.
**Robert Berry** for a letter to Barbara Bell 1938.
**Robert Clinton** for great support and practical help with local contacts.
**Bill Day** for details about Justin Brooke Ltd and memories of Francis.
**Jill Flack** for details about Jack and Nesta Loader, and Wickhambrook.
**Ann Gander** for information and for her research into the Bell family history.

**Nancy Whitlock (née Hardwicke)** for memories of Francis.

**Elizabeth Hollingsworth (née Brooke)** for details about her father, Justin Brooke, for memories of Charles and Edith Brooke and of Francis. Also for a copy of Minutes of Directors' Meeting 08/08/1960 and copies of correspondence between Justin and Francis, and for permission to use the photograph of the Trojan vans on page 133 and Justin Brooke's workforce on page 129.

**David Lee** for details about Justin Brooke Ltd and memories of Francis.

**Nesta Loader** for details about Jack Loader and memories of Francis.

**Charles MacNab** of Cottenham for information about Chivers of Histon.

**Dr Patricia McGuire,** Archivist, King's College, Cambridge, for access to the Rupert Chawner Brooke Papers, also for help and information regarding the Marlowe Society and the Cambridge Apostles.

**Percy Nunn** for memories and details about Justin Brooke Ltd.and of Frances.

**Bruce Potter** for memories of the Spalding days spent with Peter Bell and for information about the nationalisation of road hauliers and his father's business.

**Florrie Swann** for information and memories about Francis at Weston Colville.

**Dr Paul E. Waters** for information about F.C.O. and British Railways in Argentina.

**Wickhambrook History Society** for access to the photographs of the Trojan vans, Clopton 1929 and Justin Brooke's workforce 1930, and special thanks to Dorothy Anderson, Terence and Valerie Hurst and Roy Cutts for supplying the names of people shown in the Coronation photo on p.252.

**Willem de Vries Lensch** for permission to use the photograph of *Lucretia* on page 220, designed and constructed by his uncle's yard in 1937 – Amsterdamsche Sceepswerf, G. de Vries Lensch.

I am also grateful for the research facilities provided by

**Janus/Cambridge University Archives**: (1 – 6) From 'The Papers of Rupert Chawner Brooke'; Records of the Marlowe Dramatic Society 1907 – 1954.

**Ruskin Museum,** Coniston

**Suffolk and Cambridge County Records Office** (Bury St Edmunds), for access to Electoral Registers.

**The Women's Library, London Metropolitan University** – Biographical press cutting on 'Aphra Wilson' taken from *The Times* 17.1.76.

# Introduction

At family gatherings Francis Bell used to describe himself as the "ne'er do uncle". He was raffish, gregarious and much travelled, as his elder brother, my father the writer Adrian Bell, was not. Of the three children born to Robert and Fanny Bell, Adrian was the one most favoured by their mother. His parents helped set him up in his first farm in West Suffolk and even moved to Sudbury to be close to him. (Perhaps a mixed blessing to my mother when she married him.)

When Francis was shipped off to South America his father was there at the quayside to see him off. His mother, memorably, was not. At the high noon of Empire it was often the fate of second sons to be sent abroad to make some kind of a living. The adventures of Francis included establishing and managing an experimental South American wheat farm in conditions, of soil and weather, most unsuited to it. These were pioneering days in Argentina and much of the pioneering was done by the British-owned railway company Ferro-Carril Oeste. The railways needed destinations and the destinations needed development. Hence the experimental farm intended 'to make the desert bloom'.

Francis wrote of the place of his exile, 650 kilometres from Buenos Aires, 'It had to be the most desolate looking place on earth'.

The hidden treasures of this book, mined by his biographer with great skill, were what were known to his family as 'Father's South American papers', old photographs, notes and diaries that Francis kept of those extraordinary times. He was never known as a writer, but he clearly shared his brother's way with words. His descriptions of the living and working conditions on the dust-blown farm, where his first home was a railway carriage, read as fresh on the page as if they had been written yesterday. They are without literary artifice and written with a sympathy for the men who worked alongside him. It was 1926 and Francis had learned enough Spanish to get along. Although engaged essentially in a colonial enterprise, he was a colonist without assumptions of European superiority.

The diaries are thus of interest not only to the family but to a much wider audience. It was a time of the opening up of continents and the forced march of 'progress' through forests and deserts. Francis was an eyewitness of the process and became, through his writing, a reporter of it.

His was not an easy life. He was alone and abroad for seven years. Having taken a first class ticket out, he worked his passage back on a freighter. He later managed the huge fruit farm established by Justin Brooke in Wickhambrook in West Suffolk. He was good at the job and good with men, but it was a semi-feudal relationship with the Brooke family; and that employment did not end well either. But his marriage to Barbara brought him much happiness, as did their three children Pete, Sally and Judy.

He smoked home-grown tobacco. One of my abiding boyhood memories is of the great leaves hanging on the clothes drier over the Aga. Some of them may additionally have been contaminated by pesticides. He died of lung cancer in 1963 at the age of 57.

We the children of Adrian, Francis and their sister Stephanie owe a special debt of gratitude to Jenny for this labour of love and scholarship. She is not of the family but married into it – a potentially hazardous undertaking, as some have found – but in this case the marriage was successful. Pete got it right in the end.

With this splendid book she has done us all proud. She has revived and preserved the memory of a man of whom, as she notes, no ill was ever spoken, and who was in his own way surely as remarkable as his better known elder brother.

Francis de Witt Bell was my favourite uncle. For all the hardships and adversities of his life I would judge it to have been a short but successful adventure. There are many measures of success, and to be so much loved by so many is surely one of them.

Martin Bell

# Author's Preface

Peter had brought few legacies with him. Broken marriages are not renowned for their accompanying goods and chattels and Pete's were no exception. But he did have what were vaguely referred to as 'Father's South American Papers' - a dusty polythene bag full of old photos, files and bundles of paper that had been relegated to successive attics over the years.

Alongside Francis' extensive fruit farm diaries which he wrote from the late 1930s up until the early 1950s and tucked away amongst a jumble of old sepia photographs, school poems, weather charts and railway maps, were sheets of faded typescript. Closer observation would reveal them to be two versions of a journal. Unfinished, they spanned the years between 1926 and 1931. They were written at a time when it was still fashionable for young men to be sent to the Argentine and years before nationalisation of the British Railways in Argentina in 1948 would lead to the liquidation of Ferro-Carril Oeste - the railway company that employed Peter's father Francis de Witt Bell there in the late 1920s.

Francis rarely spoke of his South American experiences. His premature death from lung cancer in 1963 leaves many of our questions unanswered. Did he feel he had failed to make a success of things; failed to fulfil the hopes and expectations that had accompanied him on the outward voyage?

The accounts he left tell a different story. They remain a testimony not only to his writing skills, but also to a young man, whose inheritance as a younger son was a one-way ticket to South America and the gift to live by his wits, to make the best of things, and to have a little fun along the way.

J.A.Bell

**The Bell family portrait:**

**Frances, Stephanie, Fanny and Adrian**

# Part One

What to do with Francis must have been a problem. His father didn't believe in a university education despite having attended Edinburgh himself, and besides, Francis desperately wanted to farm.

His older brother Adrian had gone from London to work as a pupil on a Suffolk farm. Within a year his parents, or perhaps if the truth be known his mother Fanny, had poured a great deal of the family finances into setting Adrian up in a small farm of his own.

The remainder of the family, led undoubtedly by Fanny's recently acquired enthusiasm for all things bucolic, were subsequently moved to Suffolk. Francis, five years his brother's junior, spent most of his time at Adrian's side, where he acquired not only agricultural skills but a love of outdoor life.

But in 1924, at the age of eighteen, Francis sailed from Southampton. His destination was Buenos Aires.

Stopping off at Madeira on the way, it was a voyage that would take six weeks. It would be seven years before he returned. And yet, only his father went down to Southampton to see him off. Francis would never forget the absence of his mother at such a momentous time, but then Fanny Hanbury did come from rather an extraordinary family.

There was her Aunt Ada, who had, at some distant time, been a young artist of considerable talent. Contemporaries of Ruskin, who was known as *'one of the greatest Victorians; artist, art critic, teacher, writer, geologist, social critic'*, both Ada and her equally talented older sister Blanche had, between the years of 1875 and 1887, exhibited their work in London; the thirty-nine pictures were all studies of flowers.

In 1885 Ada had, *'with full directions by her sister Frances Ellen Blanche Hanbury'* also published a book called *'Advanced Studies of Flower Painting in Water Colours'*. Her sister Blanche would go on to publish a number of text books on teaching reading to young children.

In what must have been not only a considerable accolade to their talent, but a remarkable achievement for women of that era, two of Blanche's pictures and five of Ada's were accepted by the Royal Academy. Ada would never lose her love of the natural world and her desire to live and portray it in her own way.

In her biography *'Adrian Bell: Voice of the Countryside'* Ann Gander writes that, *'It was suggested that Ada herself fell in love with her art teacher'* but that there is no evidence to substantiate it. There is the possibility however that she did have a serious disagreement with Ruskin, and her later recorded comments indicated that she at least, had been a pupil of his. *'In 1871 John Ruskin had founded The Ruskin School of Drawing'* having become *'the first Slade Professor of Fine Art at Oxford University in 1869'* and drawing lessons for Ada as a talented young woman of a certain class, would certainly have been viewed as acceptable at the time. For whatever reason, the intractable Ada never married, but went in her later years to live at Rock Myrtle, a stone hut deeply hidden in a wood, halfway up a mountainside in Wales. Moving here in 1927, at the age of 72; Ada *'would tell Adrian that she was effectively born that year, for that was when she truly began to live'*.

Freed from the necessity of painting greeting cards depicting exquisitely painted flowers – work she had taken up to help support her aged parents and her more delicate sister Gertrude, who like herself would remain a spinster – Ada lived out her remaining years in her rural retreat, her only companions the wild birds, a few goats and chickens, and the pet rabbits she had rescued from captivity. The only remnant of her presence, left to the family of her great nephew Francis, was a painted plate, its wide-eyed yellow daisies still fresh and still evoking the legend of their painter.

**Aunt Ada at Rock Myrtle c. 1930**

The Hanburys of London were historically, brewers and bankers. Ann Gander writes of them as being, *'a complex, colourful and unwealthy family'* with a history and connections that went back to Catherine the Great. In fact there had been considerable wealth in the family in the past. It is well documented that Sir Charles Hanbury (1708 – 1759) a Welsh diplomat, writer and satirist, M.P. and British Ambassador, had inherited a fortune from his godfather Charles Williams in 1732, provided he assumed the name of Williams. After diplomatic posts as British Ambassador to Poland, Saxony, and Prussia; he went as Ambassador to Russia and became part of history, by introducing the Polish aristocrat Stanislaw to the Russian Grand Duchess Catherine Alexeyevna, the future Catherine the Great. His portrait hangs in the

National Portrait Gallery and he would be remembered for his brilliant wit and lively, biting satire. Attributes his descendants would inherit.

Yet despite these auspicious connections, Ada Hanbury and her five brothers and sisters found themselves in 1862 to be the family of a declared bankrupt. In her biography, Ann Gander writes of the possibility of there being some money around, but of their father, *'Thomas James Hanbury, son of a stockbroker ... working as a clerk to an attorney in London...and [losing] the lot by standing security for a friend.'*

Audrey Locke, in her two-volume history, *'The Hanbury Family'* published in 1912, gives us a thumbnail sketch of Thomas and Emma's six children. *'Thomas was born in 1814 and was the only surviving son of Samuel Hanbury and Frances, his wife. He had married Emma Lydia, the second daughter of Richard Parish de Witt of Sudbury, Suffolk in 1843, the wedding taking place at St. Pancras Church in London. Educated at Rugby, he later joined the Catholic Church.'* Nothing is recorded here of Thomas' bankruptcy, and it is interesting to note that despite this, the boys at least, received good educations. Their second son, *'William Frederick James, born in 1847, taking a Bachelor of Arts degree at St. John's College, Cambridge, in 1873 and a Master of Arts in 1878.'*

All three of their sons seem to have been prepared to earn their own living; *'the eldest son, Charles de Witt Hanbury, born in 1845, became an architect and surveyor'* whilst the youngest, James Augustus Sewell, born in 1851, spent *'many years of prosperous business life in Birmingham'*.

Without doubt their father's bankruptcy would have had a profound effect on the Hanbury brothers and sisters, although they were still young when it happened, with Charles being only 17 years old at the time.

Ann Gander writes of his sister [Emma] Gertrude being *'engaged to a gentleman'* at the time *'found herself having to release the panic-stricken chap from his bond'*. Although she was only 16 years old, having being born in 1846, it would not have been unusual in a well to do family of this time, for an engagement to have taken place or indeed for it to have been arranged. An additional factor, is the probability that a dowry would have been paid, and that in releasing this *'chap from his bond'*, the dowry would also have been lost to him. An adverse reaction from him would have added to the stress of the bankruptcy. On the other hand he may have felt relief at escaping from an improvident match. After this misfortune, it seems that no further suitor was sought. And so at the age of 16, it appears that her fate was sealed and poor Gertrude is recorded as remaining a spinster, for the rest of her life.

Was she embittered by the fact that this 'gentleman' did not appear to want to marry her for love? Her fragility is also referred to, though she did in fact live on until 1927 when she died at the age of 81.

Another possibility that could have been a factor within the family, at least for the girls, was their mother's influence. How much pressure did she exert on them not to marry, with perhaps her own old age in view? Certainly her youngest daughter Ada, like so many girls before her, would have felt it her responsibility not only to look after the fragile Gertrude, but also to keep her ageing parents. And so the lives and eccentricities of these Hanbury forbears would earn them a place in the family archives.

Years later, in his own autobiography, *'My Own Master'*, their great nephew Adrian would write of these Victorians – this unusual family that had helped to shape the life of his own mother, and those of himself and his siblings. Bringing to life again the children of Thomas and Emma Hanbury, those great Aunts and Uncles, he would give them added dimension both through his own memories, and through the stories of them passed down by the family.

He wrote of Charles, the architect, his mother Fanny's own father, who *'one Sunday morning pushed a wall over on his way home with his children from a walk'*. Although *'the wall had been built to his own specification ... he considered the work shoddy ... so he took a run at it, in*

**The Hanbury Family**
Back row: l. to r. Fred, Charles (Fanny's father), Gus
Front row: l. to r. Marion (Mrs Fred), Blanche, Ada, & Gertrude

*his frock coat, silk hat and lavender gloves!* And of his great Uncle William, always called the *'Rev. Fred'* by the family, who was *'black bearded, and dressed like a fisherman'*. Of how he had joined the church, moving eventually to the Isle of Wight where he *'devoted his evenings to port* [and] *for exercise, walking round the island in a day.'*

Then there was *'Gus'* (James), who was also intending to join the church until he read Darwin's *'Origin of the Species'*; but had shocked his family one day by declaring that *'Religion is a swindle'* and emigrating to, of all places, Darwin, Australia, *'there to grow pineapples for the rest of his life!'*

There was Ada in her mountain retreat on the Welsh border and Gertrude her older sister, whom he describes as *'a frail gentlewoman'*.

Only their sister Blanche it seems was able to slough off the inevitable cloak of spinsterhood for the Hanbury girls. Christened Frances Ellen Blanche, she was born in 1852 and went on to marry a house-master from Uppingham School, but not before she had been called in to help her older brother Charles, with his three young daughters, Ellen, Fanny and Katie. Their mother Georgiana had died in 1883, whilst the girls were still young, and although their architect father Charles would later remarry, he sought the immediate help of his sister Blanche in the upbringing up of his young family.

Charles De Witt Hanbury would never be a wealthy man. Though as Ann Gander records, *'He made enough money for the family to uphold its middle class status and he never lost his sense of breeding, or his eye for decorum'*. Tragedy however, never seems to have been far from his door. Not only did he lose his wife prematurely, but also his eldest daughter Ellen Mary Gertrude, born in 1872 died at the age of 24. However, his three daughters must have ensured that, in the early days at least, his house was more often filled with laughter than tears.

His second daughter Fanny (Frances Emily Jane) was born in 1873. She was both artistic and extrovert. Full of fun and sparkle, if at times a little outrageous, she loved to be the centre of attention. Like her younger sister Katie (Katherine Mabel, born in 1876), she had a great sense of style and colour, together with a certain degree of theatricality. Like her aunts, Fanny too was a talented artist, yet despite wanting to live the life of a bohemian painter, Fanny married a young Scotsman, Robert Bell in 1895.

**Robert Bell,
Leeds, 1904**

Renouncing the family ironmongery business in Edinburgh for journalism (Bell & Donaldson, Ironmongers, can still be found in Edinburgh today), Robert had first worked on the *Fifeshire Journal,* before moving eventually to the *Manchester Daily Dispatch* and subsequently to London. There he would become assistant editor of *The Observer*, a post he would hold for almost thirty years and one which his son Adrian later reflected, earned him the reputation among his contemporaries, *'as one of the ablest journalists in Fleet Street.'*

An early member of The Fabian Society, Robert was an ardent socialist as well as a republican, with a keen intellect and strong beliefs, yet despite this his head was always full of poetry and music. His family would remember him, particularly in later years, as a shy quiet man. He had met Fanny Hanbury whilst she was at Art College in Leeds. The deeply religious Bell family back in Scotland may have had misgivings at Robert's choice of bride. Not only was Fanny a fervent atheist, but she did rather startle the younger members of the Bell family by performing a series of cartwheels across the room. They were married in 1895. He was 31 years old and she just 22.

It seems that her father Charles also had misgivings about the marriage. Hearing that Fanny wanted to marry a Scottish journalist, he made the immortal comment, 'Journalists are a shady lot and seldom sons of gentlemen'. How astounded he would have been had he been able to look to the future beyond Robert, and seen what this union would generate in the world of writing and journalism.

Robert would always adore Fanny, yet they would eventually live almost separate lives, albeit within the framework of their marriage. No doubt this would be partly due to his work at *The Observer* and the pressures of getting the paper to print, but also perhaps due to their essentially disparate personalities and interests. *'What had started out as a marriage with good-humoured if opposing ideas would later become a war zone.'*

How different Fanny's life would have been had she not married but gone on to develop her very real artistic talent. She never lost her intuitive eye for colour and style, but transferred that thwarted creativity to spotting and buying up good pieces of antique furniture which would later furnish not only her own, but also her children's houses and attics besides.

As Robert became increasingly deaf and withdrawn in old age, it would be hard to imagine in later years, as Adrian would point out, that Fanny and Robert had once had the reputation of being *'a lively couple when they were young'*, and much in demand, *'their intellectual sparring* [making] *any dinner party a success.'* It was on such occasions no doubt, that Fanny would be at her gayest and most entertaining; her lively stories made all the livelier by her enjoying a drink. These were social skills that her youngest son Francis would inherit, and which would remain with her, into old age.

Years later, when she and Robert had taken up residency at 'The Four Swans' in Sudbury, she could still be seen 'holding court' at the centre of any gathering. Always attractive, always well-dressed if perhaps a little flamboyant and flowing, she would never be seen without her jewellery, her fingers full of rings. Delighting in the bar companionship, perhaps dropping in a little music hall number to liven things up, Fanny would be seen smoking a cigarette held delicately with a hairpin that she had deftly twisted to form a little loop. By placing her cigarette into her improvised holder she would ensure that none was wasted. Her long hair, now greying, would still be piled elegantly on her head This she only ever washed once a year, preferring to use 'Gloy', a starch paste that she regularly brushed through her hair, presumably taking dirt and grease with it. Her hair was renowned both for its thickness and lustre, though perhaps her method of achieving it was less appealing.

Robert would slip away as he did so often, taking himself off to the tiny house in Stour Street, that his son Francis had bought him. Here, in what would ironically be the only house that Francis would ever own, Robert would sit at his piano that almost filled the tiny ground floor room, and soon be lost to the raptures of his beloved Bach.

Of the three children born of the marriage, it would be the eldest and more delicate son Adrian, who would become the centre of

Fanny's existence. Francis, born five years later in 1906 was a robust, good-natured child whose arrival into the world seems hardly to have diverted Fanny's attention. And when another baby was born two years later, this time a daughter, it was natural that the two younger children would become inseparable.

Stephanie would always remember her adored older brother Francis as being, 'the light of her young life'. He was always to be relied upon for jokes and good fun, as well as being her saviour in times of childhood distress. Nicknamed 'Bony' by her in childhood, it would be her name for him, for the rest of his life. It was a reference to Bonaparte rather than his stature; they used to play a game whereby he was the Emperor and she the Empress Josephine.

**Frances and Stephanie**

Early married life for Robert and Fanny seems to have been set in a series of rented rooms. However, after moving to a more spacious house in Old Trafford, more suited to the needs and responsibilities of parenthood, now that they had a child to consider, Robert's subsequent move to Fleet Street dictated their eventual removal to

London. They lived in an apartment in Battersea and it was here that both Francis and Stephanie made their début into the world.

With the growing demands of a young family and the need to provide a more suitable environment for them all, another move seemed to be inevitable. This time they moved to a semi-detached house in Streatham with a garden to play in, nearby Tooting Bec Common providing a haven of adventure for young children; the house would be their home for a number of years.

Family tradition and social aspirations that were in direct contrast to those of her husband, would ensure that their three children would, at Fanny's insistence, all receive public school educations. Initially Francis followed Adrian to Glengorse Prep School in Eastbourne. There is no record of his time spent there, or whether he found the regime there any more tolerable than Adrian. Photos of the time certainly indicate that the boys still wore the hated starched Eton collars.

For Stephanie, however, it was be Ravens Croft School, also in Eastbourne – never once did she receive a letter from her mother whilst she was there and the memories of those school years would haunt her for the rest of her life.

Eventually Francis, like Adrian would attend public school at Uppingham. It was, after all, where Fanny's Uncle Fred had been, and Great-Uncle Fred Witt before him. And her Aunt Blanche had married the Reverend Theophilus Rowe, a housemaster at Uppingham. Despite, being his second wife, and having to live with her predecessor's portrait, it seems that their marriage was a productive one.

Not only did Blanche, as Mrs Blanche Hanbury Rowe, go on to write and publish a series of books on teaching young children to read; a method known as *Mrs Rowe's Rapid Method of Teaching Reading*, but two of their three daughters, were early women students at Oxford - Dorothy at Somerville and 'Benedicta' at Lady Margaret Hall. It seems that Dorothy inherited her mother's love of teaching, becoming a much loved and respected teacher at Talbot Heath School in Bournemouth, where she would teach both of Adrian's daughters, Anthea and Sylvia years later.

Although both the boys were in Farleigh House, life at Uppingham would not prove as rigorous and punishing as it had been for his brother. Adrian found his final year there a time of change for the public school and the many cruel traditions and bullying that had caused him real suffering. Did in fact the family story of the De Witt ancestor who was 'flogged through the streets of Amsterdam' actually refer to an old Uppingham tradition spoken of by Great Aunt Blanche and referred to in later years by Adrian? *'Blanche ... as a young bride of the housemaster had noticed one small boy looking progressively more pale and ill every day. She was worried and made investigations. Somehow she discovered that this boy was being persecuted by the rest of the house, being forced every night to run the gauntlet of thirty boys (fifteen a side) armed with wet knotted towels. As a result of those nightly beatings-up he got very little sleep.'*

Upon mentioning this to her husband, the Rev. Theophilus, Blanche was horrified to discover he would do nothing to intervene. This, she was told, was part of the tradition of the public school, and any intervention would result in further torment to the boy.

Was this in fact the source of the flogging story, passed down through the family, of one of the De Witt ancestors? Was 'being flogged through the streets of Amsterdam' in fact the schoolboy terminology given to the ritualistic running between two lines of boys each armed with a stinging wet knotted towel?

It was perhaps an indication of the warmth of the relationship between Father and son that, carefully kept amongst Robert's photographs and jottings, were a number of original poems written by Francis whilst at school. No maudlin or romantic verse here, but the cheerful voice of a schoolboy already showing a zest for life as well as a great sense of humour.

## Latin Prose  *F. de W. Bell*

*At the best of times I never had a brain,*
*And to try and do a prose sent me insane:*
*I could tackle Julius Caesar*
*I can work the bathroom geyser,*
*But a Latin Prose was too much of a strain.*
*I can cook myself an omelette and make tea*
*And for a man, what could more useful be.*
*I can wash up dirty plates,*
*I can learn my hist'ry dates,*
*But a Latin Prose just leaves me up the tree.*
*I would rather have six months for being drunk,*
*And stay in prison with my spirits sunk,*
*Than to work with 'ut' and 'ne'*
*And become a master's prey,*
*Oh a Latin Prose just gets me in a Funk.*

Apart from his poetry, Francis appears to have left little record of his time at Uppingham either sporting or academic. He left in 1922 at the age of 16, a practical chap who had received an excellent education, but whose sights were firmly fixed on a life in agriculture. Or at least, that's how it seemed.

Francis' future was certainly hanging in the balance at this time and it now appears there had been another suggestion – that Francis should apply to join the Indian Police. It would have been an ideal choice for him, not only offering a well-paid structured career but a colonial life-style to which he would have been so well suited. Robert too would have been very keen on the idea. Another member of his family, Roy Bell, was already in the Indian Police, and no doubt would have been consulted. It seems that Uppingham either discouraged or inexplicably refused to support Francis' application and this would further add to Adrian's dislike of the school.

Their mother Fanny's younger sister Katie, having previously been turned from an early desire for a life on the stage, had also settled for family life. Katie was a good-looking girl and, if perhaps a touch less vivacious than her sister, still managed to add considerable colour to the family history. She had married a newly qualified young doctor, William Ernest Peacock, in 1897, travelling with him to Chile, where he had taken a post as a medical officer, in charge of a region.

Katie would always say that she had never actually intended to marry him. Looking for a reason not to, she had told him that she *'disliked the English climate and that if she ever married she would have to live abroad.'* Undeterred, Ernest Peacock soon found that a doctor was needed at Punta Arenas, on the southern tip of Chile. He applied and got the post, began learning Spanish and asked for Katie's hand in marriage. How could she refuse him?

Was it Katie's heightened sense of drama or just a little vanity, that in retrospect she would always say that she was 'only seventeen at the time'? She was actually twenty-one and was perhaps more of an age to take some responsibility for the marriage.

However attractive Katie was to Ernest Peacock, he was not without attributes himself. It must also be remembered that her father was not financially secure at the time. Ernest not only had first class medical qualifications, which would, in later years give him an excellent reputation, but he also had money and he was willing to help Katie's father financially.

Life in South America was both harsh and desperately lonely for Katie. Her son Carlos in his memoirs, would later record that, *'By an ironic turn of fate,* [Katie] *who had pretended that she couldn't endure the English climate, found herself as a young married woman, marooned on the hurricane-swept, desolate peninsula that straggles out into the grim desolation of Tierra del Fuego and Cape Horn'.*

And what of Punta Arenas? It turned out to be a shack settlement, south of the Straits of Magellan. The bungalow, in which they lived with its corrugated iron roof, was a far cry from the comfortable Victorian home she had left in Leeds. It was not an auspicious beginning to married life.

**Katie (far left) and Dr William Peacock and others at Punta Arenas, a shack settlement, south of the Straits of Magellan**

Her husband's patients were from a broad cross-section of society, and were often rough and illiterate. He had to ride great distances to visit them and *'sometimes, if the remedies brought failed to give an immediate cure, his wilder patients would threaten to shoot him!'*

South America at the turn of the century was a violent and lawless place where the gun was the dominating factor. *'Age-old feuds were continually being fought up and down the long, rugged frontier that separated Chile and Argentina. Their politicians were ineffective and usually too involved in their own power struggles, to see the desperate need for social change.'* Both Argentina and Chile were underdeveloped and neglected. They offered the promise of immense riches and were subsequently wide open to exploitation.

Punta Arenas was a desolate arrival point, after what must have often been a hazardous sea voyage. It was a place where *'gold prospectors, exiles, emigrants and entrepreneurs converged, before going on to try their luck. Gambling and drinking were rife and fortunes were made or lost overnight.'*

Katie would tell of *'one family of emigrants arriving in rags and tatters, with no belongings, except a tiny stock of goods to trade. In a short time they* [had] *become landowners and merchants on an impressive scale, and ultimately one of the richest families in the Argentine'*. When, years later, she met their descendants in their great provincial estancias in Buenos Aires, she would remember the *'ragged emigrants being rowed ashore…and picture to herself that first landing, in the wind-swept Straits of Magellan'*.

It was in this atmosphere of speculation and pioneering, that Ernest Peacock began buying sheep and cattle and through this mutual interest, met Alec Cameron. They became business partners and set up a company, *'Sociedad Explotadora de Tierra del Fuego'*. Katie naturally became a shareholder.

Speculation becomes infectious, and it wasn't long before Fanny too had enthusiastically bought shares in the company. The Peacocks would return to Britain decidedly wealthier than when they had left. Fanny would treasure her unsold, worthless South American shares for many years to come; offering, as she thought, the promise of untold riches.

Cameron, an extremely wealthy farmer, was half Scottish, though originally from Wellington, New Zealand. He would remain a family associate for many years and would later play a significant role in Katie's life.

It was perhaps his dealings with the *'tough and lawless world in which he lived and worked'* that caused Ernest Peacock to develop what in his son Carlos' eyes was, *'a fierce and overriding will'*. When, after several years, the couple returned to Britain, Carlos felt that it was the domineering side of his father's character that caused him the most difficulty in adapting to an ordinary middle-class English life.

Not surprisingly, when two strong-minded people are opposing each other, the marriage became increasingly strained. So much so, that Katie, by now the mother of two young sons, Tom and Charles (later known as Carlos), felt there was no alternative other than to live apart. She and her sons lived in a series of rented cottages on the outskirts of London. *'Their father becoming a Sunday visitor, driving out to see them each weekend and returning to his London flat in the evening.'*

Later, Katie and her boys moved to the Welsh border. Here, living in series of remote rented houses in the Wye Valley, life was certainly tranquil, though Carlos would later say that they never really felt financially secure. It would be from here that he would recall walking with his mother through woodland with his Great Aunt Ada, when they stopped to admire the view – *'The River Wye in a deep gulf below us, and the high ground on the opposite bank, stretching in undulations of blue heathland. It was'* he remembered, *'perhaps this view, that made my aunt recall the time when, as a young woman, she worked as an artist… "I might have done so much better," she laments, "if it hadn't been for Ruskin's insistence on the detailed drawing of foliage. But everyone listened to him then. He was the oracle, the art lion of the age." (I remember how those words 'art lion' stuck in my mind – a small boy's vision of a lion with brush and paint box, its fur daubed with brightly coloured spots!)'*

It would not be until after the First World War, that Katie finally managed to obtain her divorce. It had been a long, drawn-out affair and ironically, having at last gained her freedom, she would once again be drawn back to South America, but this time under very different circumstances.

Alec Cameron had remained in contact, along with a number of friends and associates who had shared the Peacocks' experiences of life in Punta Arenas. It was perhaps understandable that in Cameron, now a widower, Katie felt she had found the financial security and settled life for which she longed.

Her second marriage would take her back to the Argentine, not as the young inexperienced girl who had struggled to survive the rigours of Punta Arenas, but as the wife of an extremely rich and successful rancher. Once again Carlos would say, *'it was an idealistic and misjudged step.'*

Back again in South America, Katie found herself caught up in a society whose values were measured by wealth. Of course there were aspects of the life she enjoyed - the entertaining, the entourage of servants and the money to dress well. *'But she realised too late, that back in the Wye Valley, despite its uncertainties, she had found a peace and beauty that were lacking in her new life.'*

Cameron's sumptuous single-storey house, and vast estancia 'Quinta Maori' (Maori House), were situated outside Buenos Aires. It was here, on one of the three huge estancias that Cameron owned, that Katie came to take up her role as the second wife of an extremely wealthy man.

**Alec and Katie Cameron's home in 1924**

Her new home was beautiful and luxurious, yet once she was here, Katie felt ostracised and resented by her four stepchildren. As a consequence of this, instead of settling down, she accompanied Cameron on his sheep and cattle-buying expeditions all over the world; once more becoming *'caught up in a wandering and rootless life'*.

But to the outside world, to her family and friends at home, Katie's story was one of success. After all, wasn't Cameron incredibly rich? His estancias covered thousands of acres.

It was undoubtedly on one of Katie's visits back home, when she was staying with her sister Fanny and the family in Suffolk, that the question of Francis' future was discussed.

The family had by now moved into the more spacious Seabrooks Farm at Stradishall, later to become the subject of Adrian's third book, *The Cherry Tree*. Robert was still working in London as Assistant Editor at *The Observer*, and now lodged with his brother George and wife Mabel, at their boarding house in Pimlico.

George Bell, whom Adrian would describe in his biography, as *'the last of my father's brothers to flee from the ironmongery business'*, lived a *'supernumerary sort of existence ... mostly in carpet slippers in the basement'*. Adrian describes his Uncle George as being good with his hands, spending his days mending broken furniture from the lodgers' bedrooms, and quoting Shakespeare. His wife Mabel had started taking in lodgers to supplement their income. She unfortunately also had a tendency to spend most of it on giving parties and indulging her *'passion of bead-buying'* or impulsively purchasing vast quantities of *'bargain materials'*.

It was from here that Robert would return to Suffolk once a week, to spend a couple of days with his family. Most of this time would be spent in playing his piano or wandering the lanes and byways in a poetical haze, quietly oblivious of his surroundings and the mayhem of family life.

After spending a year as a pupil on Vic and Martha Savage's farm, Hundon Great Lodge, situated at Hundon in Suffolk, Adrian, with Fanny's encouragement, persuaded his father Robert to buy him Stephenson's Farm nearby.

It was a small farm of some 35 acres; complete with its own picturesque little thatched farmhouse. Bought for a sum of £850 with a further £200 for stock, machinery and emergencies, it was no mean investment. And in the autumn of 1921, Adrian took up residency, *'his own master'* at last, continuing his farming career under the kindly tutelage of the Savage family. Despite its many charms, the picturesque little thatched farm-house, with its three interconnecting bedrooms would soon prove inadequate.

Fanny had, with her usual exuberance, decided within a year to move the rest of the Bell family up from London. Farming it seems was to be a family enterprise with Fanny herself taking a leading role. A cash crisis appears to have been an issue, and regardless of any misgivings he might have had, Adrian was hardly in a position to offer any opposition and the rest of the family needed little persuasion to move in. Stephanie would soon be leaving school and Francis had left Uppingham at the end of the Easter term, wanting nothing more than to work on the farm alongside Adrian. His easy manner, and good humour together with his ability to mix with people from all walks of life, had already made Francis popular and well liked in the neighbourhood.

With the accommodation at Stephenson's Farm proving woefully inadequate, a house was rented at nearby Farley Green and Adrian joined his family there, relinquishing his first home to his farm worker George Hempstead.

It would not be long however before the family moved again - this time to Seabrooks on the Haverhill road at Stradishall. In her biography Ann Gander records that *'on 7th October 1922, Frances Hanbury Bell ...'* purchased the farm from Vic Savage *'at a cost of £620'*. It was a much larger house and with its additional 15 acres backing onto Stephenson's, it made up a neat 50 acres altogether. *'A further figure of £401 was paid to Vic Savage for horses and implements'*.

Francis spent two years working on his brother's farm, but this was in no way ideal. The farm could barely support the family and there was simply not enough money to set Francis up in a similar way.

Katie's visit to Seabrooks must have been seen as fortuitous.

Fanny, ever the opportunist, must have felt she had found the perfect answer to their problem - what an ideal solution! Where better to send the boy and just think of all those acres. Francis would earn his keep by working on Cameron's estancia near Buenos Aires. He would gain inestimable experience and who knew what opportunity might present itself?

For Katie, so desperately lonely, to have a member of her own family at Quinta Maori would have seemed heaven sent. Her own two sons, by now grown up, had remained in England. Tom had gone into farming, Carlos was at Cambridge and, with the tension between herself and Cameron's daughters, there must have been times when she felt very isolated.

And how did her nephew Francis react to the suggestion? Being Francis he would have loved the idea. What an adventure it must have seemed in the days when foreign travel was of course by sea, and usually only within the grasp of the upper echelons of society. When the furthest journey he had made since leaving school was along the dusty road to Haverhill, a journey of some six or seven miles – a journey undertaken as a drover, walking Adrian's bullocks to market.

Of his voyage all that remains is a cracked sepia photograph. Perhaps only his father understood the ache he felt when his mother Fanny was far too busy to see him off from Southampton.

# Part Two
# South America

In the Argentine, Francis would prove to be the ideal guest.

Tall, fair-haired, charming and exceedingly good-looking, he was everyone's image of the archetypal young Englishman. His sense of fun and joie de vivre soon won the hearts of Cameron's daughters, Amy and Heather, and he must have helped to bridge the gulf between them and their stepmother.

Although perhaps never quite sure of his role, as guest or gaucho, Francis would remain at Quinta Maori for just over two years. In that time he learnt to speak passable Spanish, to ride and work as a gaucho, to shear sheep, and to make himself socially agreeable whenever the occasion arose. He had a room at the Manager's house. This set him apart from the other gauchos, yet was suitably removed from the main house.

The house at Quinta Maori was impressive in its own right, but it was the grounds that featured most in Francis' photographs. Their landscaped acres spreading out from the house were dotted with date palms, no doubt brought back from the Canary Islands by Cameron, on one of his trips.

But, perhaps the thing that impressed Francis the most was having his own car. He proudly sent a photograph of it to his father. 'this is my <u>own</u> car in the Argentine. Please feel impressed.' Whether he was actually showing off the car, or the attractive girl sitting on the running board, remains to be seen.

That he enjoyed himself at Quinta Maori there is no doubt. Why he left can only be surmised.

For whatever reason, the opportunity to work for Ferro-Carril Oeste must have seemed attractive. The job offered managerial status,

**Francis' first car in the Argentine**

whilst prospects of advancement at Quinta Maori were doubtful – they already employed a manager of long standing and Cameron did have two sons.

Although it was British, Ferro-Carril Oeste was one of the four big Argentine Railway companies. It had been registered in London in 1890 as 'The Buenos Aires Western Railway Company Ltd'.

Jobs with the Railway Company, as Francis would himself later note, were obtained through 'a little inside pull' and Cameron, as a wealthy businessman, would undoubtedly have provided that.

Cameron's two daughters were also obviously attracted to Francis. Was there a liaison developing that Cameron would have wished to discourage? Charm and good looks were really all Francis had to offer.

Back in Suffolk, Francis' older brother Adrian would continue to farm at Seabrooks for three more years, but events were destined to change all their lives irrevocably.

But for Francis, this was the start of what would be the loneliest time of his life. He had gone out to South America with a one-way ticket – first class of course. He would return, nearly seven years later, working his way back on a tramp steamer.

Naturally he had fun too - when wouldn't Francis have made the best of things? Yet, the journal he kept, showed it to be a time beset with hardship, frustrations, appalling weather conditions and recurring crop failures.

## Ingeniero Foster - 1926

**The Station at Ing. Foster**

'*It had to be the most desolate looking place on earth*'...

The opening words of Francis' South American diaries would prove to be true many times over as he lived and experienced life in the driest and harshest of environments, hundreds of miles from civilisation, striving to establish an experimental farm or, in his words, '*to make the desert bloom*'.

'*I shall never forget the day that I arrived at Ing. Foster. It was not even called by that name then, but merely had a board on the station with the number of kilometres distant from Buenos Aires - some six hundred and fifty odd. My boss and I had been travelling overnight from Buenos Aires. We had arrived in a cloud of dust, which, I later came to realise, was the usual method of travel in that part of the world!*'

ing. Foster was situated due west of the capital. Although the railway had long been established as far as the town of Pico, the branch on which Francis was travelling was an entirely new construction.

The railway, wishing to extend further, was starting an experimental wheat station, together with a colonisation scheme. They were trying to attract people up there, and Francis was being sent to be in charge of the experimental crop growing station. His boss, Graham, had come with him to show him over the place and to leave him there. Despite expecting something pretty rough and isolated, Francis was shocked by the desolation of the place when he arrived.

'*I had noticed passing through the last fifty or sixty kilometres of our journey, that the country had become wooded, and as we progressed the vegetation grew thicker and wilder looking... no vivid tropical jungle here, but a seared scrubby type of tree with stubby grasses growing in the coarse grass.*'

The trees were mostly of 'Caldene' and 'Algarrobe', rather like oak in appearance, except that the leaves were different and the only use for the wood was to burn it.

Arriving at their destination, all that was there was the railway station and one or two mud huts, with forest all round. The railway track disappeared into it, leading to one station further west, called Arizona, which was the terminus.

The train consisted of an engine, a carriage, half of which was first class, the other second, together with a goods van. This combination ran out there twice a week, and, as Francis soon discovered and appreciated, was the event of the day.

'*It did save us from being cut off from civilisation, and it was a great consideration to get your papers and mail twice a week. Later the service ran three days a week, but we were getting things into shape by then.*'

Francis was struck by the amazing manner in which the colour of the whole landscape seemed to blend into one kind of dusty grey-green; there was no sign of verdant vegetation anywhere. '*I remember wondering how we could possibly persuade wheat to grow in a desert like* this. *For though there was vegetation it had all the appearance of desert, so drab did it all seem.'*

A fellow named Jorge Crueslain met them at the station. He was in charge of the tree-felling and other work. Later Francis would say that he would come to know him better than his own brother, for they lived together for several months before his house was built, up at the experimental farm.

**Jorge's hut**

Jorge told him that he was originally working on the construction of the line up here. There had been nobody here at all then, and they had had to cut their way through the forest.

Despite the arrival of the train, there were not more than a dozen people at the station. Most of these were carters and woodcutters who were clearing the land of trees. There was one however, to whom the boss introduced him, a Russian by the name of Lesniff, and for whose company later, he would be profoundly thankful.

The first day there was little time to lose, for the boss had to return to Buenos Aires two hours later, by the same train. So they set out in Jorge's Ford, to visit the site of the experimental station and to discuss *'various ways and means.'*

There were barely fifty acres of the farm cleared of the bush or 'monte' as it was called, at this early stage, and although this had been ploughed, it looked a very depressing sight. *'The surface had been merely scratched, and the ground was so hard that little could be done without rain, and rain seemed to be very scarce up here.'*

The farm was about a couple of miles from the station, and as Francis' house at the farm had not yet been built, he lived in a railway coach on a siding and fed with Jorge in his hut. He had many a rude awakening in that old coach.

*'The goods train used to come in and shunt trucks about to be loaded with wood, and during the shunting my coach would go too!*

*I have often gone to sleep at one end of the station and awakened at the other. Until I got used to this, the crockery and the clock used to be broken and bumped about, for often the shunting was a little rough!'*

**The railway carriage where Francis lived for four to five months – it was half full of samples of wheat**

Graham returned to town, and Francis felt a little lost when he had left. It was not that he had taken any particular liking to the man, but he did at least speak his own language. Although he could speak Spanish fairly well, like most Englishmen he was a little nervous of speaking in another language, and he had never been quite so cut off before. With no letters or papers for two days, when the next train was due - he felt very lonely.

Jorge, however, soon put him at ease, and he and Francis passed a pleasant enough first evening together in his hut, before Francis set off to sleep in his railway coach. It was very cold, and he was glad that he'd brought plenty of blankets with him.

The storekeeper had told him earlier that he kept whisky and seemed disappointed when Francis told him he didn't often drink it. Francis had to later admit that a drop or two that first night would have been more than welcome.

The coach however, proved surprisingly comfortable. There were two beds, a table and a chair or two, but water was the main problem, or rather a lack of it. The station had a mill and pumping apparatus, but the supply was very limited and washing would prove to be rather a luxury. He would take a pail of water to the coach, and this would last about a week, his own ablutions being of the scantiest.

Later he suggested that a bath in Buenos Aires now and then would be pleasant, if not necessary, and the boss promised to let him go off for weekends now and then for the purpose. It was a good excuse for a weekend off anyway.

The acute lack of water really was a huge problem.

All the water for the horses on the farm and for the men who were working cutting up the wood was sent up by rail. The corral at the station would be full of mules and horses; they would all be waiting for the train to arrive with tanks of water.

*'Often as late as eleven o'clock at night, these wretched animals and men were still waiting for water, and when it did arrive, the tanks were often left a long way from the corral. This necessitated them being pushed by hand for several hundreds of yards at times.*

*The stationmaster was a bad egg, a red-hot anarchist. I fancied he had been tucked away here to be got rid of. He was clever enough to do just his duties so as to avoid getting the sack, but in a friendly and obliging manner he would help no one. Instead of getting the water tanks shunted into position, he would leave them anywhere, and the devil could take them.*

*We never realise what a lack of water means when we have it to use freely, and it was a heartbreaking sight to see some of those animals drinking when at last they had the chance. For our horses at the farm we carted water in a water cart, and naturally we had first claim to it, so were generally well supplied.'*

Wells were being sunk in various places, but it was a long job, as it was all handwork. The men had to go down as far as a hundred and fifty feet to get good water, and pass through a lot of hard rocky substance called 'tosca'; the station well had been bored, but it was not a great success. If anything went wrong with the pipes below, they couldn't get down to them to do repairs. So, other wells were being dug out by hand, about two yards square, which left room for a man to be lowered and to carry out any repairs necessary. It was a miserable job.

**Well digging**

During the first few weeks Francis went about a good deal with Jorge, as there was not much to be done up at the farm. There were three or four men there, but it was impossible to get order in the place. There were so many irregular jobs to do, such as water carting, bringing in the horses and cooking.

'One man had to go to the village every day, (I call it a village, but there were half a dozen huts in the place) to fetch the meat and stores, such as they were, and get it cooked. Another had to collect the horses every morning. This was a very erratic task. They might arrive at seven o'clock or twelve. One could never tell. You see, there was no fencing round the farm then, and when the horses had done the work, they were just turned out into the 'monte' to get their living as best they could. The consequence of this being, they wandered for miles at times, and the job of collecting them was very difficult.

Quite a number of fellows would have got lost had they been sent after them, but the old whiskered chap we had was pretty clever at the job, though that was about all he was useful for. He was named Pereyra and on foggy mornings, it was often midday before the old fellow arrived on horseback with his troop. By then it was too late to start on a day's work. So things had to drift very much at the start.'

**Francis riding with Pereyra, the old horse collector**

The horses too were mostly unfit for work. They could not get enough nourishment from the dry grass and all looked in poor condition. One afternoon Francis picked out an animal and saddled it up. He rode three paces and it collapsed under him, complete with rider. His comment, *'The R.S.P.C.A. should have been there. It would have made the old women talk!'* underlined his deep concern for the welfare of these horses.

These animals had been sent from the good camps further east, and although he continually asked for fodder for them, he never got sufficient feed to be able to work them continually. The carters used mules and donkeys for carting away the wood. These however, seemed to flourish on the poor grass and worked well. They had a tractor and plough also, which did quite good work. They had to use a disc plough, even though the land was cleared of wood, as there were always a number of roots remaining in the soil, and an ordinary share plough would soon have come to grief.

**The type of cart used on the roads…………and the disc plough**

Jorge's main job was to supervise the clearing of the land, and it seemed to be a thankless and frustrating task.

*'The clearing was done by contract, and the contractors had hundreds of half-bred fellows working, cutting out the trees by the roots and carting away the wood after it had been split into convenient sizes. We often discovered trees that had been cut off level with the ground and the roots just covered with earth. It was then that Jorge would get going. He would rave as only the Latin temperament can. But, he certainly obtained results, and they were all pretty scared of him.'*

The contractors were only interested in clearing as much land as possible in the shortest time and taking their money; consequently they could hardly be relied upon to see that the work was done properly. Jorge then, was kept pretty busy going over all the cleared land, besides having to superintend the loading, weighing and despatching of all the wood from the station. He would often load as many as half a dozen freight wagons a day.

Francis often wondered what Jorge thought of him in those early days, but Jorge was used to working with Englishmen, and besides, they seemed to get along well enough. If ever anyone dropped in to see him or he was having a 'fiesta' anywhere, he would always send for Francis to join him and they were always able to raise a good laugh between them.

**Francis and Jorge**

They never saw much of the stationmaster. Francis would write of him as being, *'Such an uncongenial fellow who had the most appalling temper when roused. He loved to get up a heated argument about the slightest thing.'*

The storekeeper, a Spaniard by the name of Alonso, used to look in of an evening. *'He did a very good trade, as may well be imagined, seeing as everyone had to buy the necessaries of life from his store, and he had no obligation about charging for them. However, he was an amusing little man and we enjoyed his company.'*

Now and then one or two from the next station, Arizona, would drop in if they were passing, and there was always the police official.
*'He had got a uniform like the President of the Republic, complete with sword and revolver. The only snag being that it didn't fit properly, and he looked less imposing than he should! However, in a little place like that we were glad of anyone for company, and spent many hours smoking and drinking maté of an evening.'*

Francis was determined to mingle with these men. After all it was either them or none at all, and once he got into their mode of life and ways of thinking, they were very entertaining and a lot of fun. It was what made an extraordinarily lonely existence for a 21 year-old young man, carrying a great load of responsibility, actually bearable.

'It was amazing what a friendly spirit prevailed in that God-forsaken spot. They all seemed curiously interested in me, being a newcomer, and were all most anxious to make me feel at ease.' One must always fit into the society in which one finds oneself, and seeing that eighty percent of their conversation was upon women and wine, I also fell in with my share!

Englishmen were usually thought aloof and stiff, but if I had kept apart from these, with whom could I have conversed? These men were my only companions so to speak, and as we must all have companionship of some kind, I tried to live in their sphere of life.'

The stationmaster flattered Francis by telling him that he was unlike others of his race, 'mas gaucho', as he called it. And so Francis drank maté with them always and took to their ways. In fact, doing everything as un-English as possible, though his appearance was against him, 'Being fair and tall, and everything these Latinos were not. It would have been horrible to have felt isolated from human beings in such a spot as that. I took their acceptance of me as a compliment, for I must confess I've met many of our race abroad of whom I have felt thoroughly ashamed. There is a type who never seems to realise that they are earning their living in someone else's country, and behave in the rudest manner.'

As for the gangs working in the Monte, Francis saw very little of them round the village. He used to go with Jorge sometimes when he went to have a look around, and was amazed to see how primitively they lived. 'Their huts consisted of holes dug in the ground with a structure of poles over them, which were covered with a grass. You could see the children bolt into them like rabbits when our car approached.'

**A woodman's family home**

Their women used to work beside the men, splitting up the wood and helping to load it in the carts. They were a very tough gang, but for the most part they worked well. All of these jobs were done by piecework, so the more they did, the more they earned.

They would get their food from the store on account and settle up at the end of the month. Anything over was spent on wine. The place was like bedlam on pay-day.

'I remember Jorge and I were having evening grub one night while all around there was a noise like a madhouse. The light from their fires could be seen all round the Monte and the most drunken shrieks and cries were being raised - it sounded for all the world like an attack by Indians that one reads of. There were often shots to be heard too, and in the morning there were generally a few casualties!'

Jorge told Francis that this was a regular occurrence on pay-day. The unfortunate policeman had to try and show his authority, but was wise and always waited till morning. It seems that this was an awkward spot for law preservation as they were situated on the boundary of San Luis and La Pampa. Anyone committing a crime on their land had but to walk about half a mile and their policeman couldn't touch him. He was then in another department and the police of San Luis was responsible for him. The police however, co-operated well and the official at the next station was a tough customer.

**Railway map showing the line out to Ing. Foster and Arizona**

Francis remembered one afternoon, *'Seeing two of the woodsmen dead drunk; they were chasing each other round the store. The pursuer had an axe in his hand, and swore he was going to split the other fellow in half if he caught him. I have little doubt he would have done so, had he been sober enough to catch up with him, for these fellows knew how to handle an axe!'*

Francis and Jorge naturally in those early days spent a lot of time together, with Francis eating with Jorge each evening in his hut down at the station. Jorge had a boy who used to do some of the odd jobs for him and a bit of cooking – but, when he was in, he always did it himself and proved to be a very good cook too.

The food was pretty ordinary, as there was little choice. Meat was plentiful but of dubious quality. *'There was a fellow calling himself a butcher working with Alonso the storekeeper. He would go away for a couple of days and return with a dozen cows, which he would kill as he needed them, and then repeat the journey.'*

Milk was obtained from Lesniff, the Russian who lived nearby, and whom Francis had first met at the station. He kept a few cows for milking, and a hen or two, who produced a few eggs in the spring. For a change of diet they would have a goat or more rarely, a pig.

*'There was one occasion when Jorge returned with a young pig in the back of his Ford. He gave everyone to understand that he had bought it, but later told me he had found it wandering on the road track and, no one being anywhere within owning distance, had caught it and brought it along. We tended that pig with great pride and watched it grow, while we tried to conjure up the smell of roast pork!'*

There were also a few partridges and hares in the camp, but they were pretty scarce. If Francis and Jorge went out in the car for any distance, they always took their guns and would shoot quickly if they saw a bird. It was for food rather than sport, and they tried most things in their quest for a change in the monotony of their diet.

*'Emus we also tried to eat, but they were pretty beastly. There were quite a number of these before the bush was cleared. On one or two occasions I saw some 'guanaco'- a kind of deer, but these soon disappeared further west, as the work around this district progressed.'*

Meanwhile Francis had been doing his best to shape things up at the experimental farm. He had about sixty different samples of wheat to sow, in small experimental plots.

*'We only had very rough ideas as to what particular classes would suit the district, and sowed a few square yards of each variety in our carefully prepared plots. We then had to repeat the process all over again, a month later, and then again a month after that. Most of the samples came from the North American dry zones, and were of the bearded variety.'*

All the sowing of these sample wheats had to be done by hand and Francis found it very tedious. The men didn't care much for this job either. Often the mornings were cold, and as each grain had to be sown separately, it was difficult on frosty mornings. *'They always called it a woman's job and I must say they were about right. I got very fed up with it myself at times, when the wind blew cold and one's back ached with the stooping.'*

**Sewing seed by hand on experimental lots**

There was always a lot of laughter and coarse jokes following the suggestion that some girls should be sent up for this work. As Francis said, *'Anything of a skirt up there was looked upon as a luxury. The only women to be seen were those of the woodcutters in the monte; we were apt to forget what a feminine figure looked like. I forget of course the stationmaster's wife. But she was kept very much indoors, being busy with three children to look after, and everlastingly bemoaning the fact that she hadn't enough water to wash the floor with.'*

Francis had been up in Foster a month before there was any appreciable rain. He had got on with the ploughing and managed to run in a little wheat after this but naturally it was a roughish job, as the land had only been scratched at the first ploughing. Graham the boss, *'full of theory'* as Francis would say he always was, had been drumming into him the principles of dry farming - of the necessity to harrow after every rain, to keep the moisture in the soil. But Francis soon realised that they were up against something rather unique there. Because the soil was so light and sandy, if it was harrowed too much the whole field was likely to blow away the next day.

**Disc harrowing with horses**

He wrote of the frightful winds they had to contend with and of the problems of having so very little rain. Until the ground had some consistency, it was very difficult to work. It seemed as though it had no body in it. They were often troubled with dunes forming during a windy spell, and what terrible 'temporales' they were. After being out of doors for half an hour or so, he would have his face all powdered with dust and eyes so full of it, they smarted with irritation. All he could do was hope for a change the next day.

*'Many a day have we spent shut up in our rooms, with the dust blowing everywhere. Dust in your food, dust in everything, until it seemed to get into a man's very soul. It made one in such a filthy mess and it was really depressing to watch. I would set the men to do a few jobs in the buildings, just to keep them busy and leaving them, would go to bed for the rest of the day. I thanked heaven for having a book or two to read, or I think I would have gone mad before long. One couldn't even lie in bed in*

*comfort. It was useless to try and wash, as the dust stuck to you more than ever when you tried to dabble it with water.'*

He could now understand why nobody there wore socks. It was useless with such dry sand about. He wore his leather top-boots, but the workmen wore rope-soled slippers, and he decided to do the same in the summer. For two days or more the wind would blow in this fashion, and then perhaps, they would have one fine day. And then it would blow for two more days from the opposite direction and still no sign of rain to lay the dust. *'I never grumbled at rain again, after having seen what a hell the lack of it could be.*

Jorge told him that rain here was a real luxury, and that for most of the year they would have to put up with the dust. *'I had to keep a temperature and rain chart and I must say I never became worn out measuring the rain.'*

Francis found the trees were very strange to watch during these winds, for they barely moved in the gale. Nature had so constructed them that, unlike man, they seemed to stand impervious to whatever was thrown at them. On occasions he would find a branch or two blown off, but that was rare.

**Francis in rope sandals in the heat of summer**

It was on one of those dusty, windy occasions that some of the railway directors arranged to come up and see the new zone and how the work was progressing. The special train arrived in due course. The wind was blowing great guns and the dust was rising hard. Several cars had been hired to convey the directors from the station to the experimental farm.

Eventually they arrived. They looked around, asked a few rather futile questions – railway directors after all are not farmers – and cleared off again. One of them, however, Francis would always remember. He climbed on to a piece of high ground, put his hands on his hips, sniffed at the wind and said, 'My God, this is worse than Egypt!' Francis had never been to Egypt, but if it was anything like Ing. Foster on that day, he had no desire to go.

They rather enjoyed these official visits. Most sections of the railway would have been on tenterhooks, but seeing as the visitors knew very little about farming, they couldn't ask many awkward questions or find fault. The managers were kind too and would often leave Francis English cigarettes and on one occasion, a large parcel of fresh fruit.

Any trip to the station made a welcome change for Francis and there was always the chance that there would be letters from home.

Robert seems to have written regularly and often enclosed photographs. Picnics with the family, Stephanie growing up, visits by Uncle George and Roy Bell, Fanny and Stephanie on holiday on the continent. Any news from home must have been greatly anticipated and treasured by him.

Soon after Francis had arrived, he borrowed Jorge's Ford one Sunday, and went along to visit Lesniff and his family. Jorge had told him he was mad, but then he always called anyone 'loco' when he couldn't understand them. Francis was sure that word was often used about himself when he wasn't present.

The Lesniffs kept three enormous Great Danes – fine specimens, but extremely terrifying when anyone entered the premises. Francis drew up in front of the house, a mud affair with a tin roof, but then remained trapped in the car, until someone arrived. A woman came from the house, disturbed by the barking, and started to speak to him in Russian. He couldn't understand a word of this and answered in Spanish, which she could make nothing of. She then ran inside and returned with another woman. She was very beautiful, and spoke to Francis in almost perfect English.

She was the wife of Lesniff. She asked him in, telling Francis that her husband would return shortly. Francis was astounded and totally charmed. *'I could never have dreamed that there would be anyone within miles of this place who spoke my own language. We conversed together until her husband arrived.'*

She told him they were all fugitives from the Russian Revolution. Poor women. What had they come to? He would often think of them stuck out in that remote isolated spot. It was a bad enough place for a man to be stuck in, let alone women.

Mr Lesniff then arrived. He was wearing the most disreputable looking hat Francis had ever seen, and his clothes were well used and torn. And yet, Francis could tell at once that he was a superior and well-educated man. He had a very charming, gracious manner. He tried a few words of English on him, but they found they could converse better in Spanish. His wife couldn't speak Spanish but understood it well enough. Francis felt very ignorant, for they tried to speak to him in both French and German, but he stumbled, and then had to fall back on Spanish. However, they managed to converse quite well, filling in the gaps in any language that came to them. They were indeed very charming people, and he would be very thankful in later days, to have their company and friendship.

The Lesniffs told him how they had escaped from Russia during the revolution, and how they had come to this desolate spot, thinking it was as far away from the Soviet world as they could get. They must have been through terrible times. Francis thought that Mrs Lesniff had a very wild look in her eyes, as if another big shock would have been too much for her. They showed him old photographs of their palatial homes in Russia, where Mr Lesniff used to keep large racing stables. Francis counted thirteen grooms in one of the photographs. Lesniff knew all about the Derby winners and classic horses for years back, and Francis found it shocking to think he had come to this. Still he knew that the family were lucky to have their lives and what little money they had managed to save and bring with them.

He had a splendid tea with these two. Home-made bread and cakes, which were good to taste again. *'What a difference a woman makes about the place, even in such a dirty old shack as they inhabited.'* They had a son too, about twelve years old. A delicate, large-headed boy, whom they adored. It was a memorable afternoon.

*'Lesniff and I played chess after tea. A game I had not played for years. Though he beat me I think I gave him a good game. I am sure they were as pleased to know me as I to know them, for they were quite lost among the other folk here, who were quite uneducated, and we at least had more in common. But there was a difference. While I could mix with the others, Lesniff couldn't, and so missed a lot – for every angle of life has its interest.'*

When Francis returned to Jorge's that evening for his meal, he found him calling Alonso, the storekeeper, all the names he could think of. He was fuming like anything and Francis was interested to find out what the row was about.

*'It appeared that Jorge was feeling pleased with life and was making a sweet omelette for supper. He thought it would look better if it was lit up with some brandy, and had sent his boy over to the store for a gill to pour over it. Well, though he had struck nearly a box of matches, the brandy wouldn't light, and he accused Alonso of watering it down. This resulted in a delicious prose poem from Jorge, cursing the storekeeper, his family and ancestors for the last three generations. He was in a real temper about it, and went out there and then to see Alonso personally and tell him all about it. I didn't go with him – I expect old Alonso just withered up in front of the storm. Anyway Jorge returned later, still mumbling, and was bad company for the rest of the evening, so I got myself off to bed early that night.'*

Francis felt his diary seemed to dwell a great deal on food, but it was of course, a most important matter. A good cook in the men's department at the farm was, he discovered, half the battle in keeping the men contented and in a good working mood. He thought he had more trouble over cooks and food than any other single thing there.

*'When I was eventually installed in my bungalow on the farm, I tried four boys at cooking, but eventually had to do most of it myself. Then again, if the men couldn't get their meat ration for some reason or other, there would be no end of fuss. After all, in a place like that, food was the only thing to occupy the men's minds. They had no entertainment and nowhere to go, so if their bellies were not well filled there was bound to be trouble.'*

On feast days and holidays he and Jorge would buy them a goat or sheep and a few litres of wine. *'The carcass would be roasted whole out of doors and we would eat it together and laugh and joke, and they would all be as happy as kids at a school treat. And, to be sure, I enjoyed it as much myself.'*

It would be some four or five months before his bungalow at the farm was ready. During all of this time, he was living in his railway coach and feeding with Jorge which would not be without its moments of hilarity. *'One evening Jorge found the most revolting spider in his kitchen - an enormous thing, as big as an egg! He poured some petrol on it and lit it up - rather a cruel proceeding, but that seemed to be the way they killed them. After all, one could hardly stamp on a thing that size!'*

During those months the village had changed quite a lot and outside the station there was now what could almost be called a road. Several more shanties had gone up, and they had heard that someone was going to start a bakery. Perhaps that would mean fresh bread? It would be a change from the 'galleta', half bread, half biscuit, that the storekeeper sold, which must have been rather like the unleavened bread of the Bible. It wasn't too bad when fresh, but that was seldom.

**The new baker's at Ing. Foster**
*'Please admire the Avenida, we had 7mm. of rain the night before'*

'The newly arrived baker has started to build his house in the village. He is using bricks, so it will not be the usual dried mud affair. He got his bricks from a fellow who lives in the 'monte' and made them. There was a disused well there, which must have been years old. He managed to fish up some water at times, which served for making bricks, though it was hardly fit for drinking.'

There was also a sawmill at work, put up by one of the contractors who were given the job of digging the wells. The last twenty feet of these had to be boarded up and they used to cut the planks out on the sawmill. Short planks, a yard or two in length, could be obtained from the trees, but nothing longer. For carpentry purposes the wood was really useless.

'Our boss was very keen trying to invent uses for this wood, but its only real use was for the fire. The traffic engineer told me that during the [First World] War they used to burn it in the engines, but it was a terrible nuisance as it ruined the boilers and they were all glad to see the last of it.'

**The sawmill cutting up the cleared wood**

Francis had about a couple of hundred acres cleared on the farm by this time, and owing to a little rain, had been able to get it ploughed and sown after a fashion. They had put some earlier wheat in, and some oats, and now all they could do was hope for the best.

He had taken on another couple of men by now, an Italian and an Argentine, both quite good workers and this had made their number up to six. There was always plenty of work for them to do. Francis was planning to tidy up the newly constructed farm buildings and corrals, which were already looking impressive when one considered they had been started from nothing.

The men were all more or less good, except the tractor man. Francis didn't care for him. *'He was always looking at his watch and had a nasty habit of talking of his companions too. He never had a good word, always a bad one. It was a nasty trait and I knew we would fall out before long. In fact a month or two later I sacked him, and taught an unskilled boy to drive the tractor. That was the worst of those fellows. They thought they knew too much and were indispensable. He was a lazy fellow too, and no loss when he went.'*

Francis had got the men more or less settled to a routine. The old horse-keeper who brought in the horses in the morning used to cook for them. This arrangement worked well enough, provided the horses could be found easily. He was wonderful at finding them. They were usually in by about seven in the morning. Francis couldn't imagine at what hour the poor old fellow must have set out to find them.

As a cook he was not so good, but filled the gap. His main trouble was his liking for wine. He used to be drunk most weekends, but Francis didn't say anything. He felt they were rather in his hands as far as the horses were concerned. He was born and bred in that part of the world and knew the 'monte' well.

The other chaps they had were not much use on a horse. Had they been, they wouldn't have been there, as a good horseman could usually get a job on an estancia at that time. Anyway, in spite of his failings, Francis stuck with the old horse-keeper until the farm was better established, wire fences were up and they had their own feed for the animals.

He had a row with the boss over the old horse-keeper one day. The old fellow used to go to the village every day to buy the necessary provisions for the men, and must have stopped off at the store to have a drink. When he returned he was definitely the worse for wear and could hardly keep his seat on his horse. The unfortunate part of the affair was that the Boss and Francis happened to be passing just at the precise moment when he was trying to dismount. It was obvious that he was quite drunk.

Francis tried to get Graham away, but he saw him and started making a fuss. He thought the old man should have been sacked on the spot. Francis thought so too, but it wasn't quite as simple as that. The trouble was who could have done his job? None of the men working on the farm knew the 'monte' well enough, and how could they have found a substitute at a moment's notice?

After much argument Francis managed to get the boss to see his point, and he kept the old horse-keeper for as long as he was needed. He did however, go and give the old fellow *'a devil of a talking to, but he was much too far-gone to take much notice. A most unwholesome spectacle he was, so I told him to shut himself up and I sent another of the fellows to cook the evening meal for the men that night.'* The men complained that he often came in like that and Francis knew he would have to get someone else to do the job of cook. 'If the men didn't get their grub there was sure to be trouble.'

Graham used to come up every couple of months or so to see how they were getting on. He was not so bad at the beginning, but later on Jorge and Francis used to dread his arrival. He was so bumptious and loved to throw his weight around. *'He spoke Spanish, but with a very English accent, but was not ashamed or shy of it, like most of our race. He was always full of plans and ideas, directing Jorge and me about our work as if he was a general and we were his lieutenants.'*

Some days, when Francis had started the men on their daily jobs, he would come out and tell them all to do something completely different. He found himself resenting this, for he had left him in charge of the place and Francis felt he should have been consulted before he made these changes.

Time would usually be lost in the end and then he would say the men didn't work long enough and make another fuss. Francis would say that he didn't wish to presume that he knew more than him about the work, but that there were ways of setting about it.

*'One morning I had set a man to plough up a piece of land for a garden. He was using a small plough and a couple of horses. Out came Graham just as we were well started - all hell and bustle, insisting that the work should be done with one horse. The ploughman and I looked at one another and although I argued with Graham, it was useless. We had to untie the horse and try to plough with one. Of course it didn't work, and we had eventually to catch the other horse and continue as we had begun.*

*I merely give this as an example, but there were hundreds of instances. No doubt Graham's theory was perfect. He had plenty of letters after his name. But, when it came to practice, he should have kept his mouth shut.'*

But this was not his worst fault, unfortunately. He was also very fond of whisky and Francis had the embarrassing job of trying to hide a fellow-countryman from sight of the workmen.

*'I felt so thoroughly ashamed of him at times that naturally I lost all respect for him, and I fancied Jorge did too. A pity indeed that he was thus, for it was the only chance I had of speaking to an Englishman, and I came to loathe the sight of him, instead of enjoying his company and discussing the work good-naturedly.*

*I don't ever wish to assume that I didn't make mistakes, for surely I did. I'm no technical man, but our job was difficult, trying to grow crops with only twelve inches of rain a year. The climate too was disagreeable and the living far from luxurious, so that the one hope one had of existing, was a certain satisfaction in the work accomplished. But Graham did his best to make that a misery too, though he didn't entirely succeed.*

*He was very unpopular with the maté pot too* [a South American infused drink served from a hollowed gourd], *I noticed. He never joined in our circle as the communal maté was passed around, everyone taking his draw in turn. He preferred bringing one of his own and sticking to it. It was a small thing really I suppose, but it was just enough to make him a bad mixer and not one of us.'*

Perhaps Graham's only saving grace was that he did bring Francis and Jorge some good cooked ham and fruit, which were very welcome, and also tobacco for Francis. It was good wet English stuff for a pipe and not the dry, black kind that was smoked locally.

Several months had passed before Francis' bungalow was built. It was simply constructed with just two rooms and a kitchen. The company sent him up some odds and ends of furniture and it proved to be quite a comfortable little place. But the dust there was no avoiding.

**'My little grey home in the West' – Francis' newly built bungalow**

It entered everywhere if the wind was blowing at all. He tried plugging the windows with felt, but it was all hopeless. *'It was most uncanny how it got everywhere. You put your spoon into a plate of soup and it grated on the bottom of the plate. The cook's fault perhaps? But no, I've cooked for myself and had it the same.'*

The company gave him a boy to look after him, but the trouble was finding one. He tried three altogether, and at last gave up in despair and cooked for himself.

*'The first boy I had when I was settled in my bungalow at the farm was a young Italian. He was a character - full of talk and filthily dirty but I must admit he amused me, which I think was the only reason why I kept him so long. He told me all his history in broken Spanish, mingled with Italian. I used to laugh when he brought in the soup with a flourish, standing back with his dirty dishcloth on one arm, explaining how good it*

was. I nicknamed him 'Mussolini', though he was far from being his counterpart. He slept in the men's quarters, but would be at my bungalow most of the day, cooking and doing odd jobs and a bit of gardening.'

Yes, a garden was planned. Some plants were going to be sent up from one of the company's nurseries, and set around the house to make the place look a bit civilised. Francis found it interesting to watch the place grow. When he had first arrived at Foster there was practically nothing, but now it grew almost day-by-day, and this was one of the things that kept him going.

Various people had been enquiring about land up here too and the company would soon be sending some of them up to have a look round. Francis was told to push the place for all it was worth and he wondered if they would get any settlers. *'If only we could get a harvest and some results, it was quite possible that people would settle here and the railway would achieve its object in extending in this direction.'*

By the map, Ing. Foster was just about in the most central spot of the Argentine, situated halfway between the Atlantic coast and the Pacific on the Chilean side. Perhaps one day the company would extend the line right over to Chile if things went well up there, as they had on the Pacific Railway further North.

Francis had a 'christening party' at his house soon after he was settled in. He bought a young goat and planned to roast it out of doors. He chose a good evening for the party; the night before the 25th May, which was a national 'fiesta' and when no work would be done. They could lie quietly in bed all the next day if they liked.

He and Jorge spent an afternoon interviewing the storekeeper. They were down in his cellar looking over all the wines he had in stock. Francis suggested a bottled wine for the occasion as being more fitting than the usual barrelled stuff. *'We spent a long time there nosing around, and Alonso, the storekeeper took much interest in the affair, as he was one of the invited guests. We loaded a dozen bottles of something Spanish into the Ford, (Alonso assured us it was something extra special), and several litres of common wine. I also bought a couple of bottles of gin, together with some vermouth and cognac as well as some soda water - Alonso* had a small machine for making this. We likewise borrowed sundry glasses as my stock at the farm was very limited.

We borrowed a gramophone from the newly settled baker, who had also been invited, and some records. All tangos and guitarists of the real 'Criollo' type. Our only regret was we couldn't muster any women to come and dance with us.'

A table was rigged up on the veranda and the goat was cooked directly in front of the house. Jorge's boy was put in charge of this, as he had a reputation of being a good hand at a roast. It smelled delicious as it cooked over a huge fire, being soused now and again with spices from a bottle. It turned out to be excellent. It is no mean achievement to cook out of doors like this, as the carcass must be at least two and a half hours in cooking to be really done to a turn, and this one surely was.

It proved to be a very merry party. 'My special gin fizz was the cause of much comment and speculation, as no one knew just what it was. I assured them it was greatly appreciated by the 'Ingleses' and, sure enough, I very soon had to mix more. Our two bottles of gin disappeared like lightning, and we straight-way forgot all our troubles and set to on the roast goat. Jorge was to the fore, as usual on all festive occasions, and the police official came up with a friend. Then there was one of the contractors, Alonso the storekeeper and another one or two odd fellows - I think we were eight in all. Anyway, we cleared up the goat and drained the demijohn of wine. I can see them now, sitting in the firelight eating. It was a wonderful moonlight night though a little cold, and the trees behind them looked very vivid. These 'Caldene' trees looked so weird at night - stiff and stark and gnarled like oak, but without their dignity and beauty. A wonderful picture it made and I longed at that moment for someone to appreciate it with.'

Francis hadn't asked the Russian to join them whom he felt would have appreciated the scene, as he didn't think he would have fitted in with them, although he would have been a welcome visitor. It was Francis, however, who more often visited him, and he was very grateful for his company and that of his household.

It was really Jorge who started the horseplay. '*He was continually bantering Alonso and after one of his quips, Alonso picked up a soda-siphon and let fly at Jorge, soaking him well and truly. We then began to get uproarious and the surplus soda-siphons came into play. These didn't last long and someone suggested throwing Alonso into the water tank. The poor fellow was carried bodily out and we had got him right by the tank before the police official interfered and suggested he might be spared. We extorted a promise from him however, not to adulterate his brandy, and held him perilously near the water, before releasing him.*

*We thought a race to the village would end the evening appropriately - there were four cars present, and as I remained up at the farm, I was to be the starter. So we lined them up and I got my revolver - after much parting and thanks, I set them going with a shot in the air. They went down the farm road safely with a lot of roaring of engines, bawling hard at each other as they raced, with the dust rising in clouds behind them. Jorge won I believe, not because he had the fastest car, but because he was the one who knew the bumps in the road best.*

*I thought how we used to grumble at the woodsmen in the 'monte' when they got fresh on the nights after they received their pay. We made as much, if not more noise, that evening.*'

The next day being May 25th, and a 'fiesta', a horse race had been arranged for the afternoon. Francis was not feeling at his brightest after the celebrations the night before, and stayed in bed till late. His boy brought in his 'maté' at about eleven, which bucked him up no end.

The race was to be between their two best horses and two of Lesniffs. The Russian would ride one himself and his young son the other, whilst Francis and one of the men would ride two of theirs. Francis' horse was one he had more or less broken himself. It was much too heavy for speed, but he told Lesniff he'd run it just for the sport.

When he eventually climbed out of bed, he got on his horse and rode off to the village to see Jorge. He was wandering about his kitchen in pyjamas with a greatcoat over them, and seemed none the worse for the previous night's debauch. Francis had a maté with Jorge, and then rode on to the Lesniffs. The storekeeper had hung out several flags to celebrate the 'fiesta'. The High Street with its few buildings and the station all decorated with flags, looked very comic.

The Lesniffs were in excellent form, but very agitated about a shot they had heard the night before, and a lot of shouting. Francis put them at ease by telling them it was only their festivities and perfectly innocuous fun. He really had no idea they had made such a row. Even though the night was still, it was hard to believe the noise would have carried all that way - it was at least two miles between the farms.

The Lesniffs pressed him to stay to lunch, but he had to refuse. The men were having a special roast and had asked Francis to join them as it was a special occasion. Lesniff promised to be round after lunch for the race, and assured Francis that he would win easily. Francis was pretty sure that he would beat him, but was not so sure about his other man. His horse looked more useful and, being his own, was well looked after. He hurried back as he didn't want to keep the men waiting for their lunch.

When he returned he found it was a lamb they had cooking over a fire, and they were waiting for him before starting on it. They had several litres of wine, which Francis had bought for them, so they were all eager to set to. They looked very clean, having shaved and donned clean neckerchiefs for the occasion. The lamb was jolly good, being almost as succulent as the goat the night before.

Lesniff and his son arrived after lunch. One of the 'peons' [day-labourers] was giving them all a song on a very battered guitar when they arrived. They tried to press a mug of wine on him, but he refused and was eager to be started on the race. So they fetched their horses and went off to the starting point. The course was the main road leading to the farm. Jorge arrived just as they were getting down there, so he acted as starter, and the police official who accompanied him, took up his position as judge at the winning post.

### Francis ready for the race

The real Argentinian race was not started with a pistol shot, but the competitors, usually only two, would gallop up to the starting point. If both men were ready, they would shout at one another to go - if not, they returned and tried again. Francis had watched them start for ages like that, often returning a score of times before they were both satisfied and were off. They were having none of this however, so they lined up, and Jorge let off his revolver and they let their horses go.

'The course was about three quarters of a mile long, and we were pretty level for the first hundred yards. Then mine dropped behind - I knew it would. My weight alone was enough to keep the animal back, and besides that, the horse was much too thickset for speed. I could see it was going to be a near thing for the others. The three of them were going neck-to-neck and hell-for-leather, and the dust was flying right up into my eyes.

Lesniff won, but our man was only about a neck behind, and the Lesniffs' boy a length behind him. I came in an 'also ran' and was cheered loudly when I reached the winning post, the others having arrived some seconds before.'

Francis was invited back to the Lesniffs for tea and supper afterwards, and passing through the village on the way, he saw two of the carters having a wager - both a little the worse for drink. It appeared that one had bet the other that his best donkey could pull better than any belonging to the other. They both brought forward their champion animals and, setting them back to back, harnessed them together. On the word, the two animals started to pull against one another. It was an amazing sight to watch, though it struck Francis as rather cruel.

'The manner in which the donkeys got down to it was uncanny. The animals put all their weight into it, as if they knew. Just a steady pull till at length one began to give, and although the owner urged it frantically, it was unable to recover itself and was forced backwards for several yards. The champion won his bet, but it was not a pleasure to watch. The men never once laid a whip to their donkeys, but merely coaxed them and it was amazing how the animals responded.'

Lesniff, however, thought it was a great joke, and laughed about it all the way back to his farm. He was not content until he had explained it all in Russian to his wife.

About the time Francis moved up to the farm, the well there was just being completed. Water had been reached some hundred and twenty metres down and they seemed to have a satisfactory supply.

They started drawing it in a most primitive method. A cowhide fashioned like a bucket was attached to the end of a rope, and this was arranged on a pulley over the well. At the other end of the rope were two horses. A man was mounted on one, and they pulled each skinful to the top of the well, where a man emptied it into an Australian tank that had just been constructed.

The scene reminded Francis of biblical days *'for such a primitive method was indeed rare in these modern days.'* They were not long with this arrangement however, for an engine and pump were soon installed, and later, a windmill. But it was by this same bucket and horse method that all the wells on the farm were dug out.

'A man would go down the well, pick-axing his way down. He filled the cowhide with the nibble, and when it had been drawn to the daylight by the horses, his mate at the top would unload it. Thus they proceeded, taking about six months or more to reach water, and every day risking their lives. It only needed a small stone to drop on the head of the man below to kill him, for a stone falling some hundred and twenty odd metres would soon gather speed.'

Most of the men working on these wells were Basques. They would go up and down the well while they were working on it, in the same cowhide, putting their feet into it and holding the rope in their hands, but it was a dangerous occupation.

'A man who was working on our farm told us how he once got stuck halfway down. I think he had gone down to fix some boards into a crumbling portion of the side, when the horses at the other end became restless. The consequence was that the cow skin disappeared from beneath the fellow down the well, and he was left clinging for dear life to the side'.

Another strange thing about the wells was that the water always came up warm. On cold mornings it could be seen steaming as it was being brought up. Later, when they had installed a mill, they built a larger Australian tank, where they used to bathe in the summer.

**The pump house, windmill and Australian tank**

**Francis having a bath – picture taken from the windmill**

*'This was very pleasant - being able to plunge into cool water after a dusty day's work. We valued it greatly, always keeping the tank as full as possible. It was about six feet deep and about twenty feet in diameter, so we could have a comfortable bathe. Though the bottom was earth, it never troubled us much, as it was fairly firm, and not soft mud. Many a time I have been bathing in our tank when the men who had been working in the 'monte' would come and ask permission to take a load away - for drinking too.'*

In the village there was an old Spaniard who owned a water cart and a few horses. He would cart water to these men, charging at a rate of a dollar a barrel, which gives some idea of the respect they had for water. And as for rain - they waited and watched for days for it and were constantly disappointed. The crops would wither and wilt and the soil turn to powder underfoot, before a drop would come. Then, maybe, one night there would be a heavy shower, and the following day a terrible wind would dry it up in twenty-four hours. But the joy of feeling that rain when it did come...

*'I've stood purposely in the rain at times and got soaked through and enjoyed it. The dryness of the atmosphere was excessive. One's nails would become brittle and skin dry up. One's very self would become dry, both physically and mentally.'*

Actually the annual rainfall was sufficient for dry farming, but what beat them was the infrequency of the showers. Given the right quantity at the right time, all might have been well, but what usually happened was nearly half the rainfall would come just as they were harvesting, and the greater part of it would be wasted.

They did, however, get some astonishing results with certain types of wheat, considering the climate. Although the results could not possibly have shown a profit, the data collected and experiments that were carried out were not worthless, and provided a great source of interest in the work.

How interesting it must have been for the Bell family too back in Suffolk, reading Francis' letters about the heat, the dry dust, the terrible winds and the constant lack of rain. Being in the southern hemisphere all the seasons were reversed, winter being from June to August and summer from December to March with temperatures sometimes soaring to 40C. How longingly too Francis must have studied his father's photos of the deep snow recorded at Seabrooks in January 1927, and yearned for the cool English climate and the crisp coldness of that snowy January.

**Francis sewing grass seed on his 21st birthday, 17th February 1927**

The one bright spot in Francis' existence of course, was when he and Jorge could get off to Buenos Aires for weekends every two or three months. He used to make his need for a bath the excuse for going to town, but later, when they had a plentiful supply of water and had fitted up a primitive bathroom, he had to think of more honest excuses.

He and Jorge had free passes on the railway, so the journey didn't cost very much. It was when they arrived that the spending began. *'After all, with three months' salary in your pocket and a rather caged existence during that period, can a fellow be blamed for letting things go a bit during a couple of nights in the city.'*

Francis used to enjoy the journey too, once they had finished the dusty part, which was from Ing. Foster to the junction at Pico. From

Pico it was comfortable. They boarded the train there at about five o'clock and arrived in the city next morning about nine. They could dine well en route and had a comfortable sleeper to turn into. Then there were often people they knew on the train, engineers and others.

Naturally the return was not so bright. *'But one felt more sober then, what with a depleted pocket and a rather weak-kneed feeling for a day or two afterwards!'*

Francis and Jorge used to look forward to these jaunts. They would sit for hours discussing what they should do and what they had done. Jorge had a mother and father in town, where he always used to stay. They were French and Francis did meet them on one occasion. As soon as ever they reached Buenos Aires, however, they had to go to the office and be criticised by the Boss. He would ask a lot of silly questions and keep them hanging about, whilst they were itching to be off.

Francis used to put up at a hotel called Dirty Dick's – at least that was the name it always went by. It was mostly English people who stayed there, and these for the most part were fellows like himself, who came up for a few nights from the camps. So he usually met a pretty cheerful crowd there.

**Caricature of Francis at Dirty Dick's, Buenos Aires**

*'The trouble with being shut off at Foster for a month or two, was when one did break out for a weekend, one naturally tried to make up for lost time. A fortnight's normal existence, and then the longing for another weekend in town would get hold of one again. Until that longing was gratified, you were not satisfied, and so it went on. If one stopped to think about it, it could have seemed a rather pointless existence, but one didn't. It's all very well in theory, to be living where 'men are men', but when it came to the point it was very futile and I found myself*

*inclined to get narrow and cabbage-like. There was not much comfort either, with the wind and the dust blowing every other day. And nothing to see, and nowhere to go for an evening's relief from the monotony. If I had not been interested in the work, I would not have stayed long. Though in those days I knew I should be thankful to have a job and a roof over my head.'*

Signs of spring at Ing. Foster were slight. The trees, it is true, would put on fresh leaves and the grass grow to a certain extent, but the green was such a dull colour that you could hardly notice the change. The few birds that inhabited the district would become more visible. *'One was called the 'Calundria', which had a very pretty song. Besides these there were the common sparrows, which always seem to follow man wherever he goes. There was also a pretty little white bird called the 'Viuda Blanca', the white widow. Why it had this name I never knew, for there surely must have been an occasional widower as well as a widow. But the real sign of the coming of summer was the parrots. Quite a common green variety they were, and if one caught them young from the nest, they were easily tamed. At one time I had several about my bungalow, and a nuisance they were, although they made a bit of company. Mussolini my cook, used to take more trouble about feeding them than he did me! Those and a mouldy dog he picked up seemed to be his chief delights in life.'*

Francis had tried eating parrots on one or two occasions, but they weren't too good, being a very coarse, tasteless meat. They also used to catch an animal called a Peludo on moonlight nights. They were a type of armadillo, and were very tasty when well cooked. The meat was rather similar to pork, with perhaps a little more flavour. It did however have rather disgusting habits.

*'The 'Peludo' lived on rotten carcasses and was a dirty feeder. We often caught them running out of the carcass of a dead horse or a cow, yet in spite of their habits, they were none the less tasty for that! There were two varieties of armadillos to be found there and we would eat both kinds. The other was called the 'Molita' and was the smaller and cleaner of the two. It was vegetarian, feeding only off grass and vegetation and made very good eating.*

*Being so small though, one had to catch several of them to make a satisfying meal.'*

Several loads of plants and young trees had been sent up to plant around the farm during the winter months and most of these now looked fairly promising. It involved a fair bit of watering of course, but it did begin to look as though the desert might bloom if they persevered. The wheats too, were looking fairly well, considering the hurry in which they had been sown. Some varieties of maize were also showing signs of health, and the general aspect certainly cheered them up at that time.

**Experimental wheat plots**

Francis had managed to get the work more regular by this time, and the men were working to a timetable. The only snag was the old horse-keeper. Francis knew that as soon as ever they got the farm fenced round and had sufficient feed for the horses, he would have to go. He had taken him off the cook-house work, and got another boy to do the cooking for the men and that arrangement seemed more satisfactory.

The new cook was a dab hand at catching sparrows. He would catch about fifty of them and make them into a pudding. He was an Italian and said that this was a great dish in his own country. He seemed to be a good cook and the kitchen looked much cleaner than when the old fellow was there. Francis thought he was a bit of what they called 'Compadron'. In other words, he liked show and swank.

There were continual but inevitable rows amongst the men as they had to pay for their own food which was a very unsatisfactory arrangement. At the end of the month when they drew their money, they had to settle up, and there was nearly always trouble.

'I heard such a row in the cook-house one evening that I went to see what the matter was. I believe I was just in time to stop them from fighting. It was the usual row over the paying for the stores, each afraid he would be paying for more than his share!

I calmed them down and settled it for them, going through the bills with them and doing what I could. Then one of them suggested I should do their accounts regularly for them and collect the money from each and pay the bills. They all seemed to agree to this, so I had no alternative, and anyway I would have done it for the sake of peace, even though it had nothing to do with me. They were just like children, these men, and I suppose they found the arithmetic too much! At least they all agreed they were feeding much better now owing to the new cook in the kitchen.'

Francis would say that he treated the men too humanely really, and that Jorge's methods were much more effective. But he could never work himself into a passion over such small provocation. Jorge got into such rages sometimes, that the men were afraid to come near him, and even Francis wouldn't talk to him when he was like that. He envied Jorge his gift of managing labour. He just hadn't got his temper, which had a lot to do with it. He was always inclined to be too kind. He knew it was a weakness, but couldn't help it.

There was only one occasion when he did really lose his temper with a man and got his revolver out, and that was with one of the cooks they had. 'This fellow had been pilfering the men's stores and taking it off to some woman he kept in the village. We caught him at it one day - I told him to clear out in half-an-hour and he turned a bit nasty. It was a good thing that I didn't lose control altogether. He annoyed me so much that I could have plugged him with the greatest of pleasure, but I was glad I didn't afterwards.'

It was not long before the company sent up a prospective settler to visit the farm. Mr Piludski arrived by train one afternoon and to their surprise spoke English. By his name, Francis thought him to be a Pole or a Russian, but though he must have had some Polish blood in him to get a name like that, he was American. *'He was a regular Tom Mix of a fellow, complete with sombrero and all his belongings tied up in a spotted handkerchief!'* Francis and Jorge took him round to have a look at the settlement that afternoon, and as he wanted to stay for a day or two, Francis offered him a shakedown at his bungalow.

*'He was an interesting fellow to talk to, once you had got over the American accent. He had tumbled about all over the world and knew quite a lot about farming, though he didn't seem over-impressed by this district.'*

Francis took him along to see Lesniff and they conversed in German together. Francis had tipped the wink to Lesniff about this, and asked him to be very optimistic about the land and what a fortune could be made out of it. Judging from the conversation, he thought that Lesniff did his best, *'though heaven knows he had little reason to be optimistic.'*

*'The visitor seemed quite impressed by our wheats though, especially the experimental plots. They were all coming on quite well after some rain we had a little while back, and didn't look at all bad.'*

That evening Piludski saw Francis' revolver and showed him how one ought to shoot. Francis stood three bottles up for him at about forty yards distance, and he knocked the necks off them all. It seemed a clever feat to Francis who could only succeed in breaking one out of three, at about thirty yards range.

He took Piludski round the farm the next morning on horseback and he seemed very interested in it all. He thought the company was charging too much for the land though, and so did Francis, though it wouldn't have done to say so. Anyway, they were prepared to lend a big mortgage on it for a period of thirty years, so that should have helped a would-be buyer.

Piludski was very interested in the well-sinking. One of the men working on the job, showed them a fossil they had found, about forty yards down. It looked to Francis like a 'Viscacha' [a rodent of the Argentine Pampas closely related to a chinchilla], having the same shaped body, head and teeth. It was evidently some prehistoric relic, as it was impossible to account for it otherwise.

Piludski and Francis went for another round that afternoon, with Jorge in his Ford. Francis took his gun as usual. They always hoped to bag a partridge or something, but seldom got the chance. However, that day they were luckier. They shot three. A partridge was such a luxury and a welcome change of diet. On the way home they ran into a flock of ostriches wandering about the dirt track. Jorge let his old Ford go full tilt out into the middle of them, and Francis sat tight in the back and shot a brace. It was rather good shooting as it was difficult to aim from a car, going at forty miles an hour on a very bumpy road.

The birds were both dead when they picked them up. Francis and Jorge took the skin off their necks for tobacco pouches, and pulled a few of the best feathers off them, then let the carcasses lie as they fell. Before they left them, however, one of the carters came by with a load of wood, and whipping out his knife, cut two legs off one of the birds. He told them he was going to eat them. Francis was amazed.

*'Personally I thought the meat beastly. It was very coarse and of a peculiar flavour; not at all pleasing to the palate. I didn't think these men would have eaten it, but apparently they did, as this fellow seemed quite pleased with his joints. The eggs were worth finding in the spring though, as one went further than a dozen hens' eggs.'*

Piludski was rather enjoying himself and said that he was sorry to be leaving the next day. He and Francis called in at the store that night, and he got very talkative after he had downed several cognacs 'to keep the cold out', as he put it. In fact he kept refusing to come home, until Francis told him he was going without him, which brought him to his senses. He turned in soon after supper that night. The riding all day had made him sleepy he said, but Francis knew it was the cognac that had had the desired effect.

One afternoon when Francis went over to see Lesniff, he found him puzzling over his Ford tractor. He couldn't get it to start. So Francis took a turn at trying to crank it and after a while they got it going. The carburettor was blocked and that seemed to be its only trouble.

He had finished sowing his wheat and Francis hoped he would have a good harvest that year. Every time he saw him, he felt sorry for him. He was so impractical, like a fish out of water. He seemed fitter to converse in a salon, than to grapple with a tractor. Francis didn't suppose he had lifted anything heavier than a pen before he left Russia, and now he had to shift for himself. It was a similar story with his wife. He was quite sure she had never touched a cooking utensil before, but now she was highly practical from the domestic point of view.

He didn't stay to tea that day, though he was pressed, but arranged for some more chess in a day or two. Madame gave him some bread to take home – one loaf of black bread made from rye. He didn't care much for it, but took it with many thanks. It was glutinous stuff, and one mouthful he found, was a meal in itself.

Francis had taken on a man to do the fencing that had to be done. The fellow had been working at the saw-mill, and he had told him he could come along to the farm, when he had done there. He'd been told he was quite a good worker and as there was a good deal of fencing to be done there would be work for him at the farm for a month or two.

So Francis spent one afternoon doing the work of an agrimensor [Spanish for a surveyor] marking out lines for the fencer to start work. It was no easy job as the fence line was about half a mile long. Jorge came up to help him. He was used to the job. He had had a lot of it to do when they were initially clearing the land in the forest. As yet they only had a boundary fence all round the land. Now, seeing most of it was clear, they were going to divide it up into a dozen different lots, to facilitate the growing of different classes of wheat. It was quite a long job, measuring and marking the different points where the fences had to run. The problem was if you started a little out in your calculations, you found yourself a long way out at the finish.

A good deal of harvest machinery had been sent up in the early summer, much more than they were likely to need for the harvest, and also a new Diesel tractor. It was a Swedish company that supplied this, and a very decent young Swede called Scofter, came up to hand it over and put it in working order.

**'Our new Diesel tractor with two ploughs'– Jorge walking behind**

*'I gave him a shakedown in the office and he stayed two nights with me, and I was very pleased to have him. Funny how different these northern folk are from the Latin blood so prevalent about here. We talked and drank beer till quite late into the night. He told me he was engaged to an Italian girl and had good prospects in his business. He deserved them, for he was a good fellow.'*

He wanted Francis to look him up when he next went to town, so that they could spend an evening together. He, like others, wondered how Francis could stick it up here all alone. Francis argued that to live in town on his salary would be misery. Whilst here, he was free from monetary troubles for the most part. But Scofter refused to accept his point of view, saying it was like being buried alive.

*'Though I did not live in luxury by any means, I did prefer this existence a hundred times to one in a hot city. At least when I went to town,*

*I had money to spend and would enjoy myself for a couple of evenings to the full. An existence in the city, counting every cent before one spent it, would have incurred much worry!'*

As they had no mechanic on the place at this time, Scofter instructed Francis in the workings of the tractor, so that when they got a man Francis could show him the ins and outs of it. It had been an enjoyable couple of days. *'I was sorry to say goodbye to Scofter. He was good company and a good fellow.'*

Francis used to go ploughing with the new tractor himself quite a lot in the slack season. He'd get all the men started on their jobs and then take the tractor and plough for an hour or two, if it wasn't too far from home. He didn't like to go off for too long a stretch at a time, as the men would soon get to know if he wasn't about and slack off in consequence. In some ways, it was actually quite relaxing and made a change from his usual routine. Later when they were once again left without a mechanic for one of the tractors, and they were particularly busy, he took it on for a bit.

*'I rather enjoyed ploughing with the tractor, though one would think it was a monotonous job. I ploughed a mile stretch at a time, with the dust rising all the while, but there was a certain fascination about it, especially as one got to know the machine.'*

Several acres of alfalfa had been planted on one side of the farm, and there had been terrible trouble keeping a herd of goats off it. Francis thought they belonged to some of the woodcutters working nearby. He had it fenced round with wire, but they still got in. It needed a good fence to stop a hungry goat, especially with so little else for them to eat. He got pretty fed up with these goats and having found out who owned them, sent word to tell the owner to look after them. When he saw them in the alfalfa again one afternoon, he told his boy Mussolini to go and scare them off. *'You can shoot them if you like, but just get them out of there!'*

Sure enough he did shoot one. He took the gun from Francis' room, and came back with a young kid slung over his shoulder.

Francis had only meant him to just pepper them a bit and frighten them off, but Mussolini had done the job properly. He did get a bit scared when Francis told him the owner would probably come and have a great row with him. He never came, however, and they ate the goat and enjoyed it, and the rest of the herd never appeared on the alfalfa again.

He found Mussolini one day, bargaining with a dirty looking villain in the yard. He was trying to sell him some pork. Pork being quite a rarity, he did good business both in the men's kitchen and with Francis. Francis told Mussolini that he didn't mind him buying some, provided he knew how to cook it. Mussolini was deeply offended and took it as an insult to his cuisine. So, they had a deal with the vendor and bought various parts of the pig, including the head, which the cook assured Francis, he would serve up 'deluxe.'

Francis looked forward to 'pig's head deluxe' with eager anticipation, thinking it ought to be something very special and very out of the ordinary. He was in for a big shock. Coming in for 'grub' one day at midday, Mussolini brought Francis lunch with his usual flourish. To Francis horror, it consisted of the entire pig's head they had purchased. Mussolini had cooked it whole, and put it down in front of Francis, the whole head grinning malevolently at him. He was frightfully pleased about it. Francis didn't really know how to start it, so had a cut at a cheek. It tasted more or less as pork should taste, so he didn't complain, but he hated its teeth. *'They looked as if they were going to bite you at any moment!'* He told Mussolini that they had better keep it till it was cold, and then they could hack pieces off it for breakfast. In the course of a few days they did manage to take the smile off its face.

Francis used to see a good deal of Lesniff, his Russian friend, in the early days. He went round there once or twice a week, usually on Sundays, as they used to be deadly dull. Except during harvest, they didn't work on Sundays, and he was pretty bored with the day generally, as there was nowhere to go and nothing to do.

*'I was glad to be able to go round to Lesniff's in the afternoon. I would go there about teatime and stay till ten or eleven in the evening. They were as pleased to see me as I was to see them, for they never saw anyone else and must have got tired of their own company.'*

Lesniff and he would play two or three games of chess, and were quite well matched, which was a good thing. Lesniff won more games than Francis did, but Francis would always give him a good fight. They must have discussed every subject under the sun. The Russians were great talkers and Francis got to know a lot about their past life. He found them charming and cultured people, but very simple and unworldly. *'I marvelled sometimes at their simplicity, and I am afraid I often showed the red rag to the bull by mentioning the Jews or the Bolshevists. Either of these never failed to raise an argument, and the Lesniffs refused to see two sides to a question. When the discussion became too heated, we would adjourn to look at his crops and return to supper, which his wife had prepared for us.'* They did try to play bridge once, but it was rather difficult, as Francis had to call his bid in Russian, and got very muddled. He never cared for bridge at the best of times and they didn't try again.

They had a colleague of Lesniff's living with them at this time; a doctor apparently, who was shortly departing for Europe. They told Francis a queer story of how a man working on the farm had cut himself very badly. This doctor had naturally attended to him, dressing his wounds with what little remedies he had at hand. Three or four days later the police official came along to see the doctor, and told him that as he was not a qualified doctor in this country, he should not have attended to the injured man. He then tried a little blackmail, threatening to expose the doctor unless he paid a certain sum for hush money. Anything more preposterous could hardly be imagined, as the doctor had merely done the humane thing, which anyone would have done. Luckily the Russians got angry with the police official, who saw there was more likely to be trouble than money forthcoming, so cleared off with as good a grace as he could.

The Russians were flabbergasted that anyone should have tried such a trick, but they were such innocent people and not up to the ways of the world, least of all in this corrupt country. Francis often wondered what sort of world they must have enjoyed in their own country before their exile. *'They must have had so much money that they never gave it a thought, and they could never have come in touch with the business of life and living. They seemed so impractical and so surprised at everything that was quite commonplace to us. Like travellers on a trip for the first time, seeing new sights and encountering new wonders at every turn. Lesniff was always telling me about someone or something which he thought extraordinary and which to me seemed quite natural. I supposed he would never be able to shake off his old self. I liked him immensely, but he was rather childish at times and I could quite see why Jorge thought him a little mad.'*

One Sunday, just before harvest, it was very hot, and Jorge, Francis and a police official from the next village of Arizona, went off in the Ford to a lagoon. It was due west of them, and a good sixty kilometres ride on the roughest of tracks, but they looked forward to it for days ahead. The lagoon had the reputation of never having been dry. It was also salt water, though horses would drink it at times. There were wild duck to be had there too, so they loaded the car up with some food and shotguns, and off they went.

The police official was called 'Pascual' and a *'good fellow'* in Francis' eyes. He did a lot of good in his district, which was more than could be said for the man they had at Foster.

*'We arrived about midday and I must say it was a wonderful sight for us to see water in this fashion. In Ing. Foster we would seldom see a puddle, so you can imagine how we enjoyed this stretch of water. We had undressed almost before the car had stopped, and the three of us went running into the water stark naked. Not that it mattered, for we never saw a sign of a living soul all day!'*

There was thick mud at the bottom of the water, and it was very shallow. They waded right across, which must have been about two or three hundred yards, but never got out of their depth. Quite a number of duck, some swans, and a flock of flamingos were disturbed, but they didn't trouble about trying to shoot these yet. It was enough for them just to be in the water. *We splashed about like children paddling in the sea, and would then come out and lie on the edge in the sun and dry. We had brought no towels with us, and didn't need them, for the sun soon dried us. We cooked our grub and ate it, just as we were, and never thought of putting on our clothes again till evening, when we planned a campaign to shoot some duck.'*

Francis told Jorge that he would go and stand in a spot where they had watched them flying, while Jorge waited with Pascual around where they would land on the water. Jorge wouldn't believe that Francis would be able to kill them flying. He liked to be sure of them on the water. However, he was wrong, for Francis bagged several as they came over, and also brought down a wild swan and a flamingo, that he would regret shooting for the rest of his life.

'*I didn't know why I killed the flamingo, for they are pretty and harmless creatures, and useless to eat. It came gliding so temptingly overhead that I couldn't resist it, though I was sorry afterwards. I did skin it however, and a wonderful sight it was. I still have the skin, although the colours have faded and it hasn't the brilliance of the living bird.'*

They returned home with quite a number of duck and the swan, and were very well pleased with the day. They went back there several times, but somehow that first day always seemed the best.

'*I shall never forget how we revelled in that filthy, muddy water. We enjoyed it a hundred times better than the most select bathing pool. One's environment does indeed make one appreciate the things one lacks. I only recall that Sunday's journey to the lagoon because it figures as one of my happiest days in that part of the world. We three seemed so care-free that day, and as we bathed and lay in the sun, nothing seemed to matter. Perhaps the solitude helped, but I always recall it with the greatest pleasure.'*

They planned to make a grand feast with the wild swan Francis had shot, and Jorge took great pains in cooking it, but it was a big disappointment. Francis had always imagined a swan to be a delicacy, but after tasting it vowed that he never wanted to eat one again. It seemed so pungent. He only ate a little piece, but the taste lingered in his mouth all day, and not a particularly pleasant taste at that. The fault was not in the cooking either, for Jorge was an excellent cook. Francis felt that he could have got a job as a chef anywhere. Where he picked it up from Francis didn't know, except that Jorge had roamed the whole country from the heat of the Chaco to the cold of Patagonia, and must have learned the art during his wanderings. Just before their first harvest, there were three days of the most frightful wind and dust.

**The lagoon where Francis shot the flamingo, and spent one of his happiest days**

The first day it was so bad that no-one could get about at all. The men were doing odd jobs in the barns and everyone was thoroughly miserable. Francis fell to cursing Mussolini about the dust in the food, but knew it really wasn't his fault. It was the sort of weather that put everyone in a bad temper and grumbling at someone relieved matters a little. It was most depressing when these winds set in, and the clouds of dust that accompanied them made one wonder where it all came from. The growing corn kept a certain amount of it down, but still it came, and entered everywhere.

At nights when it blew in this fashion, Francis never troubled to get into bed or undress, but would just lie down and get what sleep he could. If you passed a cloth over a table to clean it, in a couple of minutes it would be covered with dust again. You could go nowhere and do nothing except read and then one's eyes would smart with the dust and become bloodshot, and one's teeth would grind grit. Sleep was the best remedy, but it was difficult to sleep twenty-four hours on end.

The wind at this time of the year was hot too, and burnt everything up as it came. The poor plants and young trees, which they had been so pleased with, were in a sorry state. Some of them were showing their roots, the wind having blown the soil from around them, and the leaves that they had, were shredded and tattered by the driven sand. After all their work and hope, it was such a depressing sight. The wheats, which a few days before had been about 'milk' ripe, were dried up and beginning to shale out.

But worst of all was the maize crop. This had looked so very promising, sown a little thick perhaps for this dry zone, but the plants had looked strong and healthy. After the 'temporale' it looked as though it had been passed through an oven. Francis would never have believed that the winds could have caused such devastation in less than a week, had he not seen it with his own eyes.

It was therefore, in a rather depressed spirit, that they started harvest. A mechanic had come up to take over the new tractor and large harvest machines, while the smaller binders were worked with horses. All the experimental plots Francis harvested by hand, with a couple of men. This was quite a business, as the sheaves all had to bear labels and great care had to be taken not to get so much as an ear mixed.

Graham came up for a couple of days just to see things were going according to plan. There was a lot of fuss as usual, and more whisky than there should have been. He got very drunk one evening, and instead of staying indoors, would parade about the place. Francis was furious. *'I don't say I never got drunk in Foster, for conditions at times were very conducive to alcohol. But I guarantee that neither Graham, nor any of the workmen, ever saw me in that condition.'*

He had it out with Graham that evening, and told him that if he must get drunk up here, he might keep out of sight. *'I tried hard on occasion to save the man's face, but got so fed up with him at length, that I gave it up. My cook boy would come laughing away in the morning, telling me how tipsy the Boss was. Well, that is a bit awkward to deal with, so in the end I didn't try to.'*

Graham came up twice during the harvest, and on one occasion he brought the editor of the Company's magazine. The man was a German-American. He was very good company and Francis enjoyed his visit. He stayed for about a week, though Graham wanted him to return with himself, the day after his arrival. He had come to do some photographing and to write up some propaganda for the place. The Company owned a lot of the land and as their ultimate object was to colonise the area, they were trying to get people to take up the farms. Lesniff had done this, getting a mortgage from them on easy terms. Jorge and Francis had some great fun going about with this fellow while he photographed things, and they had many a good laugh together.

The new mechanic Francis had got was proving to be a pretty useful fellow at his job and knew how to manage machinery. The trouble was he was *'a rather bad-blooded sort, a Uruguayan by nationality'*, and Francis soon noticed that he became boss over the men too. That didn't matter; he was good at his job, which was the main thing.

Towards the end of harvest Francis would go with him on the harvest machine and sew up the bags. They would take it in turns to drive the tractor sometimes, for it can be a monotonous job on a hot day, with plenty of dust about. When Graham was down, Francis would often do this, as he preferred to be out of the way.

When they had finished cutting their own wheat, they went and did some for Lesniff. *'These big harvesting machines could cover the ground, and Lesniff was very grateful for the help. We only charged him a nominal figure for doing the work.'*

**Harvest, using the tractor-drawn mechanical harvester**

Often in the heat of the day, it was difficult getting about the machine for greasing up, as the metal got so hot. It even came through the soles of your shoes, though of course the soles were only rope. A singlet, a hat, a pair of trousers and rope-soled shoes were all they used to wear in the summer. Francis was only too well aware of the dangers of baring himself in the sun too rapidly, having suffered some agonising sun-burn early on. Interestingly the few native Argentines they had working for them always used to wear their shirts well buttoned up, and a scarf around their necks even in the hottest weather.

Being an experimental station, they had numbers of different varieties of wheat and each little piece would have to be cut with a binder and stacked separately. It was a terrible fiddle and the men thought them quite mad. The machine had to be thoroughly cleaned before starting the next piece and Francis always had to be there to see they didn't make a mess of things or take any short cuts. The men's idea of harvest was to begin and get finished as soon as possible. As for cutting little plots by hand, they thought it was a great joke, until their own backs ached with the stooping. Francis ended up putting two

Italians on that job, because they had been more used to intensive cultivation at home.

As a harvest, it was a failure. They consoled themselves by the reflection that it was the first year, and they hadn't had time to prepare the land properly; it had suffered from the lack of rain, which they didn't realise at the time was to be the usual thing up there.

There was quite a lot of trouble over the men at harvest too. In most places they did the harvest on a piecework system. The more they did, the more they earned. But here that was quite impossible. The row was eventually settled by giving them a bonus when the harvest was finished, but it was not really a very satisfactory way of doing things.

Just after harvest, Francis had a final row with Mussolini and kicked him out. Perhaps it relieved his frustration and depression about the poor harvest. Mussolini had really become impossible. *'He had worn one vest all the summer and never changed it. You could actually smell him every time he came near and his cooking was pretty appalling too.'* They had taken on a couple of Russian emigrants for the harvest and one looked quite respectable. He assured Francis that he could cook, so he took him on.

He certainly was an improvement on Mussolini, but his really strong point was as a barber. He used to cut Francis' hair quite regularly and even offered to shave him too, though Francis drew the line at that. As a matter of fact, shaving had become a rather promiscuous affair with him.

*'I used to try and grow beards and moustaches at odd moments. I would let my beard grow for a few weeks and then suddenly shave it off, only to start again a week later. This seemed to relieve the monotony of life here somewhat, though what the men thought of my changing appearance I never knew.'*

Thus he lived, working, sleeping and eating, with an occasional trip to Buenos Aires to look forward to, and a weekly visit to his friend Lesniff. And then, one day, the Boss arrived and dropped a bombshell on them.

It appeared that he was sending another fellow along to take charge of everything. He was going to live on the experimental farm, but was to take charge of all the work up there, and he and Jorge were to be under him to do his bidding.

'I quite understood the idea, especially as far as the experimental farm was concerned. There was a lot of technical laboratory work to be done and I had no experience of this. However, I didn't relish the idea. I asked him if there was anything I had done for which he could blame me. But he explained that I was not a technical man with a laboratory education. After harvest, there would be the various crossings of different breeds of wheat, and other experimental work to be done. With this I could not argue, for technical knowledge I had none.'

Francis did argue, however, that if Graham could but spend a day or two up there, and give him a start with the detailed work, he could have easily picked it up. However, Graham said that he didn't have the time, so that was that. Francis faced the change with some trepidation.

'Perhaps I should have been glad to have company up here, but the unknown rather frightened me. I had become used to living alone, and was not anxious to share my solitude with another. When two people live alone in this fashion, there is nearly always trouble. They are bound to get on each other's nerves. When one is alone and feeling on edge, there is only the furniture to break and thin air to curse at. But if there is another present, it is quite different and puts a constraint on things. Those frightful winds we used to get were very trying at times. I wondered what would happen with two of us cooped up together in a room for days, with the dust choking us.'

Jorge too was very fed up about the whole idea. The new man being sent up was a German, and he had a particular dislike for that race. However, they could do nothing but wait and see. They had been on their own for over a year, got the farm up and running from absolutely nothing and neither liked the idea of someone else being brought in. So in order to boost their spirits, in classic style, Jorge and Francis decided to have a final farewell 'fiesta' to their independence. It was arranged for Francis' birthday, the 17th of February. This fell in a week or two's time.

*'Jorge and I made big preparations for the 'fiesta' on my birthday. Once again we ransacked Alonso's store. We borrowed crockery and glasses from him and had Jorge's boy up at the bungalow all day, preparing things. We had managed to get hold of a lamb, as well as a turkey, and prepared to roast them both. One might think that would be plenty for about ten of us, but believe me, there wasn't much left, when we had done with it.'*

**Ready for the party – Jorge centre with Macchi in his pinstripes**

All the old friends came, including the two police officials, and the chemist from about thirty miles distant. Of course they had Alonso the storekeeper and one or two others, but Francis would never forget how incongruous Macchi the chemist looked. He was immaculately dressed in Piccadilly striped trousers and dark coat, and a very neat collar and tie. Jorge and Francis of course, just wore their usual things, a pair of trousers and a shirt, with a scarf round the neck. Macchi, however, was on top form, and kept everyone roaring with laughter. He came out with joke after joke, until he faded out later in the evening. The poor chap had drunk a bit too much and was horribly ill. Jorge dumped him in the back of his car, and left him there until they had done with their merrymaking. Macchi kept groaning about his mother being all alone at home, and that he would have to go back to look after her. This was all they heard in the intervals, when he wasn't being sick.

He didn't get back to his mother that night anyway, because Jorge kept him at his own hut for the night. The rest were not too much worried by his troubles, and continued the evening in the highest spirits. About half way through, the mechanic Guaraglia came to see Francis. He had been scalded with a plate of hot soup, which someone had slopped over him. As he knew Francis kept a few medicines in stock, he wanted something to put on it. It was a nasty burn, but they gave him a bottle of wine, and he soon forgot his troubles. It was a great party.

### 'I played the banjo'

*'It was amazing how the time passed. I played the banjo, and we sang, laughed and drank till the early hours. As they all drove home, laughing and calling to each other, I didn't like to think how Macchi came off, riding in the back of Jorge's car. Even when cold and sober, it is no mean job to keep oneself from hitting one's head on the roof. Macchi must have been shaken like a pea in a box, at the speed Jorge drove home that night.'*

It was about a week later that Graham and the new man arrived. *'I remember how Jorge and I waited at the station for them. We speculated as to what Herr Carl Krebs, for that was his name, would be like. We had both shaved and donned clean neckerchiefs for the occasion. Although Jorge was definitely depressed, I was more curious than anything else.'*

They arrived at last. The Boss jumped out of the train almost before it had stopped, as was his custom, and they were introduced.

'*Krebs was nothing like I had expected. I suppose hearing he was German, I had looked forward to seeing the square head and short hair, which was my characteristic idea of a German? But no, he was a small man. He had a rather congenial face, a pince-nez and a moustache. He must have been about forty, and had a very intense way of speaking. So this was the man, I thought, with whom I was to share my solitude now. And I remember that my first impression was that it might have been a great deal worse.*'

**Carlos Krebs 'the German wheat man'**

Graham was returning by the same train, in a couple of hours. As usual they all had to rush round receiving his instructions as he put it. He also assured them that he had several colonists coming up here to take farms and wanted to know how Jorge was getting on with the land-clearing work. So, for the next two hours, they were all on the run. It was not until Graham had been seen off on his train again, that peace and quiet were once more restored.

Krebs and Francis returned to the farm together. '*I showed him the bungalow and we sat down over the 'maté' pot to talk. He knew pretty well what Jorge and I had been thinking of his arrival. He was most anxious to assure me that all he wanted was for us to work together in a friendly way. 'And let us not get on one another's nerves', he said. 'I know what it is to live in a place like this, just the two of us together'. He called me 'Don Francisco', and I called him 'Don Carlos'. We shook hands on it and began to investigate the ways and means indoors.*'

As the bungalow only had three rooms and a kind of shed for a kitchen, Francis and Don Carlos arranged to sleep together in one room. The second room would be as an office, and the other, as a sitting room. If Graham came up for a night or two, they would put up a camp bed in the office for him.

Life was certainly going to be different from now on.

The first night of Don Carlos' arrival, he and Francis talked together till long into the night. He had a wife and two children in Buenos Aires and had been working on a big camp in Mendoza, vine-growing as well as the usual ranch occupations.

**Don Carlos with his wife and daughter and assorted pets**

A few months after his arrival, the company built him a bungalow next to Francis', where his family would join him from time to time. And although Francis missed his company, he too enjoyed their visits. Don Carlos told Francis that he'd got this job through a little inside pull and because it interested him. He was a real 'laboratory' man, most accurate and calculating in all his work. That indeed was his real line. Later on he came to leave all the outside and more extensive work to Francis, whilst he would interest himself in the small experimental plots of wheat. He loved this meticulous work and taught Francis a good deal about it.

'I discovered Don Carlos was really more Russian than German. Though his parents were German and he had studied in Germany, most of his life had been spent in Russia. He had even fought with Russia in the War. He had also taken part in the Revolution, and had only saved himself from the Bolsheviks, by the skin of his teeth. He spoke both Russian and German fluently and he told me that during the War, they had tried to get him to do spy work. But, he had always refused, preferring to be shot in open combat rather than up against a wall.'

In a few days they had thoroughly settled down together – Don Carlos would always come and consult Francis about the work before he began doing anything on his own. And Francis much appreciated this. *'It did much to make the work more interesting and life in general more congenial. We would discuss the jobs for the day, in bed in the morning, and then I would go out and see the men, just as I always used to. Don Carlos was very interested in this zone. He was very optimistic at the start, but it broke his heart before I eventually left him.*

*I often recall the eagerness with which he started, though I did my best to cool him down a bit. You see, he hadn't seen our harvest as I had, and neither had he swallowed so much dust as I had – yet. But, above all, the thing that really finished him was Graham.'* The problem was that Don Carlos was infinitely more scientific than Graham, and Graham became very jealous and thoroughly unpleasant.

A kind of small laboratory was put up a little later on for Don Carlos to work in, though only of the most rudimentary sort. One can imagine the kind of place it was in that climate, with the dust blowing four days out of seven. As for the actual rough work out of doors, Jorge and Francis continued to manage that. *'We could do it far better than either of them could. This is not a boast, but both Graham and Don Carlos were technical men, and Jorge and I were – well just rough. I still continued to see the men on the farm, as Jorge did with his land-clearing gangs. It was much better so, and Don Carlos realised this too.'*

**Don Carlos in his 'laboratory' with his wheat samples**

The first Sunday after Don Carlos' arrival, Francis took him along to meet the Lesniffs, and realised from then on, that he would always be a back number there. *'In fact I felt very out of it, for Russian was the language of the day. And how they talked. I don't think there can be a nation on earth that talks so much as the Russians. We went round there soon after lunch and didn't leave till about ten o'clock at night. And I'm sure they didn't cease talking for ten seconds the whole time. Mrs. Lesniff tried to say a few words to me now and then, out of politeness, but she was always talking to Don Carlos, who was talking hard in Russian to Lesniff. Poor folk, I cannot really blame them. They had been shut up here so long with no-one of their own race to speak to, that it was only natural that they should want to talk. Anyway I made a mental note that I would let Don Carlos go alone next time, and I did.'*

Don Carlos and Francis got along together very well, especially during the early days. He was a wonderfully interesting man to talk to as he had wandered about such a lot. He'd been through the War, been lost

## Lesniff and Don Carlos

for four years in Russia during the Revolution, worked in a coal mine to earn his bread, been out of work for a couple of years and had finally emigrated to the Argentine.

In those days they had plenty to talk about, but little by little, they exhausted their conversation. So to drive off boredom, they started to learn English and German. *'He wanted to learn English and I thought that to learn German would be useful. And so, we made good progress together, though I picked up German from him quicker than he learned English. Had I been able to go to Germany at that time, I am sure I could have got along quite well, and in six months have spoken quite fluently.'*

They found it useful to converse with one another in front of their cook-boy and the men. As they could not understand, it was possible to talk of anything they did not wish them to hear. With Francis' musical ear he certainly seemed to have a gift for languages. To have picked up and be able to speak Spanish fluently, albeit as he would later say, *'the rough, working Spanish of the Argentine,'* was no mean achievement and it did him great credit.

Perhaps more poignantly Francis did also try hard to learn a bit of Russian. *'I thought I might then be able to join a little in conversation at the Lesniffs, but although I bought a Hugo's course, I made very slow progress. And they would roar with laughter over my pronunciation.'*

Francis and Don Carlos played chess together regularly. Francis usually beat him, but it passed the time in the evenings. But how Don Carlos used to annoy him by humming to himself as they played. *'There were moments when I felt like hitting him over the head. I expect it* was merely that we were cooped up together and got on one another's nerves a bit. Thus, we amused ourselves, and if I was impatient with him at times, it was really only natural. You see, I was twenty years younger than him, and while he would be content to sit and study, I would be longing for the movements of youth.'

Francis would always feel that he owed much to Don Carlos. He taught him a great deal. Francis would later take a scientific approach to his own work in fruit growing, saying that he had learned so much from Don Carlos. He was always willing to explain his work to him. He never stopped him from going anywhere or doing anything he wished, and Francis was really grateful for his company. He had been living alone for over a year by this time, and did come to realise that his company meant a great deal to him.

By the second year that Francis was in Ing. Foster, the town, village or whatever one cared to call it, had begun to expand considerably.

When he first arrived, there was little more than a station and a store but now there were real signs of growth. In fact, there was almost a High Street. They had the newly arrived baker who had set up business, but now they also had another store and a place that called itself an 'Inn'.

'It was a gruesome looking place, though the landlord was cheerful enough. It was mainly built of mud, with a tin roof. I don't like to think what the beds were like. I did feed in there one day however, and the food was quite good, which was something to be thankful for. Thank heaven I never had the pleasure of staying there for a night!'

**'The type of country here, with houses the railway has put up for colonists'**

Practically all the movement in the place was due to the company's activities. What with the preparing of thousands of acres of land for farms, the clearing of land and the digging of wells - it all made a lot of work. Men had begun to settle there, bringing their families and what goods and chattels they possessed. And also at this time, quite a number of people came up by train to look at the farms. Some with a view to buying, others from mere curiosity.

Free railway passes were given to anyone who wished to visit the place. This seemed to have been greatly abused, for many people came up just for a couple of day's outing. They were always advised of anyone coming up, and had to show them round. They knew in the first five minutes whether they were interested or not, and gave them a reception accordingly. Don Carlos often cursed the people for wasting his time. But, if they were genuinely interested, he would take great trouble to show them round and explain all they wished to know.

Letters might have been a life-line to Francis, but they didn't always bring news of fun and family picnics. It would have been about this time that Francis would have heard the news that Seabrooks was to be sold. With his access to the world news through the newspapers, he would have been fully aware of the deepening agricultural and world depression, quite apart from hearing news from the family. Christmas 1928 would be the last one the Bell family would spend there, with the farm changing hands the following June. Bolstered up by Robert's income, the farm had survived longer than many of its beleaguered neighbours, but now the decision had been made. For the time being at least, Adrian's farming dream would have to remain just that, and another source of income would have to be found.

The news must have been a shock; it had been Francis' home too, and must have stiffened his resolve to stick it out in the Argentine for as long as he could.

Don Carlos and Francis would usually go down to see the train come in. It now came three times a week, and they would go, not so much from idle curiosity, though it was indeed an event, but to get the mail and newspapers. Although Jorge had a wireless set, it worked very badly. You could seldom hear the news on it. So, they looked forward to reading the affairs of the world in the newspapers, and there was always a paper-seller on the train.

Francis used to like to go and greet the train too, because there would sometimes be an engineer on board, or the traffic inspector. As these were both English, it was pleasant to have a little chat. The sectional engineer always used to greet him with, '*What, still here? I'm blowed if I know how you stick it.*'

One day he was in the station, and the train was about to move on to the next station of Arizona. '*I happened to be reading a paper I had just bought, when I suddenly felt someone tapping me on the head. I turned round quickly, for I thought it was probably Jorge up to a practical joke. I very nearly swung my fist into his stomach and I am glad I didn't, for I was amazed to find that a bishop was blessing me!*' He had been travelling on the train, descending at every station, and laying his hand on anyone who looked as if they needed his redemption. '*I felt very embarrassed, and Lesniff, who happened to be present, roared with laughter. Jorge hoped I felt better for the benediction, but I can't say I did!*'

There was also a day when the train arrived and ran into a mule. It happened just as the train was drawing into the station. No-one seemed to know whose it was, and, to Francis' relief, some kind person cut its throat. *And kind-hearted folk were rare up there, as far as humanity to animals was concerned.*

The train arrived three hours late one day owing to the permanent way being covered with sand. All the passengers and people on board had to get out and clear the line so that the train could proceed. The engineer told Francis that thistles too sometimes stopped the train. This was a frightful nuisance at times. They became entangled in the wheels of the engine, making further progress impossible until they had been cleared. *'We used to call it 'Cardo Russo' and it grew in the form of a small bush. When it was dry and full of seed it then became uprooted by the wind. Being round in shape, it was blown along like an enormous football sowing its seeds hard all the way, until it came to rest against a fence or some other obstacle. I noticed after such a wind that the fences were packed with it. In fact one could hardly see the fences at all for the masses of the stuff. It burned like tinder too.'*

The curious thing about this weed was that it only seemed to come after the land had been in cultivation. It was seldom seen on virgin soil, but once the plough had been at work, up it would come and be a plague forever afterwards. Unlike their crops, it always seemed to thrive, rain or not and was an endless source of trouble.

It did not take Francis long to find out that Don Carlos was an expert at the experimental work. His experimental plots for the different varieties of wheats were very different from last year. Everything was minutely planned out beforehand. They had a special frame of wood made to assist in the sowing of the varieties of wheat, so that each plot should be exactly to measurement. All the grains were sown by hand, one by one. In fact, it looked like a well-kept garden. These experimental plots didn't occupy more than about an acre in all, but the work they entailed was endless. *'Don Carlos would always occupy himself here, for it was the work he loved, while I would first of all saddle a* horse, and get out after the men who were working extensively on the other 500 hectares of the farm. But I used to spend a lot of my time with Don Carlos and his trial plots, and found it very interesting to work with him in this manner. A hopeless task one might think, trying to grow wheat where God never meant wheat to grow, but as our livelihood did not depend on what we grew, it became very interesting work.'

They spent much time comparing the different classes of wheat, crossing the one with the other and improving the breed to suit the zone. But for a man like Lesniff, who was trying to gain his living by growing wheat and keeping a few sheep, Francis was truly sorry.

'Even Don Carlos and I, who received our salaries, wheat or no wheat, were frightfully depressed at times. Just the sight of the crops thirsting for rain, or being burnt up by the searing winds, or ruined by hail, would send us into fits of hopeless depression. But, for a man who was trying to earn his living, it must have driven poor Lesniff almost mad.'

It was odd, for though they had a great deal of sunshine there, yet everything seemed so depressing. The people were poverty stricken, the animals looked permanently hungry, and the constant dust was the worst of all. These, and the lack of companionship, were really arduous to cope with, especially for anyone as gregarious as Francis and he was still so young. Then they were being continually harassed and nagged by Graham, and in nine cases out of ten, without cause. It was a pretty tough existence and there must have been many times when he wondered how long he could stick it out or what future it held.

'Life however, had its pleasant moments, and we would delight in the simplest of pleasures. I remember how much I would look forward to a long lie in bed on a Sunday morning. To lunch eaten in a clean shirt and a different pair of trousers. But there were no women here, and when one is young, one needs at least to look upon one of the opposite sex. When a chap is hermited away like this, he gets longings. Quite out of proportion I admit, but until one has to do without anything, one never really appreciates it.'

Francis would often wonder why Don Carlos and he didn't get on one another's nerves more than they did, there were enough opportunities. But as for Jorge, he was by far the most temperamental and volatile of them all. He didn't have to live with Frances and Don Carlos, or heaven knows what might have happened. *'There were days when he wasn't fit to speak to. He would perhaps be in a raging temper one day or another time, be as full of joie de vivre as a schoolboy.'*

Jorge never had a high opinion of Don Carlos. It was mainly it seems, because he didn't understand him or his work. It was all too precise for Jorge. But, they would get along well enough together, as Don Carlos wisely interfered very little with Jorge, the gangs, or his clearance work.

The weekly visits to Lesniff would continue, although Francis would sometimes let Don Carlos go alone. When he was there, they would always talk a bit in Spanish for his sake, but he knew they preferred to talk in Russian among themselves.

As a matter of fact, there was a soccer team being raised in Ing. Foster about this time, and Francis would sometimes go and play for them on a Sunday. They were very keen. They just managed to raise eleven men who could play, and to muster a very few reserves. Jorge used to referee, and it seems, he was a very good one at that - never going on the field without his gun. It was not to use, he said, but was just to show who was in charge. He did stop the game on one occasion, however, owing to the two sides nearly coming to blows. This happened nearly every time they played, but they still continued to play.

Sunday afternoons was the time when they would play, and they would go miles for a game. There were two or three villages nearby, up and down the line, and matches were fixed with these. *'I've often been twenty or thirty miles for a game, and I didn't enjoy it a bit. I can't think really why I played; except that once I started it was hard to stop. And they liked having me in goal. It was being English and being rather tall, I think. The English were always admired as footballers. As a matter of fact, being in goal was a cushy job, because in the Argentine it is forbidden to charge the goalkeeper, once he has the ball in his hands. So, unlike my fellow players, I was quite safe. I often used to think what my old school-masters would have* thought of me, after all their careful tuition, and their 'play for the side' slogan. Here was I, playing football for a village in the Argentine, which was too insignificant even to be included in a map of the country.'

Francis found it funny to watch them play; dust flying everywhere and enough shouting as he would say, 'to raise the devil. And I don't think they ever had a game without a row. Still, I expect they enjoyed it in their way'

**The Football team at Ing. Foster with Francis as goalkeeper**

One morning, while Don Carlos and Francis were busy sowing wheat on the experimental plots, Jorge came up to the farm. He had had a telegram from the Boss saying that a special train was coming up the next day, bringing the general manager and some of the directors. They wanted to have a tour of inspection. They had received notices like this before, but usually with plenty of warning.

This was rather short notice - not that there was much preparation needed, except to clear up a bit and hire a car or two in order to escort the directors about. They set most of the men on cleaning the place up, and arranged to have everything 'on show' as it were, for the next day. By now they had several new buildings put up, with a barn and a shed for the machinery. They decided they would have tractors working conveniently near at hand, and one or two other machines doing useless jobs, just so as to have something to show them when they arrived.

**Several new buildings had been put up – and the beginnings of a garden round Francis' bungalow**

The visitors on the special train duly arrived and just for a change, had picked a very pleasant day this time for their tour of inspection. There was a brilliant sun and no wind. There was the usual cloud of dust behind the cars, but for Ing. Foster, the day was definitely pleasant. Francis didn't go down to the station to meet the company this time; just Don Carlos and Jorge went. Jorge was always there, as he had to act as chauffeur. Francis remained to stage-manage the farm.

About ten minutes before the party arrived, one of the tractors broke down. He had had it working close to the entrance, just as a kind of demonstration, but it suddenly stopped work and threw all his carefully staged plans into disarray.

The mechanic and Francis did their best to get it going again, and managed to make it crawl a few yards at a time. Something was wrong with the fuel feed, but if the small starting tank was filled with petrol, it would run a little while before giving out. So, they filled the tank up and Francis told the mechanic to wait until he saw the party arriving. Then, he was to start up and do his best to keep going as long as they were in sight. As it happened he managed well and the tractor just kept going for the necessary time.

There were a crowd of visitors this time, about eight or nine of them and also two women. These latter were very amusing, for when they had all unloaded at the farm, one of them asked Francis if she might see round his bungalow. Showing great interest in all their domestic arrangements, she called the general manager over, and said she considered they should have more domestic utensils, which amused them greatly. Francis had told their boy to polish up a bit and make their beds; so fortunately, things did look a little cleaner than usual.

Don Carlos and Francis escorted them all round the buildings to examine the various items of interest, such as the water supply. They asked a lot of foolish questions as was usually the way, and one old fellow scanned the horizon and said, 'Who wouldn't be a farmer – what a wonderful life.' Francis felt very tempted to tell him a thing or two, but refrained, as he naturally felt a little awed in the presence of these important dignitaries.

Just before they left, Graham, who came up with them, suggested going to see the tractors at work. Francis suggested that the newest would be the most interesting. This was not the one that had broken down, and luckily they all marched off to see it and left the disabled one alone.

The managers left Francis several packets of English cigarettes before they left and the promise of some further cooking utensils. They were always very good in this way, and if they were in need of anything reasonable in the way of furniture or such like for the house, they would usually get it sent up sooner or later.

As soon as the visitors had left, they reverted to their regular work again. But they all rather enjoyed these official visits - they made a change, and there was little anyone could get hauled over the coals about, as it was all rather out of their line of business.

A couple of days later, Don Carlos went off to Buenos Aires to see his wife and family. Francis was left alone for the weekend, and it proved to be a very dramatic one for him; in fact, something more akin to being in the Wild West.

He had gone to bed at about nine o'clock and was having a quiet read before going to sleep, when he heard running footsteps outside. A moment later the door was burst open by their cook boy. He could hardly speak for fright. *'Having one's door suddenly burst open in this manner is a little alarming, so I had caught hold of my revolver, which I always kept on a table by my bed. This I suppose had scared the boy more than ever, for it was some minutes before I could get a coherent story from him.'*

It appeared that the mechanic Guaraglia had been shot by accident and the cook-house was in pandemonium. Francis clawed on a pair of trousers and a jacket and ran out to investigate. *'I got as far as the cook-house door, when a young Italian who worked for us, threw himself at my feet. He was weeping and howling and calling on all the deities for mercy. I've never seen a fellow in such a state.'*

Francis did his best to calm him and find out what had happened, but it seemed a hopeless task at that moment, so he went back to find the mechanic. The poor chap had collapsed just outside his room, and blood was running down his face from a wound in his forehead.

Now Francis had no idea what to do. Guaraglia wasn't quite conscious, but by the look of the bullet wound it looked as though he could be a dead man at any moment. With the aid of one or two of the men they got him onto his bed. Francis then sent a chap over to his bungalow for some bandages and a bottle of brandy he kept there. One of the less excitable men present then told him how it happened. It appeared that the Italian boy had a little revolver and he was playing about with it. He jokingly aimed it at Guaraglia and the thing went off. All the men who saw it said it was quite an accident.

Francis bandaged the man's head up as best he could, and poured a good dose of brandy down his throat. He then went off to get Jorge and his car, for it seemed to him that it looked very serious and he would have to be taken off to see the doctor.

'Jorge listened while I told him what had happened, and then burst out with an oath, 'Pity it wasn't your revolver he was playing with. That would have blown his head off, and we shouldn't have to turn out like this.' His revolver happened to be a long-barrelled Smith and Wesson and Jorge had always coveted it. 'I must admit I felt rather the same way myself. One can't leave a wounded man, whereas had he been properly dead, the job would have been finished with by now.'

Jorge and Francis went back to the farm with the car and loaded the wounded man as best they could. They also took the Italian who had done the shooting and then drove to Arizona, where there was a doctor. Jorge had to drive very slowly because of the bumpy road, and twice had to stop, as the poor chap was violently sick in the back of the car.

They eventually arrived at Arizona, which was about twenty kilometres distant, and then had to wake up the doctor and the police official. They hadn't been able to report the shooting to the police in Ing. Foster, because the farm was a few hundred yards within the San Luis boundary. This meant they had to report such matters to the authorities of that province, and the nearest happened to be in Arizona. Francis described what happened next.

'There was a most gruesome business at the doctor's, as the police official tried to extract a statement from the wounded man. This was to show that it was an accident. It was a ridiculous business really, as the injured man was practically unconscious and had lost the power of speech. There they were, bawling at him to try and make him speak, when he was quite incapable.' They gave it up eventually, and the doctor, after examining the wound, said that the bullet was resting in the skull. It would be necessary to take him to hospital immediately, so that he could be operated on at once.

'This made us curse even more, for the nearest hospital was at the junction of Pico, some two hundred kilometres distant. It would mean hours of driving over rotten roads at a snail's pace. However, there seemed to be no alternative, so off we set, taking it in turns to drive. It was half past four in the morning when we eventually arrived in Pico. We had banged on the doors of two doctors before we were able to rouse anyone and it was then that we discovered that the hospital had been closed. So, we decided we would have to take the sick man to his home, and let the doctor attend to him there.'

They had another difficult time trying to find out where the poor fellow lived and eventually extracted the information from him by signs. It was odd because, although the man was conscious, he was quite unable to speak.

'We got him landed at last however, and very thankful we were to be finished with the job. We were pretty well done in ourselves, and jolly thankful to get some grub at a nearby café, which happened to be open early. I returned by train to Ing. Foster, as it happened to be a day there was a train running, and Jorge brought the car back later.'

The affair did not finish there by any means. Some days later, Francis was called into Buenos Aires to make a statement about the matter, and he also had several visits from odd police officials. As for the young Italian who had done the shooting, he had to square the police at Arizona with a hundred dollars, before they left him alone. Francis found such corruption pretty despicable. 'It seemed rather wicked to me, because it was plainly an accident, but that was the way things were done in that country.'

Don Carlos returned from town a couple of days after this affair, and was rather surprised to hear what had happened.

They were now left without a mechanic for one of the tractors and as they were particularly busy at that time, Francis took the ploughing on again for a bit which he thoroughly enjoyed. He didn't record whether Guaraglia made a full recovery or indeed if he actually did recover, but it didn't sound as though he returned to work at Ing. Foster again. It would be the last major incident that Francis recorded whilst he was in the Argentine and perhaps one of the most dramatic.

They got hold of another fellow eventually; he wasn't a skilled mechanic, but was good enough to drive the tractor. Francis felt that often these skilled mechanics were more trouble than they were worth, as they seemed to get big ideas as to their value. In that country, they really needed people who could turn their hand to anything. They were too remote and isolated. When a problem arose, albeit mechanical or otherwise, a fellow on the spot was essential. Someone who could deal with most things, rather than having to wait days for a specialist to appear, losing valuable windows in the weather and holding up the work schedule. There was no practical alternative. They had to do all own repairs, as well as blacksmith's work, etc., but Francis was able to fix most of the machinery and would always say that he found a little common sense went nearly as far as a smattering of technicalities.

It was the dawning of the mechanical age of farming. Although Francis would soon return to Britain, it would be to a farming world still dominated by the use of heavy horses. Within a decade all that would have changed.

That bit of common sense and practicality would always be an essential part of Francis' character, the ability to adapt to any situation and to excel in whatever line of work presented itself. But he would also carry a keen sense of his lack of academic qualifications and a feeling of being the poor relation, despite his not inconsiderable achievements.

Francis returned to Britain in the summer of 1931, working his way back on a cargo boat. His luggage, failing to disembark with him, continued on its way to France, from where it was later sent back to join its owner.

His journal lay unfinished and forgotten for over 80 years. Why he returned can only be surmised.

**Working his way home on a cargo boat**

Among Francis' papers, were found copies of reports of the experiments undertaken at Ing. Foster along with comparative studies of rainfall. Written by Carlos Krebs, they cover the period up to the end of 1930 and indicate that Francis was still at Ing. Foster then. Final reports show the disastrous failure to grow crops. Did this finally persuade the Railway Company to abandon its colonization scheme? Also brought back was a photograph taken at Ing. Foster, dated 29th June 1931, written on by Jorge, which suggests that he left at the end of June, in time to help with the harvest at Vic Savage's, late that summer.

We do know that the line from Pico was never extended beyond Arizona. It still exists today, but the service remains that of a goods train, running out to the area twice a week as it did originally.

The constant annoyance and aggravation with Graham that both men felt, was certainly a factor. Did this tension become unbearable?

Later photographs also show a young man, identified as Graham's brother, sitting on Francis' bed. Was he living alongside Francis in his bungalow? Francis tells his father that, *'Our boss's brother,* [is] *just down here for a while.'* Was Graham trying to oust

'Me, ready for town! The German wheat man (awfully good fellow), our boss (Graham)' and 'our boss's brother, just down here for a while.'

Francis from his job by bringing in his younger brother? Or was he simply fed up with the whole situation – desperately lonely and seeing no future in the job, did he decide to come home?

Alongside these considerations, and perhaps more importantly, the worldwide economic crisis of 1929 was beginning to have a serious effect both politically and socially in Argentina. Unemployment and hardship were causing deep unrest, which would manifest itself in a political uprising in 1933.

Added to this, the news from home had not been good. Britain was gripped in the stranglehold of the depression. Farming prices had slumped to an all-time low; house and land prices had plummeted, and some farms were even being abandoned.

Back home in Suffolk – the Bell family had not remained immune from the economic pressures of the time.

# Part Three
# Home to Suffolk

1929 had been a bad year. Seabrooks along with Stephenson's Farm and the precious 50 acres had been sold. Like so many others at the time, Adrian had had to concede that, even with his father's continual monetary assistance, the farm was not financially viable.

Seabrooks farmhouse would eventually be bought by a local Suffolk brewery, Greene King's, and become The Cherry Tree Public House, the name by which it is still known today.

Stephenson's Farm was sold to Will and Annie Lunnis, who lived there until 1937. Ironically a member of the Bell family would once again live in the cottage, yet despite his dreams of farming the land again, it would not be Adrian.

Ann Gander writes of the plan put forward to move the family nearer to London, *'to find a small house from which Robert could commute to the Observer and Stephanie could try obtaining a little job'*. This plan was soon abandoned when Fanny found a large empty house to rent in Sudbury that was quite perfect. Draughty, old-fashioned and big enough to house her antiques and her family - The Gables at Number One, Stour Street, would become their future home.

Once here Fanny would create an exquisite home; placing her furniture to its best advantage and buying more whenever she had a space to fill or could afford yet another irresistible bargain. It was here that Adrian began writing up his farming experiences and where Francis would finally meet up with his family again.

Adrian had first come to Suffolk in 1920 as a farm pupil on Vic Savage's farm, Hundon Great Lodge. These memories would become the subject of *Corduroy*, his first book, and from this beginning a literary career was launched. Although he would return to farming some years later, it was as a well-loved East Anglian author, that he would most be remembered.

Vic Savage and his wife Martha had moved from the farm at Hundon some years earlier. Living for a short while at Great Bradley, they now farmed Hall Farm at Weston Colville – a large farm they rented from the Six Mile Bottom Estate and situated just over the border into Cambridgeshire. The Swann family had moved with them.

Arthur Swann was a rather individual sort of farm worker. He lived with his wife Margaret and two daughters Winnie and Florrie at Hall Cottages next to the farm. Whilst Margaret helped Martha in the house, Arthur looked after the electricity plant at The Hall and carried out any general maintenance. Then if time and weather permitted, he took himself off to help on the land. His hours were never really fixed, and whereas Vic could be seen in the yard, early each morning, watch in hand, checking the arrival times of the men, as far as Arthur was concerned he seemed to turn a blind eye.

Of course it worked both ways, and if the Savages were away, Arthur and Margaret would be up at The Hall at any time of the day or night, ensuring that the fires were made up and the house was in readiness for their return.

Vic and Martha Savage had no children of their own, and the Swann's daughter Florrie became a particular favourite of Martha's. The little girl would often be at The Hall helping her mother and remembered receiving kindly instruction from Mrs Savage on how she should dust. 'Shake out your duster Florrie. Don't take dust from one place to another'.

Another time Martha asked the little girl if she would like to be 'her little girl'. Florrie didn't think she really would, but it was very difficult for a little girl to be able to tell her so.

When Messrs Knight, Frank & Rutley offered the Six Mile Bottom Estate for sale in 1912, the Auction particulars advertised it as *'a Very valuable Sporting Estate, noted for its exceptional Partridge Driving'* and this could still be said to be true when Vic Savage moved into Hall Farm. He loved nothing better than a good day's sport whether it was hunting, of which he was very fond, or organising big shooting parties for friends and family.

Martha too enjoyed entertaining, with tennis parties during the summer and large dinner parties throughout the winter months, as well as being involved in various activities and fund-raising in the parish.

The Bell family, both when they were living at Seabrooks and later when they moved to Sudbury, remained part of their circle of friends - often being invited to join Vic and Martha for dinner at The Hall, and most memorably, at Christmas. And what fun those parties were. Fanny always enjoyed them – loving, as she did, any social event. But it was not for her gay wit that she would be remembered at these times, but for her kindness.

Florrie's mother Margaret was often called upon to wait at table, whenever there was a dinner party at The Hall, and Fanny would always stop and speak to her. The Swann family remembered Fanny's concern on one particular occasion, when she asked, 'How are you Mrs Swann? You look very tired.'

How poignant those words must have seemed when, in 1946, Margaret Swann died at the untimely age of 49 years. And what a mark of respect and appreciation, when Martha and Vic Savage insisted on paying for her funeral.

Like many other large houses, they kept peacocks at The Hall and Martha couldn't bear them. Eventually, to her relief, Vic agreed to take them to the weekly market at Bury. To Martha's dismay he returned home with them later that day, having found no one to buy them. Undaunted, she sent him back the following week and the week after that. In fact this exercise was repeated four times before they were sold at last.

Perhaps it was a natural progression of events that, when Francis returned to England in the late summer of 1931, it was to Vic Savage that he turned. But not of course before trying his luck in London, where he presented himself at the Hanbury's Brewery, offering his services and no doubt hoping to trade on his family connection. Here he received a less than appreciative reception - or in Francis' own words, *'I was sent off with a flea in my ear.'*

Francis was now a mature 25 years old. His spare frame was tanned and lean - not only from spending long hours in the searing heat and winds of the Argentinian plains, but also from working his passage back home. He must have thrilled more than just his adoring sister Stephanie's heart by his arrival back home in Suffolk. And how exotic his luggage must have seemed with his broad brimmed cowboy hat and boots? The faded feathers of the flamingo he had shot, his empty leather holster, (did he give his Smith & Wesson revolver to Jorge Cruselain when he left?). His banjo, his sheepskin *numnah* that he had placed under his saddle, his *chaparejos* or cowboy chaps, the pair of patterned gourds with silver rims for drinking maté – that infusion of leaves from a shrub that made the distinctive Paraguayan green tea that he so enjoyed. The sharp well-cut foreign-looking double-breasted brown suit with its waistcoat and stylish tight-fitting trousers, complete with triangular tear that told tales of nights out in Buenos Aires and of a particular young lady with a fork. A suit which he would later wear to his own wedding and pass on to his teenage son.

By the time Francis arrived home, Adrian had at last managed to move away from the over-possessive clutches of his mother in Sudbury. By now a published author, he had married in January 1931, and after a short time of living together at The Gables, had taken his young wife Marjorie to live first in a tiny rented cottage close by and later that summer to Princes Risborough in Buckinghamshire.

Stephanie, who had recently returned from a two-month trip to India, was greeted as she stepped through the door, by her mother's tragic face as she melodramatically told her daughter, 'He's gone.'

Of Fanny's greeting to Francis, we have no record.

Stephanie had actually gone out to India in December 1930, to stay with her father's nephew Roy Bell. Unmarried, he was a

Superintendent in the Indian Police; he was 17 years older than Stephanie.

Roy had stayed with the family at Seabrooks before they moved and Ann Gander suggests that *'Fanny had known there was a chance that Roy was interested in Stephanie as a potential wife, and counselled her daughter to go and see if she might like the life out there.'* In fact it is interesting to trace the slightly complicated relationship between her father and Roy Bell, which does cast some doubt on the possibility of such a marriage being legal or at least advisable.

However, Fanny does seem to have been obsessed with getting Stephanie married off and although Stephanie was barely 23 years old, there was a hint of Fanny taking things in hand.

Robert's father, who was of course Stephanie's grandfather, was an ironmonger, Alexander Bell Jnr of Bell, Donaldson & Co. in Edinburgh. A deeply religious man, he was an ardent disciple of Calvinism with its belief that to labour industriously was one of God's commands. He took this edict to extremes, as also the Calvinistic view that luxury should be shunned and life lived thriftily. All this hard work and austere living resulted predictably in his business prospering. Alexander must have felt a distinct personal conflict, as his business success took him up the ladder of capitalism.

Perhaps in a determined effort to produce a succession of sons to take over the ironmongery business, Alexander married three times. His first wife died within a year marriage, as did the second, but not before giving birth to a son, Alexander Brown Bell in 1861. He survived and went on to marry and have a son of his own in 1891. This son was called Roy (Robert Wallace) Bell. Having lost his first two wives in quick succession, Alexander was luckier with the third. He married Catherine M'Crie Hay in 1864. She was 24 years old, the daughter of a shoemaker from Prestonpans and nine years younger than her husband. Catherine went on to survive not only the birth of their first-born child, Robert Bell, born in 1865, but also the births of another six children. Of the seven brothers and sisters, only Charles died in infancy.

This slightly difficult line of descent made Robert's father, Alexander (Jnr.), not only Roy Bell's grandfather, but also Stephanie's. And so if not in Fanny's, then perhaps in Stephanie's mind at least, Roy could never have been much more than an avuncular figure, rather than a prospective lover.

### Roy Bell

Escorted by him, Stephanie's time in India rather than that of a tourist, was spent in a whirl of social occasions more befitting a 'coming out'. Amongst her keepsakes was a seating plan of a banquet, which included Miss Bell's name as a guest of the Viceroy and Governor. Fanny would most definitely have approved. But perhaps more precious to Stephanie, were the little pair of exquisite Indian slippers; everyday items that were later sent to her at her request, as a gift.

Despite Fanny's matchmaking plans for her daughter being thwarted, it soon became obvious that, whilst in India, Stephanie had met and fallen in love with a young army officer, Gerry Scott. Marriage to him was apparently out of the question, despite his titled connections, due to army rules about his rank and marriage. Yet despite this and her subsequent and happy marriage in 1934 to Jack Thorpe, a Suffolk farmer, she and Gerry would remain friends for many years.

Later, when Gerry came to Britain on extended leave, it was to stay with Jack and Stephanie at their farm near Lavenham. Whether it was the idyllic setting of Priory Farm or the radiant presence of Stephanie, by now the mother of a little boy, and expecting another, remains to be seen but, for whatever reason, Gerry stayed on for the best part of nine months. And Jack for one, soon found his visit beginning to pall. He seemed to be running after the chap all the time.

Gerry, used to having a batman, would place his shoes outside his bedroom door each night and Jack felt obliged as his host to clean them. There really wasn't anyone else to do it. And what with the shoe cleaning and arranging shoots and other entertainments, he was getting rather fed up. What he really wanted to be doing was getting on with farming. It was therefore with a sigh of relief that Jack finally said goodbye to his house-guest, and no doubt with a further sigh of relief that he greeted his new-born daughter into the world. Luckily she looked the image of him although Stephanie did insist on calling her Geraldine.

Stephanie had always loved horses and was a keen rider, and after the family had left Seabrooks and prior to her marriage, a horse was kept for her to ride at Vic Savage's farm at Western Colville. Without children of their own, Vic and Martha had in a way adopted the Bell family.

And now with Francis arriving back home, full of energy and with no thoughts of languishing at The Gables, they were quick to offer him their help. He readily accepted their suggestion that he should live with them at The Hall for a while and assist with getting in that year's harvest.

Francis also had some ideas he wanted to discuss with Vic about starting a business - a business that needed planning, capital investment and accommodation. It wouldn't be long before he had met two of these, but as for capital – that would always be a problem and would eventually prevent him from really fulfilling his potential.

The men on the farm soon became accustomed to young Mr Francis being about the yard. And it was with much merriment that they greeted him each morning, for Francis had quickly become a popular addition to that year's harvest workforce.

With harvest behind them and the thrashing nearly done, it was time for Francis to think about the future. He would always be a man of innovative ideas and this period of his life was no exception.

Francis' idea was to start a chicken-breeding business, to set up the hatching and supplying of day-old chicks. A common enough practice nowadays of course, but in those days he would actually become the first chicken-breeder in the district.

His father was still working at *The Observer* and lodging with Mabel and George in London. Robert's time spent at The Gables was hardly more than that of a weekend visitor, but there was still the rent to be paid and Fanny and Stephanie to support. It is doubtful whether he would have been able to offer his son any more financial support now, than he could have done in 1924, when Francis first went out to South America.

Francis had saved very little of his salary in South America, indeed there hadn't been a great deal of it to save. Being able to live at The Hall with Vic and Martha, and working on the farm during that year's harvest, would have ensured that he had just enough capital to buy a modest amount of equipment.

**Francis (centre) loading sheaves at Vic Savage's farm**

Like so many other rural villages, Weston Colville in the early 1930s had seen few changes. A row of council houses had been built it is true, but for the most part life there continued at much the same self-contained leisurely pace that it had always known. Its ancient church was still the focal point for much of village life, whilst for those who sought more secular enjoyment there was always the Three Horse Shoes or The Fox and Hounds.

The Hall was situated at the western end of the village, and with almost a 1,000 acres of farmland, would have offered employment to a large number of men in the parish, as well as part time work during busy periods. Vic Savage was known as a strict, but fair employer and all the men liked and respected him.

A little further along the street on the right hand side and opposite the parish church, was a yard together with a range of sheds and barns. These were known locally as 'Church Farm Buildings'. Later they would exist only in the memories of the oldest residents, as with one exception, the buildings were pulled down in the 1960s and two new houses built in their place.

Day's Cottage or Linden Cottage as it would later be known was situated a hundred yards further on, opposite the village school. It had originally housed a foreman and later a shepherd. The cottage was part of the farm Vic rented and when it became vacant, he agreed to rent it to Francis for a peppercorn rent.

The cottage had a meadow at the back of it, and along with the buildings and yard opposite the church, which Vic also let Francis use, it was ideal for his purpose. Here was a roof over his head, and plenty of land and buildings - enough to house his hens and set up his incubators. What more could a man want? It suited Francis' needs exactly.

It was a picturesque cottage with a large old plum tree in the front garden and a pond that bordered the lane. It was here that the traction engine had stopped only that autumn to fill up with water before going on to The Hall to start the thrashing. It wouldn't be long before Fanny had furnished the cottage with a few items of furniture she had picked up locally and Francis had moved in.

He was his own man once again.

**Linden Cottage, Weston Colville**

Laughter and fun would always be a part of Francis' character and after so long without contact with young people of his own age, it is not hard to imagine the pleasure he must have felt to be back home.

Of the many friends he met and made that first summer, one young man stands out. He would become a constant companion and drinking partner. Together they would trawl the local pubs, flirt with the same girls, ride and play cricket, tennis and chess. It would be a friendship that would last a lifetime. He was a cheerful young man with a resounding laugh, ruddy complexion, and a great love of hunting. His name was Bob Berry.

The son of a local farmer, Bob had recently returned from working away as a farm pupil. He had gone first to Warwickshire and then to work on a farm in Denmark, before finally finishing up back on a farm in Norfolk. And now he had returned to 'Wadgells', the farm at Thurlow, Suffolk that his father rented from The Vesty Estate. It was situated just over the border into Suffolk and only a mile or two from Weston Colville.

The Berrys were a large and lively family, Bob being one of six children. Francis soon became a regular visitor there - calling for Bob and often staying to play a game of chess or tennis.

Late one evening, after a particularly enthusiastic drinking session at The Royal Oak at Little Bradley, Bob and Francis returned to Wadgells a little the worse for wear. Mike, one of Bob's younger brothers, challenged Francis to a game of chess. As Francis usually won, undoubtedly Mike saw this as an opportune moment. The challenge was well timed and with a slightly inebriated Francis it would prove to be the only time that Mike ever beat him.

Horses were Bob's life, and when not out with Francis he rode with what was then called the 'Newmarket and Thurlow Hunt'. Of course after working as a gaucho when he first went out to South America, Francis was an excellent rider too, though perhaps not quite in the style that the local hunters were accustomed to see. On one occasion, Bob asked if Francis would like to accompany him on a day's hunting. A horse was selected from Bob's stable and Francis duly invited to tack up. This he did, having brought with him what he felt were the prerequisites for the day. It was unfortunate that the by now, decidedly strong smelling sheepskin that Francis threw over the horse's back, and the equally strong smelling chaparejos he wore proved more overpowering than the fox.

What his fellow huntsmen said throughout the day, when the hounds refused to leave Francis' side, is not recorded. What we do know is that it was Francis' first and last experience of fox-hunting. He was never asked again.

Another friend at this time was Carl Long. He was a year or two older than Francis, and lived at Church Farm, Carlton, at the far end of the village. The Longs were a musical family and Francis was a frequent visitor and enjoyed their company.

Whilst a pupil at Uppingham, Francis had learned to play the cello, and although he would never become the gifted musician that his father was, he did have a certain degree of musicality as he had demonstrated in the Argentine. Unlike his father's, his taste was far from classical; besides which he had never really enjoyed reading music. He preferred picking out tunes by ear on his banjo, which he could play with great competence. This had proved popular in South America and now with Carl playing his guitar, the two set up a musical duo touring the local pubs, playing and singing. And whatever Francis might have lacked in his singing voice, his ability to yodel must have given their performances great panache.

Carl's young cousin Betty Ford remembered them playing, although only a child at the time, and also how well liked they were in the neighbourhood. In fact musical evenings were always popular in the village and before the new village hall was built, concerts and dances were often held in the school, opposite Linden House.

With Carl's father playing the piccolo together with Francis, Carl and others from the village, it was a merry party that made up the band for a concert one evening. With grave attention to detail and honouring the formality of the occasion, the band all wore 'white tie and tails'. Carl's father, being rather rotund at that time, became a source of secret mirth to the 14-year-old Betty, who watched the strain on his starched shirt-front, as her uncle puffed out his chest and cheeks to play his instrument. All was going well, and a sister of Vic Savage's, Mrs Wilby, who had a lovely singing voice, captivated the audience with her beautiful rendering of 'Come under my umbrella, girlie do'.

As the band struck up again, Carl's father took up his piccolo and, with renewed vigour, took a deep breath, swelled out his chest and blew, but at that moment there was a ping. In a final protest, and to the utter delight of his young niece, one of his shirt studs could stand no more and shot off like a bullet across the floor.

Poor Carl had always suffered from poor eyesight and many years later, long after they had lost touch, Francis, revisiting The Three Horseshoes in the village, saw his old friend again. He was sitting at the far end of the bar, and Francis, delighted to see him, rushed over to shake his hand. Carl seemed unaware of who it was, and Francis going right up to him, said, 'Carl, you remember me, it's Francis.' Carl's face lit up at the sound of Francis' voice, but as he lifted his head, Francis realised that he was now totally blind.

Despite Francis assertions during his school-days that he could 'cook an omelette', and indeed he could, it would seem that his limited culinary repertoire soon palled. Not through lack of ingredients, for he had plenty of eggs, but as Mrs Swann had offered to take him up a hot meal, there was no contest.

Fanny often expressed her appreciation of the way in which Margaret Swann 'looked after' Francis and would give her a 'nice tip' whenever she came over to the village. Not only did Mrs Swann send up meals for him, but she also tidied up the cottage, darned his socks and did his laundry. Florrie was usually requisitioned to collect Francis' washing and to take it back to him on a Saturday morning. And how her young arms ached by the time she had reached Linden Cottage.

Carefully walking up to Church End with the crisply ironed and folded laundry, which her mother had laid onto her outstretched arms, with the strict instructions to, 'take it back just so' - it was always with some relief that Florrie reached the cottage and was able to lay it on the kitchen table. She liked it when Francis was there, for he always had a kind word and a smile for her, although usually he was working outside.

Francis now had a large number of laying birds, which he kept on the meadow at the back of Linden Cottage. The hatchery business was going well and expanding; it wasn't long before he felt the need of some extra help.

He employed a young local lad from the village called Jimmy Taylor who also worked as a gardener for the School Mistress, Miss Wormell. He would later work for Vic Savage at The Hall. Neither Jimmy nor his sister Olive ever married – both would live well into their 90s and, until extreme old age, would never move out of Weston Colville.

❧

In the spring of 1932 Francis' solitary occupancy of Linden Cottage came to a temporary end.

He had heard from his older brother Adrian; he and Marjorie desperately wanted to return to live in East Anglia. Adrian was partway through writing his third book, *The Cherry Tree*, and although they later hoped to be able to find a house to buy, the idea of returning to live with the family at The Gables was out of the question. Did Francis know of anywhere locally they could rent?

Francis, who would have given the shirt from his back if he thought it would have helped anyone, was quick to reply, 'Know of anywhere?' Of course he did.

'There's plenty of room for us all here – I'm only using the one room downstairs and one up; we could divide the house and you two could be quite separate and I'm sure Mrs Swann would help us out'. And that in effect is what they did.

In fact there was plenty of room at Linden Cottage – it even had an upstairs bathroom, which was quite an innovation for a farm cottage in the early 1930s. No indoor lavatory of course - there was a closet outside; and no running water either - that still had to be carried up to the bathroom, but it had to be first heated in a copper that stood in a shed opposite the back door. And as for Mrs Swann, she now did the washing for all three of them.

Adrian and Marjorie were soon settled, and it wasn't long before he was able to get down to his writing again. And of course, there was always the deadline of *The Times* crossword to be met. In all the years of its compilation, few people outside the immediate family circle would know of the compiler's identity.

In late 1929, Robert had been approached by a friend from *The Times*, Robin Barrington-Ward, who was later to become editor, asking him if he knew of anyone who would be prepared to compose a crossword puzzle for the paper. Crosswords were all the rage in America, and *The Times* thought they ought to try out the idea here. The problem was he couldn't find anyone who knew anything about crosswords, let alone compile one. Did Robert have any ideas?

Yes, Robert did. He had immediately thought of Adrian back at Stour Street and suggested that his son might be interested. Possibly the regular income of three guineas was the deciding factor – it was certainly hard earned and took a great deal of ingenuity on Adrian's part, but when he met the paper's deadline and *The Times* published their first crossword 'on 1st February 1930' it was an immediate success. And as three guineas was later increased to five, little would Adrian realise that he would become a legend, earning a place in *The Guinness Book of Records*, as the original and longest compiler of the crossword, continuing as he did, through to the 1970s.

It was probably whilst they were living there together during those few months at Weston Colville, that Francis showed his brother the manuscript he had written up whilst he had been in South America.

Whatever Adrian thought of it at the time we don't know, but he certainly never forgot it and must have seen within it some of the skills of penmanship that seemed inherent in the Bell family. Years later, after Francis' untimely death, he asked Barbara, Francis' widow, if she knew where it was - he could do something with it, he thought. But Barbara had no idea where it was and Francis had never mentioned it to her. And even now, Francis was too busy with life and work to spend time finishing his manuscript; events had moved on and, besides, his evenings were filled with far more immediate demands.

Adrian spent a lot of time whilst he was at Weston Colville, either pacing up and down the garden or sitting writing under the old plum tree at the front of the house. Its leafy shade no doubt protected him from the effects of the sun's rays, for he was regularly prostrated by blinding migraines, which would keep him lying prone for days in a darkened room.

Here in the garden of Linden Cottage, situated as it was, opposite the village school, Adrian was often seen by the children and was becoming something of a novelty in the village, for they all knew he was writing a book.

He always enjoyed hearing the children singing and often paused to listen. On one particularly bright and beautiful morning, he was greatly amused as the children's voices drifted across to him, and he heard the words of the hymn chosen,

'The day thou gavest, Lord, is ended, the darkness falls at thy behest;'

It was just the sort of incident that Adrian would take delight in and write about with such humour and empathy; little incidents that made up the pattern of everyday life.

It was at about this time that Francis began to be overrun by rats and mice. The proximity of chicken-food and water were no doubt an attraction, and it wouldn't have been so bad if the rodent population had been content with staying outdoors. But when he found that they had moved into the house too, he knew that it would only be a matter of time before they were completely inundated.

When even the artful setting of cunning traps failed to make any significant difference, desperate measures were called for, and once again the resourceful Swann family were able to help. A cat of course was the answer, and it so happened that their mother cat had just had seven kittens; but which one to choose? And how could he convince the younger members of the Swann family of the pressing nature of his need, when they were loath to relinquish even one? Adrian, calling at their cottage one day, had been charmed by the sight of what he described as their multi-coloured fur rug, which lay against the kitchen range. He further delighted the children by his pretence of amazement when he discovered that the fur rug was really alive, and was actually the mother cat and her family of kittens.

However, kittens weren't the only pets that Florrie and her older sister Winnie were loth to relinquish. Vic Savage had two dogs at the time, Jock and an old black retriever called Don, which he kept at the

Hall. And Old Don, or so it seemed to Florrie and Winnie, had always been part of the fabric of their lives. They couldn't remember a time when Don hadn't come visiting, putting his foot on the latch of their door, and letting himself in. But old age had inevitably taken its toll, and eventually the day came when Vic knew that his old friend was suffering too much and he would have to be put down. But could he find him? He searched everywhere.

It was several hours later, when he called at the Swanns on a quite separate matter, that he found poor old Don. How his arthritic old legs had got him there he would never know, but get him there they had, and once there, the girls had hidden him away. And what persuading it took to convince them that it was all for the best.

**Vic Savage with Jock (left) and Don (right)**

Francis however, did manage to persuade the girls to let him have a kitten – in fact he ended up with three. Whether they felt his case was that desperate, or whether the two girls found it easier to think of three cats being company for each other remains to be seen. Whatever powers of persuasion were used and on whom, the end result was the same, and although he would never be totally free of rats outside, at least life inside Linden Cottage was a great deal more tranquil.

The Swann family played a significant role in the Bell family at that time and Adrian included them in his book, thinly disguised as 'The Martins'. And after *The Cherry Tree* was published, he gave them a signed copy, which they greatly treasured.

And years later, when Winnie married and had a daughter of her own, she called her Anthea as a tribute to the Bell family. For Adrian and Marjorie had also had a daughter by then, Anthea, who had been born in May 1936. Although they had by then moved away from the village, they had still kept in touch.

In a little over a year they had found a dilapidated old house that suited their needs exactly. Creems was situated amidst the beautiful and much-painted countryside of the Stour Valley and Adrian and Marjorie moved there in the August of 1933. And by the time the renovations had been completed, the house was idyllic.

By 1934 the hatchery business was beginning to show a downturn. The trouble was that too many people had started up and the market had become flooded. Seeking to diversify, Francis decided to keep some pigs and, at Adrian's suggestion, he went over to nearby Wickhambrook to talk to a local farming entrepreneur called Justin Brooke. It was a decision that would change the rest of his life.

# Part Four
# Wickhambrook

In 1928 Justin Brooke had come to Suffolk with his second wife Edith with a view to starting a fruit farm. He had been in charge of distribution within the family tea firm of Brooke Bond, and had originally lived in Somerset, before moving to Fingringhoe, near Colchester. Leaving the board of Brooke Bond for personal reasons, he had eventually bought Clopton Hall, situated in the village of Wickhambrook – its accompanying 150 acres seeming ideal for his purposes. Whilst he was living in Essex, Justin had planted up a Cox orchard in 1926, and interestingly this orchard, being farmed till recent times, would become the oldest Cox orchard in the country. But right now Justin wanted to grow fruit on a larger scale.

Justin Brooke was a man with radical ideas, some more successful than others, and one of these was that he thought it ought to be possible to grow fruit successfully, *'by planting on north-facing slopes in a cold district in order to avoid the damaging effects of late frost'*. His idea was that the trees would be that much later coming into blossom, and should in theory miss the worst of the frosts at that crucial time in their development.

As far as competition went, Burrells of Risby near Bury St Edmunds, were the only other fruit farmers in the immediate area at that time. Fruit was not generally thought suitable for that high, open Suffolk land with its heavy boulder clay and exposure to the east wind. In fact the heavy land would prove ideal.

Justin Brooke was born in November 1885 and was one of eight children born to Arthur Brooke, the founder of the Brooke Bond Tea Company. Although the family weren't Quakers, Justin's daughter Elizabeth would say that her grandfather's household reflected the ethos of the Quakers, with its strict code of moral values and dislike of ostentation.

Justin took his degree in Maths and Law at Emmanuel College, Cambridge, at a time when like-minded undergraduates would have been inspired by the ideals of the great philanthropists; people like George Cadbury, who had gone on to create the garden suburb of Bourneville near Birmingham in 1897. It was a form of socialism that had sprung from the Arts and Crafts Movement of William Morris and others in the 1880s and was about getting values back into working people's lives. It was about people living and working together with a communal spirit for their mutual benefit, and taking pleasure and pride in that work.

Being a student in Cambridge, he could not have failed to be aware of the development and structure of the family firm of Chivers at nearby Histon. Here they had farms given over mainly to the growing of fruit trees and bush fruit, which was sent at first to the markets in London, before they realised that their best customers were the local jam-makers. Later in a glut year the sons of Stephen Chivers William and John, persuaded their father to start jam-making and this he reluctantly agreed to do, *'the first jam boiling being made in a small barn at Impington in 1873.'*

Animals were kept to maintain a healthy soil; with chickens roaming the orchards to keep down insects, horses to help in cultivation and transportation, and pigs and cattle to make use of by-products. Soon Chivers became known not only for its fruit production but also for its rearing of prize livestock and world-renowned dairy herd.

But it was the family's policy for its workers that ensured that the welfare of the workforce was always foremost in their thoughts and that any problems were sorted out in a friendly atmosphere. Working conditions were both congenial and healthy with a canteen and a light, airy, well-lit factory with good rates of pay, sickness benefit and insurance. And this paternalism was extended to the outside community through educational programmes, the provision of a fire brigade and housing. All this inspired great loyalty.

Justin's years at Cambridge were spent with an illustrious group of fellow students, amongst them Rupert Brooke, the First World War poet, who was also a close friend. They had met through mutual acquaintances and through the Marlowe Society, which Justin had co-founded in February 1908. *'The society existed to produce Renaissance plays, particularly those in verse or those which were little performed.'* In November 1907 they had put on their first ever production at the ADC Theatre, Cambridge, of *Doctor Faustus*, by Christopher Marlowe, in which Justin not only played a leading role, but also directed. *'The Marlowe remains one of Cambridge's most historic societies, which, to this day, still focuses on producing high quality, innovative student drama.'*

Although Justin himself wasn't a member, a number of his friends, including Rupert Brooke and John Maynard Keynes were members of the Cambridge Apostles, a secret intellectual discussion society that had been founded in 1820. *'Leonard Woolf, Lytton Strachey and his brother James were all members and the Apostles became well known at this time before the First World War, with the rise to eminence of the group of intellectuals and artists known as the Bloomsbury Group. Keynes, Woolf and Lytton Strachey subsequently gained prominence as members'.*

Justin was very much within the coterie of the Bloomsbury Group; among the papers of Rupert Brooke held in the Archives at King's College, Cambridge, are fascinating glimpses of Justin's life, spent within his circle of eminent friends whilst at university there. Photographs show him to be part of that famous group, sharing a picnic by the river at Grantchester, watching a wrestling match between Rupert Brooke and Donald Robertson, again at Grantchester. Another shows him with Brynhild Olivier camping at Clifford Bridge, 'Dartmoor with the Neo-Pagans – Bloomsbury under Canvas' and yet another as the Pythian Prophetess in a Greek play put on with Rupert Brooke in the winter of 1906.

There are letters and postcards dating from 1908 and 1913 between Justin and Rupert Brooke, as well as correspondence dating from 1911 and 1915 between Justin and Maynard Keynes, who would go on to become Britain's most influential economist.

*'In the wake of the Versailles Peace Treaty'* ... at the end of the First World War, Maynard Keynes who had joined the treasury, *'published 'The Economic Consequences of the Peace' in which he criticised the exorbitant war reparations demanded from a defeated Germany and prophetically predicted that it would foster a desire for revenge among the Germans.'*

This bestselling book was written whilst Keynes was at Charleston Farmhouse in East Sussex, which was to become the country home of The Bloomsberries, and where at the time, he had a permanent room set aside for him. A further letter, also in the Archives, is from Justin to David (Bunny) Garnett, written in 1915. Garnett, who was bisexual, would later move to live in a ménage a trois at Charleston along with the artists and fellow Bloomsberries, Vanessa Bell and Duncan Grant. All very scandalous for rural Sussex at the time, though Justin didn't condone their lifestyle.

With the effects of the depression biting deep into the heart of the Suffolk countryside and no money to be made in crops, many of the surrounding farms had become victims of a collapsed rural economy. Unemployment was high and the poverty among farm-workers and their families was heart-breaking. Justin and Edith would say in their book *'Suffolk Prospect'* that they were deeply affected by what they saw - with no unemployment benefit or social security, *'many wore clothes that were little better than rags.'* They felt they had a mission to *'find employment for everyone in the district who wanted it'*.

The planting up of an orchard had to be viewed as a long-term project. First the young fruit trees or 'maidens' as they were known had to be planted out and then there was a wait of some four years before they started to produce fruit. Of course during this interval they had to be pruned and watched over carefully for bugs and pests, and the orchards would have to be hoed around, but none of this would employ vast numbers, so Justin and Edith changed from their original plan.

Justin, in those early days, was a man of great personal energy and drive. With no money being made in the growing of crops, land was being sold at rock bottom prices. It was a buyer's market and an opportune time for a man of business with enough money behind him, to add to his acreage. With the purchasing of two further farms, which Justin would say he bought for as little as *'five pounds an acre'*, it became possible for him to expand his business venture and at the same time provide employment for most of the surrounding area. He not only started planting his fruit trees, but also went into soft fruit – this would give a quicker return of course and also ensured that there was plenty of casual work available.

**Justin Brooke's workforce in 1930**

Albert Mould, Bill Day, Alf Brown, Harry Mott, Arthur French, Freddie Johnson, ?
?, Bill Gooch, Bob Nunn, Les Offord, Cyril King, Bill Cockle, Ted Argent, Fred Nunn
Tom Coe, Alf Hicks, Mrs Brooke, Justin Brooke, George Mills, H.McCartney,
Ted Hicks

It was at this time that Adrian became friendly with Justin and Edith Brooke. He went over a great deal in those early days, having initially gone to pick fruit and later to be taught how to prune. He was missing being in farming and, like everyone else, seems to have been fascinated by the whole enterprise that was developing over at Wickhambrook.

In *By-Road*, Adrian wrote about Sundays spent at Clopton Hall, Sundays seeming quite different to those that Adrian had experienced when he lived and worked in the district. The people who came to see the Brookes were *'quite different from the social groups that* [he] *had met and mixed with through the Savages'*.

Here people would descend on the Brookes 'unannounced' and *'talk about everything … they came to see the latest things – milking machines, the nursery, a mechanical plough'*, and they would arrive in various states of dress and undress - *'sandals, week-day garments and bare legs!'* Quite unlike the formal Sunday best that was still so strictly adhered to amongst the farming fraternity that Adrian knew.

His parents, Fanny and Robert, were still living at The Gables in Stour Street, Sudbury at this time, and it would seem that Fanny at least had become a regular visitor to the Brooke's house. Of course she would have loved it all. Here she would have found herself comfortable and stimulated by the mix of intellectual people from all walks of life and would have no doubt regaled them with her own experiences of farming. For as Ann Gander points out in her biography of Adrian, Fanny had been disappointed not to have been on visiting terms with *'the local gentry'*, but as she also points out, *'as they* [the Bells] *were merely farmers who laughed and chatted with the tenantry, they were "persona non grata" to the upper class.'* It had been a bitter blow to Fanny's aspirations for marrying Stephanie off.

Fanny and Edith would go for walks together round the farm with the Brookes' dogs and one occasion as Edith climbed over a stile, Fanny noticed Edith's legs. Never one to keep her counsel, Fanny was heard to remark loudly, 'Oh Mrs Brooke dear, your legs are far too thin for a farmer's wife.'

'In Rayner, a thinly disguised portrait of Justin in *By Road,* Adrian captures his sheer energy and the different ideas that kept emanating from him – likening the growth of the enterprise to that of a tree, thrusting its branches up in different directions. Each scheme seemed to initiate another, layer upon layer. Surplus fruit meant jam production and fruit bottling; planting orchards required nursery stock, so a nursery was started, and so it went on.

Locals were somewhat sceptical and bemused at first, and of course it was understandable. In that sleepy Suffolk countryside where traditional farming practices had hardly changed in centuries, Adrian wrote of the area being, *'transformed in a year from solitude to activity,'* and that *'he'd* [Rayner] *already planted fruit … to the amazement and amusement of the village.'*

And of course Vic Savage too, having so recently farmed the adjoining land at Hundon Great Lodge, was one of those who expressed his doubts. 'If they can't make fruit pay in the West and in the Fens, how does he think that's going to pay here?'

The first trees to be planted were ten acres of plums, and these were interspersed with rows of soft fruit. Soon the countryside had taken on a quite different appearance with large fields and wire fences to keep out the rabbits and hares. And with *'sheds for vans, sheds for fruit bottling, sheds for jam making, an office, a store'…* And with more and more people working there, Adrian would describe it as becoming *'something like a colonial township'.*

At the time there were a number of small farmers locally, who were selling their milk from the farm gate. As one of the recently purchased farms, Wickham House, had a cowshed and yards, Justin also decided that he would go into the milk production business as well.

He soon had his own herd of pedigree Guernsey cows grazing on the meadows below Wickham House – a dairy was established up at Clopton Hall, making butter and cream and then a modern bottling, sterilising and pasteurising plant was built. Justin had the idea of buying up all the locally produced milk from the small farmers, bottling it and selling it direct to the housewife on her doorstep. And in those days before the establishment of the Milk Marketing Board, he was able to undercut the other retailers and provide a market for all the locally produced milk.

A new, much larger milking parlour was then built at Wickham House, and great pride was taken in the herd, some of which would later take prizes at the Suffolk Show and also at The Royal. The milk business expanded rapidly, not only by the development of local milk rounds, but also by delivering to a number of milk depots in Cambridge and the surrounding towns. From here roundsmen on bicycles or driving yellow Trojan vans would take out the milk to the housewives.

The roundsmen really became the elite workers at that time. Much importance was attached to their jobs and their ability as salesmen. They often carried chip baskets of soft fruit to the door to tempt their customers with, and were encouraged to tear off half the cardboard lid ostensibly to show them the fruit. Justin himself took great pains to demonstrate to his salesmen how they should approach their customers, complete with theatrical flourish and ingratiating smile; the theory being that the housewife would feel so guilty that the covering had been torn off for their benefit, they would feel obliged to buy the contents.

Selling the fruit and milk locally was very much at the heart of Justin's philosophy. *'Decentralisation, that's the thing .... retail what we can grow in the district to the district. Send only the surplus away.'*

The brightly painted yellow Trojan vans were soon to be seen dashing about everywhere in the district and would become synonymous with the Justin Brooke enterprise – yellow being the company colour. Written on the vans were the words, *'J. Brooke – Milk, Roses and Fruit Trees'*.

For a rose nursery had also been planted, together with a field of roses beside the main road and the milk roundsmen took orders through the year, for delivery of both fruit trees and roses the following autumn. Justin was not one to miss a sales opportunity.

**Justin Brooke's milk roundsmen with their Trojan vans, Clopton, 1929**

It is interesting to see how closely this echoed the ideas of his father, Arthur Brooke, who had so successfully built up the Brooke Bond tea business by introducing a van distribution system in 1907. In later years, long after a serious fire up at Wickham House in 1939 had brought the milk business at Wickhambrook to an end and the yellow Trojan vans had really outlived their lives, they were still in use on the farm, being put to a variety of purposes. These would include housing chickens, storing bicycles and the delivery of churns full of drinking-water to houses and cottages around the farm. Driving one of these was an art form in itself – the starter button being placed on the floor and requiring the deft use of the end of a stick in order to start the engine. Their arrival was always noisy, heralded by the grinding of cogs and the rattling of bodywork as they made their way through the Suffolk lanes.

Bill Day from Lidgate was a lad of 14 years of age and had just left school when he started working with the cows at Brookes. He remembered how there would eventually be 60 stalls at Wickham House in the 1930s before the war, with 120 cows being milked in two shifts. Four men worked in the cowshed and milking was done by machine rather than by hand, powered by a Lister engine.

Justin Brooke had always liked mechanisation and in this was considered to be quite a pioneer. Even in those early years he would often prefer to use old cars instead of horses to pull implements - in fact anything around was commandeered. He would even say that he actually disliked horses, finding them uneconomical and too labour intensive and that 'tractors were more beautiful'. Interestingly, it was Vic Savage, who still saw the value in traditional farming practices, who bought up the last of Brooke's heavy horses.

Speed of cultivation and production were Justin's criteria, and it was not uncommon to see a lorry being filled with hay and taken to an elevator to be stacked, or an old Armstrong Sidley Saloon with a hay turner hitched on the back, being furiously driven up and down one of his fields turning the hay at high speed. Of course a lot of the cars were ruined in this way, but now and then the men would be allowed to borrow them and take their families to the seaside.

It would be several years before any of the men working on the farm would own a car of their own, but the first of these was always remembered. The car itself was black and as age and mud soon encrusted the bodywork, rather than wash it, its practical owner, Willy Wade, repainted it with a good coating of tar, covering mud and rust in one glutinous coat. This process was repeated on a regular basis, whenever the rust or mud seemed to be getting the upper hand. Presumably the novelty of actually owning a car outstripped any discomfort experienced in the summer as the tar grew hot in the sun.

Despite the lack of traffic in those pre-war days, driving was not without its hazards and tragedies. Bill Day still remembered how, as a young lad, the day after he started work, he had been driven to Bury in a Trojan van. There had been a terrible accident on the way home on the Bury/Haverhill road, when a motorbike and side-car had come out of a side road and run straight into the path of the Trojan, tragically killing the woman and child who were travelling in the side-car.

Another young lad, Percy Nunn, had started his working life at fourteen years old, as a back'us boy at Wolfe Hall in Barrow, near Bury St Edmunds, cycling each day from his home at Hargrave a few miles distant. He was earning a wage of 9/4d per week.

Now a back'us boy, or 'back house boy' was literally what it says – a boy employed to work at the back of the house, fetching the coal, chopping sticks and firewood and perhaps feeding the chickens. Percy would say that, 'I was probably the worst ever back'us boy there was', but for whatever reason, it was felt that he would probably do more good helping on the farm. This he did for nearly two years until he began to feel a bit disenchanted. Although his employer was quite good, Percy did feel that he was being rather exploited. At the age of sixteen he was being given jobs on the farm that really should by rights have been given to a much older man. He decided that he could do better for himself and made up his mind to pay a visit to Mr Justin Brooke.

Percy had never met Justin before. Knocking at the front door of Clopton Hall with all the assuredness that a sixteen-year-old has, having just spent the past two years of his young life as a working man, Percy would say he was met by a pair of eyes like gimlets, 'Well, what do you want?'

'I want a job.'

'What are you getting a week?' Percy told him.

'You'll have to give a week's notice.'

Well, it frightened the life out of Percy. He daren't say he didn't want the job. Those eyes seemed to bore right through him. A week later saw Percy arriving for the early morning shift at the pasteurising unit. It was 1934.

With the ripening of the soft fruit, the summer would see hordes of pickers coming onto the farm. The pickers' fruit season would start in early June with the first strawberries ripening under cloches; the main crop strawberries, with loganberries, raspberries, blackcurrants and blackberries following in quick succession.

Transporting and marketing the fruit in those early days was always a close-run thing owing to its perishable nature and the lack of refrigeration. Any surplus fruit that didn't make it to the railway station at Clare in time or hadn't been sold locally would be brought back to the farm to be bottled or made into jam. Edith organised this up at Clopton Hall, with a band of about a dozen women and girls. The jam was made in a shed specially equipped for the purpose, and years later, long after the jam-making activities had ceased and the shed was used for other purposes, it was still known as 'the jam shed.'

In the early days, gypsies used to come onto the farm to pick the soft fruit, and at one time Justin would write of there being as many as seventy working alongside the local women. It was all piecework and pickers who were experienced could earn good money.

Later on, students from universities and schools all over the country would come to pick the plums; accommodating and feeding the vast numbers of pickers, presented an ever-increasing problem. They were billeted everywhere.

Eventually a canteen for the pickers was built on the site of the old dairy up at Clopton and dormitories were built above it, but that would come much later. The fruit picking attracted people from right across the social strata and seems to have been a hotbed for romances. One of the more famous pickers was a young man called Kenneth Riches. He was a theological student at Corpus Christi College, Cambridge and would go on to become Bishop of Lincoln. He would always say that he met and courted his future wife up a plum tree.

Pigs were also kept on the farm and were *'originally planned to complement the milk business'* by being fed the surplus. The sows were housed in outdoor farrowing pens made of zinc and wood; each had its own attached run and these were moved across the field to a fresh piece of ground each day. Justin's idea was that the sows could be put on the field after the cows had grazed it down, and they would then be followed by chickens who would scrap the field about.

A system was devised whereby the back end that housed the pig was first of all lifted onto a sort of two-wheeled cart. A small crane, which was attached to the back of a Trojan van, and which in turn was attached to a carthorse, then hoisted the front end of the run up. This procession then proceeded across the field to a new location - all this of course being undertaken with its occupant at home at the time.

Later, when nearby Home Farm, Hill Farm and Rolfes were bought up before the war, the pigs were mostly kept at Home Farm.

And later still, when Appleacre, near Stradishall, and Seabrooks were added to the estate, there were fattening houses up at Appleacre, but the farrowing sties remained a feature for many years, although their movement had by then been greatly facilitated by the addition of skids and the use of a tractors to pull them.

It was a question of pigs that had first brought Francis over to Wickhambrook sometime late in 1934 or early in 1935. Whether it was at the suggestion of his brother Adrian we don't know. There is no evidence that it was, and certainly Francis never said so, but it does seem highly probable, given the fact that Adrian already knew the Brooke family.

After his meeting with Justin Brooke, Francis would return to Weston Colville, not with the advice he had sought about going into pigs himself, but with the offer of a job. It must have seemed a very attractive offer – attractive enough to overcome any thoughts or misgivings he might have felt about losing his independence and once again being on a company payroll.

Justin had a driving ambition to plant up hundreds of acres of fruit trees and eventually these would far outstrip the soft fruit. He felt that arable farming hadn't got much of a future and that fruit had – in fact time would prove the opposite. But in 1935, the job that Francis was offered was that of helping with the management of the fruit, as well as taking overall responsibility for the pigs. He had no experience of fruit farming and didn't actually know a great deal about pigs. But, he did have skills and agricultural experience that must have convinced Justin that here was a young man who would become a great asset to his business.

Francis' credentials were colourful to say the least. Not that he would be needed to roast a goat out of doors or to round up cattle, but his experience of working in South America was something out of the ordinary. And he had set up his own business when he returned. His accomplishment in developing the experimental station in the Argentine was considerable; he had proved himself adept at learning new skills and adapting to his environment, at being a shrewd judge of character and a good manager of men. He was also popular and well liked in the neighbourhood with his sense of fun and the easy way that he had with people. Besides which, the whole set-up at Wickhambrook would have appealed to him immensely.

Justin seems always to have enjoyed having younger people about and would, over the years, have many agricultural students around the farm. Perhaps at times looking more like a medical consultant doing the ward rounds with a bevy of student doctors, than a fruit farmer, he would march about the orchards with a group of students fluttering about him, the latter eagerly pointing out various infestations or problems. Once noted, the students would tie a handkerchief around the offending bough, to be dealt with at a later stage, and hurry after their mentor.

Although Francis was by now 29 years of age, he was lively, innovative and full of enthusiasm and Justin must have felt that he would fit well into the ethos of the farm. Justin was only too aware that he couldn't do everything himself, and had spoken to Adrian of needing men to develop their own initiative. In other words the farm was growing at a phenomenal pace and Justin needed to be able to hand over much more of the day-to-day running to managers. He would say he had started with one man and a boy – by 1935 he was employing one hundred and fifty three people, and this didn't include the seasonal fruit pickers.

Also in his awareness of the need to hand over more responsibility, Justin was concerned with the continuity of his enterprise, telling Adrian, *'I want the idea to be transferred from me to them as a whole, so that if anything happened to me it would go on.'*

By now Justin and Edith had their own small son Charles, who had been born in 1931. By his previous marriage, Justin had had four children, a son Justin, and three daughters, Pleasance, Elizabeth and Jennifer; of these children, only Elizabeth would show a lasting interest in the farm. Although Pleasance did come to stay with

Francis and his family occasionally, when she visited her father, it seems that she preferred to stay at Hill Farm, rather than at Clopton Hall. But now, with the birth of Charles, Justin must have felt that his baby son gave him an added purpose and that the future of the farm was secure.

It was agreed in the first place that Francis would start working at Brookes on a part time basis. There were still his chickens to attend to at Weston Colville; these he would eventually sell off, but it would seem that he stayed on at Linden Cottage for another couple of years.

When he left, the cottage was empty for some time and became quite run down. One or two people would occasionally rent it short term, but then it was finally sold off to a Mrs Stevens who used some of Francis' old sheds to keep chickens of her own.

How ironic that the Electoral Register shows that by October 1937 Francis is recorded as having moved into Stephenson's, his brother Adrian's first little farmhouse at Stradishall. Until that date the cottage had still been the home of Annie and Will Lunnis. He must have felt that his residing at Weston Colville had become a very temporary business, for there is no record of him on an electoral register in either district in 1935 or 1936. But now by 1937 he was living at Stephenson's, and sharing the cottage with him was another young man called Ian Charnock.

Ian had been taken on at Brookes at around the same time as Francis, and was put in charge of the arable side of the business, although he never really took to farming in quite the same way as Francis. This was reflected later when Justin promoted Francis over Ian, but this fact never caused any animosity between the two men; they were both far too good-natured.

To many on the farm Ian would always be remembered as 'George' Charnock due to Francis re-naming him. In fact, just to make things really complicated, Ian had been christened John Phythian Charnock so perhaps Francis could be forgiven for making things a little more straightforward.

In a moment of hilarity, of which there would many, Francis had said that, 'You couldn't call a chap Phythian', and promptly re-christened him 'George' and George he remained to most of the men.

Another young man on the farm at that time was Hugh McCartney. He too met his future wife at the farm. She was learning jam-making and preserving. Eventually using the knowledge she acquired to good advantage, she went on to join the editorial department at *Good Housekeeping*.

Hugh was an Ulsterman and was remembered as being a 'military looking chap' and, though quietly spoken, he did have the reputation of a rather quick temper. He had come as a pupil at the beginning of the 1930s to learn about fruit growing. He lived up at Clopton Green and the house had few amenities, like most houses and cottages at that time in Suffolk. Thus it was with much laughter and leg-pulling that Hugh, along with Francis and Ian, used to go along to Clopton Hall each week to take a bath.

Those irreverent young men used to call Justin 'J.B.' or 'the Old Man' and at times 'the Old man' would become extremely angry when things weren't going quite as he thought they should. There was one such time when he was talking to Hugh about something or other and had become extremely agitated. So much so, that he had got to the point of actually snatching off his hat, flinging it to the ground and jumping up and down on it. At this Hugh, for once the calmer of the two men, didn't say a word. He just smiled at Justin, waited till he had finished, then bent down, calmly picked up the battered trilby, dusted it off, re-shaped it and placed it neatly back on J.B.'s head - and then continued to press on with his argument.

When Ian married, he went to live at Wickham House up at Clopton. And some years later, when he decided, much to Francis' amazement, to train to go into the church, Justin Brooke paid him for two years and let his family remain at Wickham House whilst he was at theological college. Justin said at the time that, 'Ian wasn't a very good farmer' and that 'perhaps he would make a better vicar' and indeed this proved to be the case. Besides which, Ian had had his responsibilities cut considerably by this time, and with a promising and ambitious young agricultural student, David Lee, waiting in the wings, it was a satisfactory way to terminate Ian's employment.

Francis' records for 1935 show that by April 20th he had started working at Wickhambrook on a part-time basis and was going over there several times a week.

**Francis organising young fruit-pickers from the back of a Trojan van**

Being Francis, he threw himself in with a great deal of enthusiasm and got involved with every aspect of his new job; although Justin said there was one thing he would never make, and that was a strawberry picker, as his back was too long. Francis must have been relieved at that.

He was initially involved with the spraying of apples up at Clopton but, with the early strawberries ripening under cloches in May, it wasn't long before the picking season had started, and what with weighing and paying the pickers, learning how to bud nursery stock, pruning and planting, his first year rapidly drew to a close on what would become his lifetime's work.

From the time he started working full time in January 1936, he kept a scant daily hand-written record of the work each day, along with a record of the weather conditions. But by 1938 he had begun to keep meticulous records of spraying and work undertaken, together with costs, and by the time war broke out in 1939, each field had its own record sheet. The extent of his technical knowledge and how quickly he had familiarised himself with his job by this time, was astounding.

Back in South America, Francis had been fascinated by the scientific nature of the work being undertaken by Don Carlos at Ing Foster. Now the knowledge that Francis had gained from him would enable him to carry out his own work at Wickhambrook in a most scientific manner. He would have the opportunity to experiment with various spraying programmes and growing techniques and would eventually come to be regarded as one of the top fruit-growing experts in the country at that time.

In his keeping of the field records, Francis not only gives us an indication of the extent and application of his ever-increasing knowledge and the responsibility that his job now carried, but also provides us with a valuable piece of social history.

Some of the field names referred to people and places that went back to pre-enclosure days – some carried no more distinctive names than '40 Acres' or '30 Acres' and of course everyone knew exactly where they were, but it's interesting to see some of the old field names that were so familiar at the time and to wonder at their associations. There was Long Deadmans and Short Deadmans up at Clopton, along with Little Clopton, Stable Ley, Pond Ley, Aspley Ley, Pightle and Hookhams; others at Rolfes had names like Hop Grounds or Tinkers Hall and there was Wellington Field, White Horse Field, Mill Field, Bread Field and Bakers Ley. At Stradishall there was Sherrards, Red Croft and Dead Hill as well as Old House Field, Millands, Dovecot and Harveys Croft. Here too were Raisins, Goymers and Coopers, Clicket Field, Sand Pits and Captains. Some associations seem obvious, referring to nearby landmarks or past usage, yet how long before all these connections will be forgotten?

How many will remember where Clicket Wood once stood beyond Hill Farm? Here arable land now stretches as far as the boundaries of the old airfield at Stradishall - now Highpoint Prison. Clicket Wood was grubbed out in 1947 by the seven Avis Brothers, that formidable hedging and ditching workhorse of a family.

And who can still remember Goymers – with the farmhouse now razed to the ground? Whose farm buildings and overgrown garden would one day provide a playground for Francis' own children?

And what about the original course of the Hollow Ditch? The stream that for centuries had worn away the clay to create a wide, steep-sided gully that ran down from where the airfield used to be, to the village of Stradishall below. With its profusion of primroses and paigles [cowslips] along its banks and the little stream at the bottom, it was a heavenly place for a child to play.

Yet with modern farming practices and the use of increasingly large machinery, the need for bigger fields and straighter boundaries must now prevail and the old ditch has been filled in and piped. And the old Ice House, that was once situated in the Hollow Ditch and gave its name to Ice House field, that too has long gone, and its location just a memory.

But what is overwhelming, even in 1939, is the actual acreage; what it all added up to. And of course more would be added later – and that was only the fruit side of the enterprise.

When Francis started in 1936 he made an approximate list of the fruit tree stock; including the soft fruit (there were 34,000 blackcurrant bushes by then), they totalled some 527,093 and this didn't include the strawberries, roses or nursery stock. These figures would soon be overtaken as the relentless programme of planting up fruit trees continued up to and after the war. Francis would eventually be managing 1,000 acres of fruit, whilst the total acreage of the whole farm was something in the region of 2,000 acres.

In those early days Francis often had to use his own car as an agricultural vehicle around the farm, and could often be seen driving across the orchards with it loaded high with prunings, or carting gallons of spray. He would always say that he ruined several of his own cars in this way and in time he would be given a car with his job. In fact he would eventually have the use of two.

Just after the war an ex-army Jeep was bought for him to use about the farm, and later he would have a series of Land Rovers. But rather more splendid vehicles were handed down for his private use. Justin was in the habit of changing his own car every three or four years, and his old car, usually a Rover, was then handed on to his Fruit Farm Manager. In later years these would be upgraded to Daimlers.

1935 would be a memorable year for another reason; there would be an event that would grip the country nationally with patriotic fever. It was the Silver Jubilee of King George V and Queen Mary

Excitement had been rising for some time at Wickhambrook with the building of an absolutely enormous bonfire up at Clopton. All the prunings from the fruit trees had been kept and tied into large bundles, and these were stacked up layer upon layer, until the bonfire towered dozens of feet up, like some huge tiered castle, complete with its flag on the top.

And what a wonderful day May 6th would prove to be, with a holiday for everyone; crowds came, young and old alike, some arriving on foot, some by bicycle, some by car. The invitation was extended to everyone. The only people who had to work at all that day were those involved with milking or working up at the dairy and they had joined the party by the early afternoon.

The weather was perfect and as Francis and 'George' Charnock carefully folded the large Union Jack flag, which was then hoisted up the new flagpole erected in front of Clopton Hall; everyone cheered and threw their hats in the air in patriotic fervour as it unfurled in the breeze.

Francis and George also helped to put up a large marquee as a massive party had been organised. Sheds that had previously housed the vans, along with the bottling shed and stores, were turned into dining halls. Adrian, who was also there, would write of *'a certain solemnity'* and of the villagers being somewhat abashed at *'the sight of the ranged plates and dishes and the attendant gentlefolk'* – they stood about the doors not liking to be the first to enter. When they eventually did and the meal commenced, it was eaten only to the accompanying murmur of subdued voices.

The sight of the newly formed local Silver Band, however, seen marching past the windows in their smart new uniforms, seems to have had a galvanizing effect on the assembled diners. With cries of recognition and amazement as well-known colleagues, husbands and sons went past in all their braided finery, the dinner was finished amidst much laughter and jocularity.

This was indeed the first public performance by the Silver Band and with cries of, *'Why – why, that's Harry – that's Fred, with the big trumpet – look, you'd hardly know him,'* the audience settled back in excited anticipation as the band struck up its first tentative notes.

All the washing up was done in large tubs set up on trestle tables out of doors, amidst much laughter and unflagging good nature, undaunted by the mountains of dirty plates awaiting attention.

The children weren't forgotten either, with a tea party for them in the afternoon. This was followed by a film show that took place in the 'jam shed', which had been utilized as a cinema for the day. The film shown to the children was 'Mickey Mouse' and Edith took charge of this side of things – she was actually very interested in photography and could often be seen about the farm with her cine camera, filming various developments on the farm or, as she did on this day, recording momentous events.

After the film show there were sports with races and a tug of war, all to the accompaniment of the Silver Band who played throughout. As evening drew on the night sky was lit up first by a firework display, and then by the shooting sparks and flames from the huge bonfire. It had been thoroughly doused with paraffin that morning just to ensure the maximum effect.

Who could have known that in a little more than two years, another huge bonfire would be built and preparations would be under way for yet another royal occasion? In that brief time, the present King would die, another would abdicate and a new King, George VI, would be crowned.

On the day of the Coronation, May 12th 1937, it rained. It didn't put a stop to the festivities but it must have made things difficult. The weather had been dull and wet; the land was saturated. With tractors at a standstill, Francis had started building the bonfire nearly a month earlier. There had been a few warmer days in early May and the sun had managed to make a brief appearance, but now on Coronation day, it was raining again. The Silver Band was there of course, and Elizabeth Brooke too, aged fourteen - dancing in her Wellington boots with Francis. There was also a five-a-side football competition. It was played on the Bee Meadow at Clopton and the dairy put a team in. They were up against Hargrave, the neighbouring village, whom they beat 1-0, and were rewarded with a prize of two hundred cigarettes each.

Along with these big celebrations for national events, Justin also revived the old Suffolk tradition of the annual Harvest Horkey. This was a traditional meal given for the workers and their families, by the farmer and his wife, after the last load of corn had been brought in and safely stacked. At the Horkey the farmer and his family would wait upon the guests. Afterwards he would thank the men for their hard work and announce the bonus, and the oldest of the farm workers would reply on behalf of the men.

Now the bonus was a lump sum of money given *'according to the results of the year, at so much in the pound paid on all wages including overtime'* and this was eagerly awaited. Naturally the harder you worked, the more you earned, the greater the bonus. The men felt that Justin was a fair employer and would say that they never worked a minute of overtime without being paid for it.

Justin would record the bonus being as much as £5 per man before the war, which was equivalent to more than three week's wages and a considerable sum in those days and he paid very good wages. It was a sort of profit sharing, but the bonus did tend to vary and most people believed Justin just thought of a number.

Justin would always see the Harvest Horkey as a great event.

He would have his own family wait at table and Francis and George would help too. Some sort of entertainment usually followed and this would sometimes be a film show of events on the farm that had been taken by Edith. After Justin had made his speech and announced the bonus, Francis would be called upon to reply.

For someone as gregarious as Francis, this call to public speaking caused him quite inconceivable embarrassment. Failing to spend a little time in preparation, he would instead resort to swallowing a couple of neat whiskeys at home before making his way to the Horkey. Unfortunately this didn't have the desired effect of clearing his head – quite the reverse in fact.

1935 had also seen the building of a dozen bungalows for the men on the farm and their families to live in.

Justin had already given the council some land at the top of the lane leading down to Clopton Hall, *'and persuaded the council ... to build some cottages'* on it. However, with an ever expanding workforce, many of whom had to cycle a considerable distance to work each day, Justin felt he should provide some additional accommodation on the farm. Baileys the builders from Wickhambrook were given the job of building them.

Although they had brick footings and brick chimneys, the bungalows were built of wood and asbestos sheeting and 'were rather like glorified holiday chalets' although they were comfortable and dry. Their design was simple, consisting of four rooms: two bedrooms, a kitchen and a living room, and though there was no electricity or running water, they did have the benefit of a good cooking stove. Each had an earth closet down the garden and an outhouse with a copper for washday. Water was obtained from a communal tank, which was filled by the local council.

Later, when a retired Indian Army Captain and his wife came to live in one of the bungalows, they had a chemical Elsan toilet installed instead of the earth closet; everyone was scandalised. 'What would they put on the garden?'

How ironic it seems today, that most of the cottages around the village deemed unfit to live in then, are now are highly desirable little thatched gems. And some of the 'modern' bungalows built to provide a better alternative to the leaking thatch, are but mournful reminders of an age when asbestos was deemed a safe building material.

The new bungalows were situated opposite Wickham House on the unmade-up lane leading to Denston. Thankfully it would seem that moving-in day for at least one of the new occupants was a fine one, which was just as well, as their furniture and belongings were dumped in a heap unceremoniously in the little front garden. It wouldn't be long before the sound of a steamroller could be heard making its snorting progress along the lane from Clopton Hall.

With the building of a vast new milking parlour right in the midst of the old buildings at Wickham House and now with the new bungalows too, the traffic had increased considerably down what was once a quiet unmade-up country lane. With the transportation of the milk by van from the milking parlour to the pasteurising and bottling unit up at Clopton Hall, creating a constant stream of vehicles all day, and churning the lane into a quagmire, it had become apparent that the road would have to be done up.

At Justin's expense, the council agreed to come and tar the road. And this they did, arriving one day with a steamroller and a gang of men armed with shovels. Edith was there with her cine camera, recording another little piece of history in the making. The lane was soon widened and re-surfaced as far as Wickham House and the bungalows and the council then agreed to take over responsibility for its upkeep.

There is a great deal of handwork involved with fruit growing; this was particularly so in the early days and the organisation of this, as with everything else connected with the fruit, fell to Francis. The land around the bushes and trees had to be kept free of weeds – fields of strawberries had to be hoed.

With a continual programme of fruit tree planting, there was the ever-increasing job throughout the winter of pruning the trees, which was not only labour intensive, but the men employed there had to be taught the art. Francis spent a lot of time teaching them and supervising the work. And of course he had to learn too. Every tree had to be individually pruned; each tree was different and required different techniques.

Later Francis had the idea of giving the men photographs of pruned trees from trade journals to show them the effects he wanted, and he also took them around the orchards when the trees were fruiting, so that they could see the results of their labours. He felt that they would be more interested in their work and not find it so tedious if they understood and took an interest in what they were doing.

The fruit trees seemed to be growing well on the heavy clay land, but there would be much discussion between Justin and Francis as to the extent and timing of the pruning in order to produce the greatest amount of growth and the heaviest crops and they would seldom fully agree.

There was also the idea of planting very young trees directly into position in the fields; Justin seems to have favoured this idea feeling it saved time and labour, whilst Francis felt that a better eye could be kept on them, if the young trees remained in the nursery longer and received their initial pruning there before being later planted out.

There would be arguments about the spacing between trees. Justin favoured a 30ft. x 30ft. planting distance, whilst 20 x 20 was being recommended and was favoured by Francis as being easier to work through with a tractor, and then it was 18ft. by 20ft… And so it went on.

Discussions would usually end up with some sort of compromise, and of course much of that early work was in the pioneer stage anyway, with much to be learnt from trial and error. This was fruit production on a huge commercial scale, and always ways would be sought to speed production and marketing in the most economic way that was possible. And then there was the constant programme of spraying - a huge expense in itself and one that could not be compromised. Nothing could be left to chance. Prevention was always considered better than cure.

In the early days the sprays used were more diluted than their counterparts used today and the spraying machines required a constant supply of water. Much of the early spraying and dusting of the trees and bushes was haphazard and time-consuming. Sometimes this was done with a man walking along with a small tank on two wheels, whilst one girl pumped and another held up a thick hose through which clouds of dust was puffed up into the fruit trees. Another method, used with the blackcurrants and loganberries, was with a man walking behind a small motorised tank, whilst two other men, often running alongside to keep up with the machine, held hoses through which masses of liquid spray was sprayed out over the bushes and usually over themselves as well. Of course little protective clothing was worn then other than a cloth cap or perhaps an apron.

Men also walked up and down the rows of currants with an early version of a knapsack sprayer on their backs. Pausing at every bush, they vigorously pumped a lever up and down and a shower of dust came out covering the bush. Eventually small tractors would be used, pulling a spray pump and tank mounted on a four-wheeled harvest trolley, but the bigger the spray tanks became, the more water they needed. As with so much of farming, having a supply of water close at hand was essential – this was to ensure that time would not be lost in waiting for water to arrive to refill the spray tanks.

Justin had earlier engaged some unemployed men to dig ponds about the farm and had water piped from there, but Francis would eventually help to solve this problem by having a system of dams constructed in the Hollow Ditch and a small reservoir created at the top end. Despite all the work with pruning and spraying, so much was at the mercy of the elements.

Generally speaking the climatic conditions of East Anglia with its low rainfall and high levels of sunshine were favourable to fruit growing, but there was always the danger of late frosts and unseasonable gales. Francis would say that, 'frost would roll down a hillside like treacle, to find its level at the lower end' and with this in mind he had the Hollow Ditch cleared of scrub to attract the frost to it. And despite Justin's theory about the trees being in bud later by being north facing, there were times when the whole crop was feared to have been decimated by a particularly bitter late frost.

The spraying programme was intensive and, until well after the Second World War, continued to be a matter for scientific discussion and experimentation. A typical spraying programme would start with a winter wash of tar oil and this would be followed perhaps by a dousing of D.D.T. as the buds were about to burst. Soon after would come Lime Sulphur, then Lime Sulphur with Nicotine and Lime Sulphur with Arsenate of Lead. The Cox orchards would have Mercurated Lead used instead of Lime Sulphur after flowering. Attacks by aphids, the dreaded Red Spider Mite and Silver Leaf could devastate whole orchards and Francis kept a constant watch on all of the trees.

All this was quite general and recommended practice and there was little thought given to the consequences of using such sprays on food that was to be eaten - it would not be until 1949, that the Women's Institute actually questioned their usage and the possibility of there being any side effects.

Francis regularly received copies of *The American Fruit Grower* and learnt a great deal that he was able to adapt to the farm's own needs. He became a regular contributor both to this publication and to *The Commercial Fruit Grower in the U.K.* and was in constant communication with other growers, both here and in The United States. Talks and visits were organised to various agricultural institutions, as well as tours to other fruit farms about the country. His opinion on all the various aspects of fruit growing would soon be sought and his expertise valued.

Justin had given Francis the freedom he needed to realise his full potential. All decisions about marketing, spray programmes, pruning, and picking, in fact any work connected with the fruit, would become Francis' sole responsibility, even down to the hiring and firing. And although he and Justin would discuss daily the work in progress – Francis went each morning to have breakfast with Justin and Edith up at Clopton Hall – his responsibilities and workload were absolutely enormous. He would in time be second only to Justin himself.

Justin as *'Rayner'* had said to Adrian in 1935 that he wanted men to use their initiative. *'This is a business, not just a farm. The thing is to make the heads of departments responsible for results.'*

In Francis he had found just that man.

# Part Five
# Stradishall

Of course Francis hadn't led a celibate life. In fact one friend from that time would say with a twinkle in her eye,

'He was such a racy man.'

Yet despite this reputation, no doubt well founded, it seems that by the latter part of 1938 Francis thought that perhaps he ought to be finding himself a wife. There had been many eligible girls in his life since his return to Britain, but only one so far, that he had actually considered marrying and she was now married to someone else.

Adrian and Marjorie had recently moved from Creems to live at The Old Rectory at Redisham. The recent addition to their family of the twins, Martin and Sylvia, who had been born in the August, the marriage of his sister Stephanie to Jack and then the birth of their baby son Adrian, must all have contributed to the feeling Francis had, that perhaps he should be settling down and having a family of his own. Work on the farm and the building up of the fruit had totally absorbed him and he loved the job. His own family had by now decided that he was a confirmed bachelor, but Francis would surprise them all.

George and Francis had just moved from Stephenson's to live at Hill Farm in Stradishall – they moved in on October 12th 1938. No time was taken off work, although Francis did manage to record this event in his diary with the word 'moved'. His marriage eight months later did not merit a mention.

Situated half way up the hill out of the village, the lovely old Suffolk farmhouse had been lived in by George and Isabel Scott since 1935 and had just become available. Justin had bought the farm previously and all the land around the farmyard and buildings was being planted up with apple trees. The house, with its draughty leaded windows and gables was a typical Suffolk timber-framed farmhouse. Its pargeted walls concealed a mellow, rambling interior with exposed beams, great open fireplaces, attics, brick floors, stairs that led to nowhere and an old black-leaded range in the kitchen.

**Hill Farm, Stradishall 1940**

It did however, have the luxury of a bathroom of sorts with a cold water supply only, a bath, basin and toilet having been placed in what used to be the coal shed, just off the kitchen. Here a bath could be taken, though not too frequently, especially in winter – the water having to be heated first and then carried to the bathroom. The scullery, which you stepped into from the back door, had a pump, and the water was pumped up here by hand from a well in the garden. From here it went up to a holding tank in the roof.

Using the toilet required a certain amount of forward planning, the user having to be sure that the tank held sufficient water to work the cistern by first visiting the scullery and pumping the water up. The drainage for the house went via a cesspit to a reed bed, at the side of the garden. This reed bed would always be known as the 'sewer garden'.

For many years oil lamps and candles were the only available light for the house; a wind generator was later attached to a pole on the corner of the barn in the yard, with a bank of batteries in the dairy. This would provide a limited amount of light that would grow progressively dimmer as the evening wore on, being just sufficient to go to bed with after the oil lamps had been extinguished. In fact the wind generator only really proved to be effective when the strongest of gales was blowing.

Fanny and Robert had by now moved from The Gables to take up residence at The Four Swans in Sudbury, and the distribution of the furniture around the family did provide Francis with enough to furnish the house. A four-burner oil stove from Fanny was substituted for the range and Ian and Francis continued with their housekeeping in much the same way as they always had done. With one exception that is – the additional help of Rosy Nunn.

Rosy had been a cook in Bury St Edmunds when she fell in love with Bob Nunn. When Bob became ill with T.B. he came to work in the garden at Clopton Hall and Rosy came to help in the house and later on to help Francis as well. She used to go fruit picking on the farm with her friend Nellie Grimwood. Their conversations would often be of making ends meet and with no money left by the end of the week; Fridays were always known as Oxo days. A piece of bread and an Oxo cube dissolved in hot water was the mainstay of many households in those days, and they no doubt would be the first to say that they were none the worse for it.

Francis first met Barbara that October, just after he and Georgehad moved in to Hill Farm. He and George, together with Bob Berry, had gone to a dance that was being held in a village hall near Cambridge. In fact three local families, one of which had invited Francis and his friends, were actually giving the party.

Initially everyone was to meet up at the home of the particular family who had sent the invitation, and then to go on to the hall together for the dancing. It was a very foggy night and when everyone had gathered at the village hall, they found that the band had got lost in the fog and hadn't turned up. The hall was somewhat cheerless with a small smoking fire at one end, which was immediately huddled around by a group of shivering girls in their skimpy dance dresses. The men all decided to retire to the local pub until further news.

The band did eventually arrive, but by this time most of the men were fairly under the weather and the dance started in a rather undignified manner with George actually passing out.

Barbara Kingston was there with her cousin Olave Grain, who lived near Cambridge. They had been great friends since childhood and had come at the invitation of one of the other families. Barbara's father was Harold Abercrombie Kingston, an estate agent and auctioneer with his family firm in Spalding. Harold had met Barbara's mother, Emeline Barbara Chalk, whilst a pupil at her family's firm of auctioneers and estate agents called Grain and Chalk, which was based in Cambridge. Her sister, another Frances, had married Peter Grain and Olave was one of their daughters. Harold lodged with Emeline's father, Philip Chalk at Linton.

Emeline, who would always be known as 'Bombo' to her grandchildren, and 'Emma fat' to her brothers, married Harold (Mannie) in Linton Church. Always having a great sense of humour, even when the joke was against her, Bombo would laughingly tell of a comment she had overheard at her wedding, as she and Mannie walked back up the aisle, 'Isn't it amazing how plain girls always seem to marry such handsome men?'

Barbara would later describe her family as 'stolid and old-fashioned' and perhaps they were, but they were representative of a passing era; the good solid middle class family with Victorian values, that were the backbone of their local communities. Her grandfather Philip had been Churchwarden of Linton Church for fifty years.

Both Barbara's parents excelled at sports, her father being a first class rifle marksman and keen golfer, whilst her mother played tennis to such a high standard, that she had actually been invited to play at Wimbledon in the 1920s. The only reason she had not played, in fact, was that she had had to stay at home to nurse her children who had just gone down with chickenpox.

Barbara had attended Felixstowe Ladies College as a boarder from the age of thirteen and, hating the academic side of school, would say that she only ever enjoyed games. She had left there without distinction, but in her own quiet way was something of a rebel.

Her mother's expectation was that she would stay at home until marriage, with perhaps a little genteel flower arranging to keep her busy. Barbara's ideas were very different. She wanted to go to London to study and become a beautician under Elizabeth Arden. Bombo was horrified and permission was flatly refused. A compromise was sought after much argument, and a middle way agreed upon. Barbara would continue to live at home, but would go as an apprentice to a hairdresser in Spalding; approved of by her mother of course.

Barbara was first asked to dance by Bob, and was later introduced to Francis, who then asked her to dance with him. Whilst they were dancing, Francis put a slip of paper down the front of her frock. It had his phone number on it, and the request that she should get in touch. It would seem that he had already picked her out, for he later told Bob, 'That's the girl I'm going to marry.'

Like her father, Barbara was tall, though remarkably light on her feet. She loved dancing and had spent many years learning ballet only to be told later to her great chagrin, as she towered above her fellow pupils, that she had grown too tall to continue. An invitation to come over to Hill Farm for a weekend soon followed the dance, and was accepted. Francis had vaguely implied that his family lived there, though it would seem that Barbara's mother was perhaps understandably a little concerned. She insisted that Barbara's other great friend Nan Smith, a farmer's daughter from Spalding, should accompany her as a chaperone. And for Francis' part, Bob was always with him to make up a foursome.

In fact throughout their courtship, with a routine of meeting up at each other's houses alternate weekends, Barbara and Francis were rarely if ever alone together. So much so, that Barbara's mother actually thought in the end that it was Bob Berry who was doing the courting.

Sometimes when the girls went over to Stradishall, they would all go dancing at Great Yeldham. Dances were regularly held in a room at the back of The White Hart; one week there would be a three-piece band, another a gramophone. Francis and Bob would often end up going off to the bar, leaving the girls to dance with some of the R.A.F. boys who were based at Stradishall, Tommy Bamford being one such boy. And somehow it didn't seem to matter. Everyone was having fun - well, almost everyone.

Francis, noticing that Tommy and Barbara seemed to be getting on rather well together, couldn't help telling Tommy afterwards that he was dancing with his girl, and not to get too involved, as he was going to marry her.

Tommy told this to Barbara in some amazement, as it was the first he had heard about it. And of course it was news to Barbara too. Especially as, at this point in the courtship, she had only met Francis twice.

To say that Barbara was swept off her feet was an understatement. Of course she was – Francis for a start was that much older, thirty-two to her twenty-three years and, it has to be said, a fairly confident and self-assured character. But he was also charming, well-mannered and such good fun and quite unlike anyone she had met before. She must have felt very flattered. Here was this good-looking man, who seemed to her at the time, to be so sophisticated and so much a man of the world with his stories of South America and travel. It wouldn't be long before she began to realise that what Tommy had told her wasn't far from the truth. Francis was indeed going to ask her to marry him.

She talked it through with Nan one day,

'Do you think he's too intelligent for me Nan? Would he be bored with me?'

Nan thought about it and about Francis and told her that she thought it would be O.K. Yes, it was rather soon, but in those days with the threat of another war looming, lots of people were getting married. There seemed to be urgency somehow in so many relationships at that time, a need for life to be lived to the full whilst there was still some certainty about it.

Perhaps predictably they were in a pub when Francis asked her to marry him; it was just before Christmas. They had barely known each other eight weeks and had hardly spent any time alone together. Of course Barbara said 'Yes' and Francis then asked her to come over to Sudbury with him, to meet his parents at The Four Swans.

In later years and sadder times, Barbara would sometimes wonder what Francis had seen in her. They hardly knew each other - their courtship had been such a whirlwind and yet reading Francis letters to her at the time, he had fallen completely and utterly in love with her. He didn't marry her for money – it wasn't his way. And although Barbara came from a wealthier background than his own, he would always see it as his responsibility to keep his family. The only time he ever referred to her family's money would be to say that he always knew if anything happened to him, she would have her family to turn to.

He hadn't expected to fall in love, or certainly not as quickly, and it seems Bob hadn't expected him to either. Two confirmed bachelors, as Bob would say, *'the old firm of Bell & Berry'*. Yet even Bob would say in his letter of congratulations to Barbara, *'I've honestly never seen old Bell in such good form. I began to think he was too old for any romance but it just goes to show.'* As a man of the turf, he was utterly delighted for Francis. *'I'm sure you've both picked a winner and I know the form fairly well.'*

Francis for his part was very perceptive and always a good judge of character. Did he see an open-faced, straightforward girl who was actually a lot of fun at the time, and who, coming from a conventional if rather staid family so unlike his own, would bear his children and provide the domesticity and stability his own life had always lacked? There could be no mistaking their mutual joy and excitement at their engagement and Francis, writing to her at the time, could hardly believe what had happened.

'Hill Farm, Monday night

My darling Barbara

I wonder if you got my silly note I wrote early this morning – I just had to [write] I was feeling on top of my form.

Dearest, I can't yet believe it's true. But it is isn't it?

Bob [Berry] and I went home like a couple of lunatics – he said 'Good old Bell' and I said 'Good old Berry' and we called at all the pubs en route to celebrate. And when we got to Huntingdon, Bob said he'd ring you up. Darling it's just grand – I feel like shouting it to everybody – but won't.

I'm longing to hear if you're coming down on Friday – and we can look at rings too if you like.

I expect you'll have some more brainy ideas. I wrote Mother a bread and butter letter today – I'm afraid she's beginning not to like me so much now – still it doesn't matter – it's my Barbie that matters. Darling I do want to marry you soon. You don't know how I love you.

I'm going round to Bob's tonight and we're going to get in touch with Michael Earle.

You're an absolute brick Barbara, to take me on like this – I wish I had more to recommend me. I'm feeling I must get a move on or you'll change your mind – but dearest I do feel absolutely on top of the world, bless your heart. I love the way you say, 'We'll be alright, we'll get on'. Darling I know we shall. I've never been more certain of anything. I shall try so hard to be a decent rat. I am hoping you'll come this weekend – even if it is the last, because I've so much to talk to you about – and the future does look so rosy for me.

I haven't mentioned it to my boss yet – he's not very well today, but I will do when I get him alone.

What a bit of luck meeting you Barbara – it's awful to think I might have missed you – funny to think how near it was too, isn't it.

I keep seeing you in my mind all day – just as you were at the weekend.

Barbara, I am so happy I can't write at all coherently, so forgive me, but perhaps you can understand how I feel. Try and keep Mother in a good mood especially till I come over and tackle Pop – I will too next time I come.

*I'm longing to hear what you think about it all, especially now I'm not with you and you've got that good 'common sense' to work. And will you marry me soon darling and how long shall I have to be engaged to you? So much there is I want to know - Barbara I do love you so much.*
*Write to me won't you*
*Your very own Francis*

Barbara had never met anyone quite like her future mother-in-law before. In fact the whole family enchanted her. They seemed so Bohemian and artistic to her untutored eye, and very attractive.

Fanny of course was full of bubble and chat and thrilled to bits about the engagement, telling Barbara in a quieter moment, that she wasn't sure which of the two girls, Nan or Barbara, Francis had wanted to marry, but that she was very pleased with his choice.

Robert as always was much in the background and in fact at first Barbara hardly noticed him at all. He was by now profoundly deaf and consequently very quiet. But, like Fanny, he too was pleased. Francis had always held a special place in his heart – perhaps he had always felt he had to compensate for the attention Fanny had given to Adrian, and her apparent lack of interest in her two younger children?

Fanny would in fact prove to be 'a lovely mother-in-law' to Barbara. And if some of Fanny's ways at times were a little strange, she never criticised Barbara or interfered, always finding ways of praising her.

Her own family were not so easy. Perhaps slightly shocked would be a better way of putting it. It was all so sudden. A little reassurance was needed. Even Rosy had asked when the baby was due. A family meeting was held and concerns were voiced. They didn't know anything about the Bell family. Who were they?

Uncle Peter Grain, Olave's father, described by Barbara as 'a jolly old boy', took himself off to Thurlow to make a few enquiries on the family's behalf. To see what sort of fellow Francis was. Naturally the pub at Thurlow was his first port of call, and there he found that Francis was indeed well known and well liked – as indeed he seemed to be at every pub he called at. In fact he would later say that, 'Francis got a good write up.'

Uncle Tom Chalk, one of Bombo's brothers was also called in to give his opinion. Now he used to go about the farms in the area, doing valuations. He knew the district well and was soon able to reassure the family about Francis' credentials and prospects.

The wedding was fixed for the following May and of course Barbara wasn't pregnant. There could hardly have been an opportunity with all that careful chaperoning. Two years would pass before their first child was born, though some would watch the months leading up to the wedding with a little scepticism.

With Barbara coming from such a well-known local family, the Spalding Free Press came to interview the young engaged couple. Of course mention was made of both of her parents' sporting achievements, as well as Barbara's own not inconsiderable tennis playing. Although her mother played at county level, both she and Barbara were members of the Spalding Tennis Club.

Francis was asked what sports he played. He told the reporter that he played for the 'Odds and Sods', a mixed hockey team, which he quite enjoyed although he found the women players rather aggressive. The reporter raised a sceptical eyebrow. Francis hastened to add that he also played cricket. Ah, yes, safer ground.

A team, Francis went on to explain, had been got up from the pubs at Thurlow and Wickhambrook, with Bob Berry, Carl Long and one or two others, with matches arranged against other villages. Francis added that none of the playing was taken very seriously and to qualify this, went on to tell the reporter that the team's motto was 'Win or Lose, Have a Booze.' Bombo was horrified.

Both she and Mannie decided that they would go over to Hill Farm to see the house. They too were under the impression that the Bell family all lived there, and Barbara and Nan hadn't disillusioned them. Rosy was commissioned by Barbara to leave her coat on a bed in one of the bedrooms, to give the idea of occupancy. And as Barbara conducted her parents around, she vaguely alluded to Fanny and

Robert as she swept them past the open bedroom door. By the twinkle in her father's eye, she didn't think she had fooled them but it was worth a try.

At the end of the tour, Bombo conceded that she liked the house very much and that she thought Barbara could manage very nicely there, with two maids and someone to come in and do the rough. Barbara's reply that she would be all three must have caused her mother a few anxious moments.

Barbara could have had any sort of wedding she wanted, but she was determined to have a quiet one without a lot of money being wasted. She felt that she could put the money to better use at Hill Farm. And besides, she had never seen herself wafting down the aisle in a haze of white. Instead she chose a blue angora dress and jacket that she matched with brown accessories, together with some brightly coloured anemones in her hat and buttonhole. Did she realise that she would complement Francis' brown suit that he had bought back from South America so perfectly?

Canon Nicholas, then Vicar of Spalding, married them in Spalding Parish Church on May 21st 1939. Both sets of parents were there as well as Barbara's two younger brothers, Peter and Newy. Justin and Edith had also been asked, but declined on account of the distance. Barbara did regret this, as in her words, she 'would have liked them to have seen her home and the sort of family Francis was marrying into.' There were no bridesmaids and no matrons of honour, but Bob Berry, still a bachelor himself, was Francis' best man. And Stephanie was there. How could she miss Francis' wedding?

She didn't seem to have known about it for very long, or if she did, had not really made any plans to go. She and Jack were living at Preston where Jack farmed and it would seem that she had woken up that morning and realised that it was Francis' wedding day. She mentioned the fact to Jack. His immediate response was to say, 'You really want to go don't you?' Of course she did. So she jumped in the car and set off on her own for Spalding church.

**Francis and Barbara's wedding**
Left to right: Robert, Fanny, Peter K., Stephanie, Bob Berry, Frances, Barbara, Bombo K., Mannie K., Newy K.

Adrian and Marjorie didn't attend. No doubt with three-year old Anthea and twin babies barely nine months old, they felt they had enough to cope with.

Despite Barbara's wish for a quiet wedding, there were actually quite a number of guests and the lengthy 'presents' list no doubt reflected the affection with which both she and Francis were held. No one seemed to have forgotten them, whether it was Vic and Martha Savage or the Swann family from the Weston Colville days or the men on the farm at Stradishall; friends and family alike all wished them well. After a reception in the marquee that had been erected at her parents' house in Spalding, the couple set off for their honeymoon. Francis had bought a 'new' car especially for the occasion - new to him that is. He obviously felt the moment warranted a greater outlay or perhaps it was that he felt the length of journey to be undertaken required greater reliability – seeing as he hoped to take his bride down to the West Country for their honeymoon. And rather than spend the £5 he usually spent on a new car, he did actually purchase one for

£25. They drove as far as Rutland on the first night; Francis had booked them into a hotel in Oakham.

By the following evening they were in Wiltshire and it was from here that they both wrote to Barbara's parents,

'Angel Hotel,
Chippenham.
Sunday.
My dearest Daddy and Mum,
Everything is simply marvellous. I love being married and I think Francis is an ideal husband.

Have all your party gone yet? I bet it will take weeks to clear up but I did enjoy my wedding ever so much. Thank you for giving us such a wonderful send off.'

'Dear Mr. and Mrs. Kingston,
As I did not have to make a speech (thank heaven) I did not have the opportunity to thank you both for all the kindness I have received from you – I am indeed very very grateful and thank you from the bottom of my heart.

We are terribly happy just wandering round the country and I think you have the most wonderful daughter.

My love, Francis (& Barby)'

From Chippenham they journeyed on down to Devon and Cornwall, stopping off at the Lion Hotel, Dulverton for a night. For the princely sum of £1 8s. 9d., they had dinner, bed and breakfast, morning tea, garaging for the car and sandwiches to take with them the following day.

Apart from a couple of odd days spent visiting the Research Institute at East Malling, for Francis this would be the first proper holiday he had taken from work in four years. Except for very occasional days when there was picking, he did not work on Sundays; Saturday afternoons, Christmas Day and Good Friday were also taken off, but never a bank holiday Monday.

Working a bank holiday was normal then, though by 1938, some of the men obviously felt otherwise. In fact Francis felt it remarkable enough to record in his diary entry for Easter Monday 1938, *'several men absent'*.

The ten days of his marriage and honeymoon were his first real time off to relax and to forget about the fruit and the weather, and of course to actually get to know the young woman he had married.

**Barbara and Francis on honeymoon in the West Country, May 1939**

For Barbara, those early days of marriage could only be described as a steep learning curve.

For a start she had no idea how involved and responsible Francis' job actually was – never an early riser herself, the sound of him whistling and banging about downstairs at 6.00 a.m. on that first Tuesday morning back at Hill Farm, as he got himself shaved and dressed, must have been quite a shock. And then the water had to be pumped up and the oil lamps filled.

He did bring her up a cup of tea in bed, as he would each morning, before setting off to have breakfast up at Clopton Hall. George and Hugh would join him there, and here the work of the day would be discussed over bacon, eggs and coffee, the pouring out of which Edith made a great ritual – each man having his own particular preference for how he liked his coffee. And all this before being out ready to greet the men as they arrived for work and getting them started on the jobs for the day ...

Back in the kitchen at Hill Farm, Barbara was struggling with the oil stove. Her cooking skills were minimal in those early days, and she decided to start with the only item in her culinary repertoire – a fatless sponge cake.

She soon discovered that cooking in a paraffin oven was far removed from the modern electric cooker in her mother's kitchen. For a start the door didn't fit, and she soon found that it could only be lit after an oily rag had been pulled through the feeder pipe; by which time both her hands were covered with paraffin, which didn't improve the flavour of the cake.

But manage she did, and between them, with Francis' added expertise at omelettes to help things out, they settled into married life. Francis would always choose the joint from the selection brought by the butcher's roundsman who called twice a week. Francis felt he had superior knowledge in such matters and would always elect to 'choose the joint' as his own particular contribution to the smooth running of his household. For Barbara however, it would take several attempts before she mastered the intricacies of a perfect roast and her early efforts would cause both of them much amusement.

Before they were married, Justin had asked Barbara and Francis, if they would prefer to live at Goymers, a lovely old half-timbered farmhouse that lay down a very long drive off to the left, at the top of Edmunds Hill. Barbara was concerned that the tradesmen wouldn't call and said she felt Hill Farm would be better situated. Justin had bought Goymers Farm for the land, and the picturesque old house with its derelict outbuildings and unkempt garden, would remain empty for many years, gradually becoming a ruin before the site was finally cleared.

Most of the local tradesmen in the area delivered around the villages and farms right up until the 1960s and beyond. Bread was delivered regularly from the village bakery at Wickhambrook, and Clare, just five miles from Hill Farm, was the nearest town for shopping.

In those days, there was a tiny village shop in Stradishall, along with a pub called The Hound, a parish church, hall, and a school; but it was in Denston that there was the most amazing village shop. With its dark interior and boarded floor, it was stocked from floor to ceiling. Mops, brooms and buckets hung from above, whilst coal hods, shovels and pokers competed for space amidst candles, wicks and hatchets.

Here, by carefully negotiating a passage through, one could buy absolutely anything from an oil lamp to a mousetrap - or perhaps a sherbet dip or a few sweets from the wonderful array of glass jars behind the counter, depending on the age of the customer.

But it was from Clare that the general weekly grocery shopping came, and this by way of Mr Emerson and the Lufkin Bros' delivery van. The order would be taken on a Tuesday for delivery on the Thursday and the arrival of Mr Emerson was always a great social event. A chair would be pulled out and the kettle put on for a cup of tea. Whilst Barbara discussed what she required for the following week, Mr Emerson would make helpful suggestions as he wrote down the list. And on Thursday there he was, back again with the groceries, and just in time for another cup of tea.

On the rare occasions that Francis bought any clothes, a visit would be made to Mr Ince, the tailor and gentleman's outfitter in Clare. His shop was situated on the opposite side to Lufkin's, a little further down the street.

Here, complete with his badge of office, a tape measure around his neck, you would be greeted by Mr Ince, or handed over to his very obliging assistant 'the boy Arthur' - the name by which he would always be known, right into old age. Not that there ever really seemed a time when he wasn't old.

Once in the 1950s, Mr Ince was threatening to sell up. By now 'the boy Arthur' seemed to be very old and doddering, although he still managed to cycle the five miles to work each day from Cavendish.

Greeting Barbara with a quavering voice one day, he expressed his fears about being out of work,

'Any job that comes along Mrs Bell, I shall snap it up.'

Barbara could hardly keep a straight face. The thought of 'the boy Arthur' being able to 'snap' anything up was quite beyond her.

But the shop remained and so did 'the boy Arthur'. Here a man could be measured and fitted out in corduroys, as indeed Adrian had been all those years back in the 1920s when he first came to Suffolk; or a good suit, or perhaps as in Francis' case one day, a nightshirt.

Entering the shop, Francis was greeted in the customary way by 'the boy Arthur'. Could he help Mr Bell?

'Do you have such a thing as a nightshirt?'

Yes, he thought he had, 'although pyjama suits do seem to be becoming very popular Mr Bell.' But a nightshirt was what Francis really wanted and 'the boy Arthur' disappeared upstairs and could soon be heard rummaging about amongst the stock. Some time passed before he eventually emerged triumphant. He was carrying a flattened dusty package that must have dated back to before the First World War. Unwrapping it with reverence he proudly produced a faded cream and blue striped nightshirt, folded and held in shape by a series of very rusty staples. Never mind the staples - Francis was delighted.

'How absolutely splendid. The very thing.'

Whenever the need arose for a greater choice than Clare could offer, a trip to Bury St Edmunds was arranged. It was a journey of about sixteen miles and although Barbara drove the car in, there were still at that time, horses and tumbrels to be seen coming in from neighbouring farms and villages. These would be bringing eggs, butter, fruit, flowers and vegetables to sell in the market.

It was a journey only to be undertaken on special occasions, but such trips were anticipated with great excitement. Usually coinciding with market day, shoe shops and clothes shops would be visited and bargains sought. The one requisite that was not delivered to Hill Farm at that time was fish, and a trip to Bury always ensured that fish would be on the menu the following day.

Although Francis would never become a dedicated gardener, with the flush of early married bliss, he and Barbara did initially create a garden at Hill Farm. George Charnock had given them a lawnmower as a wedding present and Francis could often be seen after work, pipe in mouth, racing back and forth over the grass. Later the borders and trellis work would become mostly grass and a man from the farm would go over it all with a gang-mower, but in those early days, Barbara would spend hours out of doors re-creating something of the garden she had left behind her in Spalding.

With the full-time help of Elvy the gardener, the five acres of garden, tennis court and orchard at Linton House were immaculate, and the well-kept borders bloomed with an abundance of colour and variation through much of the year. Elvy had been Mannie's batman during the First World War and had remained with him ever since.

It was not that Mannie had ever actually gone to war. Playing a game of football at a training camp one day, prior to being sent to France, he had badly damaged his knee. The injury was sufficiently serious in those days for the doctor at the camp to recommend that the leg be amputated. Bombo was incensed. She absolutely forbade the surgeon to continue and insisted that she would nurse him and take the consequences. And this she did, and Mannie remained on British soil for the remainder of the war. The injury certainly prevented him from being in active service, and though in constant pain, he did keep his leg.

Some years later Mannie met an old shepherd who had something of a local reputation as a healer. Asking him to take a look at his knee, the old man did some manipulation and then asked Mannie to stand on his good leg and to 'kick yer bum' with the heel of his bad leg. This Mannie did which resulted in a loud click. The knee that had been dislocated for so long slid back perfectly. Bombo, quite justifiably, would always take personal credit for saving Mannie's leg. Not only did she have her husband in one piece, but he had also been spared what would have been almost certain death had he gone to France.

Like many men, Francis really took more interest in growing vegetables than flowers, and was soon able to keep the household fairly well supplied. He also supplemented their diet with rabbits he had shot, as well as hares, rooks, pigeons, partridges and pheasants.

Rabbits were a constant problem on the farm and were one of the reasons for the grubbing out of hedgerows and the wiring of the fields. They would nibble around the bark and kill the young trees. They were more of nuisance than hares and did far more damage. Unfortunately by wiring the fields off, rabbits did get trapped inside and of course did no end of further damage. Francis tried everything from wiring around each individual young tree trunk, to painting on an anti-rabbit paste. It wasted a great deal of time and kept men away from doing other important jobs.

At one point Francis became so incensed with the damage being caused by rabbits in a newly planted up orchard that he gathered some men and together they spread out across the huge field. They then spent the whole day 'beating' their way through the young trees and driving the rabbits to the boundary.

Although Francis would always paunch and skin the rabbits and hares he brought home for the pot, any birds he presented Barbara with, did need plucking. She found herself a little shed out in the back yard and with the help of an upturned apple box to sit on, soon became quite adept at it. The little shed rapidly became knee-deep in feathers. Once plucked however, she did draw the line at coping with the 'innards', and handed them back to Francis at this point.

Although Francis had always been an excellent shot, and used to go over to Denston for shooting parties, in later years he found it becoming more and more of a moral dilemma to shoot anything. He had never forgotten the seemingly pointless shooting of the flamingo when he was in South America and a time would come when he would say that he wished he had a camera fixed to the end of his shotgun instead.

It wasn't long after their marriage, that Edith invited Barbara up to Clopton Hall for afternoon tea. All went well until Barbara got up to take her leave. Edith smiled, 'Now you can tell your mother that the lady in the big house has taken notice of you.' What could Barbara say? Coming from the background she did, she was deeply affronted and her relationship with Edith was never destined to be a success. In fact in over twenty years, she would only ever go up to Clopton Hall one more time and that would be to a supper party not long after. The Charnocks were going and so were Hugh and Carole McCartney and Francis really felt that Barbara should accompany him. It took some convincing to persuade her that she should be there, and eventually she did agree, though with great reluctance. Informal social events were very important to the Brookes – it was the way they did things, and a refusal in Francis' eyes, would have been unthinkable. Always rather shy, Barbara hated it. She found small talk very difficult, and it was all so unfamiliar. Being offered raspberry vinegar to drink astounded her and she settled on a glass of beer as a safer option.

As a new bride Barbara felt she ought to hold one or two little tea parties of her own and invited Carole McCartney over to Hill Farm one afternoon. She had made a sponge cake, which she carried through to the sitting room, together with a tray carefully laid out with some of her new china tea service. Bringing the kettle to the boil on top of the oil stove, she poured the water into Francis' rather grand silver teapot, which she'd never used before but felt the occasion called for.

All went well until she tried to pour out the tea. To her utter amazement nothing came out of the spout. She tried again – still nothing. Rosy, who still helped out at Hill Farm after the wedding, had felt she should make a special effort with all the cleaning before Francis and his new bride came home. The silver teapot had never really had much of a clean which was probably why Barbara had never noticed it before. But now Rosy felt that it warranted some attention and she gave it a really good polish inside and out, until the old silver was gleaming once again. Unfortunately in her enthusiasm she had failed to notice that she had left a piece of cleaning cloth, well soaked in metal polish, inside the pot.

Barbara's youngest brother Newy had given a puppy to Barbara and Francis as wedding present – they called him Bow. A friend of Barbara's grandfather Kingston was very keen on shooting and bred gun dogs and Bow had been the pick of the litter.

Of course Barbara's brother hadn't been christened 'Newy'; his name was actually 'Newlyn.' It was 'Newlyn' Bombo used to say, on account of the fact that Newlyn was where her grandparents lived and she and Mannie had gone down to visit them before they were married. As Newy was their third child this connection did seem to be a little tenuous. In fact 'Newlyn' was a Chalk family name but then Bombo did enjoy embellishing her little stories. Perhaps like her account of that visit ...

Driving down to Cornwall on a motorbike and stoutly equipped against the weather in their long leather coats, Mannie had driven whilst Bombo sat in an open wicker side-car that was attached by leather straps. Stories of Mannie's driving would become legendary in the family, but on this particular occasion Bombo would recount how they had come to a sharp fork in the road. Uncertain of which to take and deciding at the last minute to veer to the right, Mannie proceeded up the road blissfully unaware that he and his bride to be had parted company. Already at their limit, this final strain on the leather straps had proved too much and Bombo, complete with wicker basket, sailed majestically on down the road on the left hand side.

Despite his noble gun dog ancestry, Bow was of course destined to become a family pet and on Saturday nights accompanied Barbara and Francis to the pub at Great Yeldon.

Sunday mornings were dedicated to Bow's retriever training. This involved Francis and Barbara sitting up in bed sipping tea, whilst

Francis threw Bow one of Barbara's new silk slippers that had been part of her trousseau. Needless to say they soon took on the appearance of a bit of chewed rag. But, as Barbara would say, they were no real loss and certainly not very practical to use at Hill Farm.

Stepping through the mud in the back yard to hang up the washing, or throwing some crusts to the chickens that pecked about there, she soon realised that rubber boots were going to be of far more use to her.

The bedroom was the scene of another drama in the first few months of their married life, but this time not nearly so amusing or pleasant.

It all started with Barbara feeling something running up her legs as she lay in bed – she gave a loud scream and flung back the bedclothes. The bed was full of fleas; they were everywhere. Sleep was impossible. Night after night they returned, and they couldn't work out where they were coming from. They tried everything they could think of – including standing each of the bed legs in a tin can filled with paraffin and burning sulphur candles. The smell was awful but the fleas seemed oblivious.

It was at this time that Bob Berry called to arrange a game of tennis over at Thurlow. Barbara caught sight of her legs in a long mirror after she had put on her tennis dress. They looked dreadful. Her legs were just one mass of red itching bites and despite the warm weather she played the entire evening wearing a pair of stockings, in an attempt to cover her legs up. She and Francis felt quite at a loss to know what else to do, and in desperation called in the local rat catcher, who seemed to cover most forms of pest control.

To his expert eye there was a simple solution to the problem. 'Really?' They couldn't think what. The fleas he reckoned were coming from the pigs. 'The pigs?' Well, that was what he thought, 'Move the pigs and the fleas will go with 'em.' It was worth a try. Anything was. The pigs, now they came to think about it, had fairly recently been moved to the buildings in the yard at the back of Hill

Farm. The dates seem to coincide. Could the solution really be that easy?

Charlie Cutts and some of the other pig-men on the farm were summoned and the pigs were moved down to Home Farm and Francis and Barbara had the first tranquil night's sleep they had had in several months - perfectly flea-free. The rat-catcher was right.

The weather that summer of 1939 was hot. Day after day Francis' diary records the weather as being fair and warm – hay-making was well under-way at the beginning of June and the gooseberries were being picked. The weather grew progressively hotter during that first week and whilst Barbara was getting to grips with married life and the oil stove at Hill Farm, another drama occurred that would remain forever etched in the memories of those involved. There was a devastating fire at Wickham House on June 7th. It totally gutted the 'state of the art' milking parlour, though, amazingly, very few cows were killed or injured and there was no loss of human life.

The exact cause seems to have been unknown or perhaps forgotten, though doubtless there would have been plenty of theories at the time. But it did effectively bring to a close Justin's dairy business, which must have been a dispiriting blow for him, for he was justifiably proud of it. And now, in the shadow of another war in Europe and the inevitable labour shortage, he must have felt that he had no viable option other than to concentrate on the fruit and the arable side of the enterprise.

Francis' diary records Sunday September 3rd 1939 as being fair and warm and that three and a half tons of plums were picked. In brackets he briefly notes *('War declared')*.

Both Hugh McCartney and Francis wanted to enlist immediately. With farming being a reserved occupation neither man was obliged to join up, but they both felt they had a duty to do so. Of course the farm couldn't operate without one of them staying on and with George Charnock remaining, Hugh and Francis decided to toss a coin.

Hugh won the toss and enlisted in the regiment of the 4th King's Dragoon Guards and Francis was made up to General Manager. Hugh went on to get the Military Cross in North Africa although he was very modest about it. He actually received it because he had captured an Italian military band complete with all the band's instruments. Later on in the war, whilst stationed in Cyprus, his own side tragically killed him. Returning home one night to the barracks, he was unaware that the password for the day had been changed. Accosted by a sentry who didn't recognise him and failing to reply correctly to the challenge, he was shot and killed.

On May 14th 1940 on the BBC's Home Service, shortly after nine o'clock in the evening, the nation heard a broadcast by Anthony Eden, the secretary of state for war.

It was addressed to *'men of all ages who wish to do something for the defence of their country.'* With fear of an imminent invasion and a growing awareness that *'bands of civilians [were] arming themselves with shotguns'* up and down the country, the War Office realised that the time had come to do something about this *'grass roots activism.'*

*'Here then'* … the broadcast continued … *'is the opportunity for which many of you have been waiting. Your loyal help, added to the arrangements which already exist, will make and keep our country safe.'*

Anthony Eden urged volunteers to contact their local police station *'Give in your name … and then, as and when we want you, we will let you know.'*

Before the broadcast had finished, police stations all over the country were inundated with volunteers. Within 24 hours 250,000 men had registered, and this would grow to a staggering 1,200,000. They were to be called *'The Local Defence Volunteers'* and Churchill would later change this to *'The Home-Guard.'*

Barbara heard it on the lunchtime news the following day.

With Hugh gone and his brother-in-law too, Francis had felt more and more frustrated. He would say he was not doing his bit. There had to be something more he could do to help the war effort? However much Barbara reassured him that he was doing important work in keeping the farm going and helping to feed the nation, it just wasn't enough for him.

Bob Berry had also been very anxious to join up and he and Francis thought that perhaps they should join the Air Force.

'We're both good shots. We could be rear gunners.'

Barbara felt the moment had come to intervene. They had only just got married. She appealed to Francis. 'Give our marriage a chance, Bob is still a bachelor.'

And now on the radio she had heard of just the job. Here at last was something they could all do on a local scale, and feel that they were making a worthwhile contribution. The moment Francis came in she told him and he rushed off to get more details. Of course Bob and Francis along with George needed no second bidding. They all decided to form platoons of *'Local Defence Volunteers'* - George at Wickhambrook, Francis at Stradishall and Bob at Thurlow.

At first, like all volunteers around the country, they had no proper uniforms and, like the immortal series on the BBC of *Dad's Army*, were armed with a startling and unusual array of weapons, from pitchforks to blunderbusses. When the uniforms did arrive, Francis being so tall, had been sent an extra large one. Presumably an assumption had been made at HQ that tall meant fat as well, and as Francis stood there with it hanging off him in great folds, Barbara cast her needlewoman's eye over it.

'Hmm. Perhaps if I unpicked most of it, I think I could make a reasonable job of getting it to fit.' And she did.

Francis' war would be spent in a perpetual state of extreme exhaustion and Barbara's, in extreme loneliness, especially at the beginning.

At barely 19 years of age, her own brother Peter had joined up almost straight from school; he had started working in Manchester before going into the army with a commission and ending up in France. At Dunkirk his unit were fighting a rear-guard action against the Germans, which enabled a lot of men to be safely evacuated.

Whilst behind enemy lines, he had captured a German motorbike and single-handedly blown up an enemy gun post. For this he was awarded the Military Cross. Missing the main evacuation from Dunkirk, he made his way along to Calais. Not daring to stop at houses along the way for fear of capture, he reached Calais just in time to be on the last boat back to England.

Later on, her youngest brother Newy also enlisted. At the time he was playing the drums in a small band, and was on his way with his fellow bandsmen to cut their first record. Passing the recruitment office on the way, they stopped and joined up instead. Newy joined the R.A.F. but never actually flew. He was sent out to India in 1942 to repair aircraft, and spent the rest of the war there, permanently short of spare parts and always short of food.

With his promotion to General Manager, Francis was now in charge of the whole farm and not just the fruit. His schedule was punishing and the responsibility enormous. Being up at six in the morning to see to the men on the farm, he would work through the day, snatching a meal before throwing on his uniform to go on duty with the Home Guard, often not returning until three o'clock the following morning.

But of course Francis, being the man he was, did have some fun too and actually rather enjoyed it all.

Manoeuvres were often arranged between villages and these would invariably start and end before closing time. Stradishall Platoon naturally had their HQ at The Hound in the village.

Francis soon discovered that he was very good at camouflage and became quite proud of his efforts. One time during one of these manoeuvres against neighbouring Thurlow, it was rapidly getting dark and he and his men had to cross a field full of cows, in view of 'the enemy' in order to 'take' the pub at opening time. Getting his men into pairs, he whispered to them to make themselves into pantomime cows, with the rear man bending forward and clasping the man in front around the waist. The chap in front had to lean forward and put his hands up to form a couple of horns. The assembled herd then stealthily made its way across the field, mingling the best they could amongst the cattle.

This they managed to do, undetected by the 'enemy' until almost the last minute, when guffaws of laughter from the Thurlow platoon told them that their cover was blown. But they were sportingly allowed to take the pub anyway, especially as it was by then opening time, though no doubt Stradishall had to stand the round.

Another time, with the very real threat of invasion uppermost in everyone's mind and the proximity of Stradishall Aerodrome, he designed a moveable hedge that he and his men constructed. This was placed down on the main Bury/Haverhill road at the Stradishall crossroads. The idea was that should a regiment of German tanks or soldiers come along, they would be confused and thinking that their road ended there, would turn down another and in the ensuing mêlée be captured. It must have been of considerable height, for one wonders why they could not have just peered over the top and seen that the road continued.

Defending the roads that might have given access to the aerodrome was of course a major priority and occupied much of the Home Guards' time. At one point a milk crate full of Molotov cocktails was delivered to Hill Farm – these were to be kept in the front garden behind the hedge. Any sign of an enemy tank division making its way along the lane outside, and these had to be lit and thrown over.

In those early days of the Home Guard, Francis decided to hold a church parade. Gathering his newly formed unit together, they set off down the road to the church. All the wives and families lined the village street or hung over their gates to watch them. It was relatively easy to get his platoon together for the church parade, but it proved to be a far more difficult task to get them all to march together in step. As they started marching in time to Francis' cries of, 'left right, left right,' he soon realised that try as he might, one poor chap at the back was hopelessly out of step. Linking arms with him, Francis did his best to get him into step but to no avail. With a step and a hop he tried to get him to change legs but he just couldn't seem to get it. Later Francis would say with great amusement that the church parade had gone really well, except for the fact that he and another chap had danced the polka all the way to the church.

It would be some time before the Home Guard received any ammunition, but when they were given some it proved quite difficult to keep dry. The brick floor in the kitchen at Hill Farm, being laid directly onto mud, was very damp and although it had the advantage of being cool in summer, the bricks never really seemed to dry out.

By the time Barbara had moved in, they were old and worn and she found washing them quite a challenge. There was never any problem with getting rid of the surplus water – it just sank down into the mud between the bricks. There was the problem, as she washed over the surface though, of it turning into a sort of muddy slurry. It was just so difficult to ever get them looking clean.

Wet washing hanging up didn't help the damp atmosphere either. And all the water had to be heated up in pans on top of the oil stove. Without a mangle, Barbara used to wring out the clothes by hand and on wet days, hang them up on lines across the kitchen to dry. When soap was rationed she found that she could make it go further if she used the soft water directly from the well in the yard. So before commencing the washing, she would first have to lower a bucket to scoop out some water. Once the washing had finally dried, Barbara did the ironing. Or at least she tried to do so with varying success.

Like most housewives at this time, she had to use sad-irons. These were made of solid cast iron and were heated up in Barbara's case, by putting them on top of the oil stove. Unfortunately by placing them over the oil burner, rather than placing them to heat up on a trivet or a solid fuel range for which they were designed, the base of the irons became black and greasy with oily smoke. They did have a cover you could put over them to keep them clean but it really wasn't very effective.

It was after one such session, when she took the clothes she had ironed to place them in a deep cupboard upstairs, that she discovered that Francis had found what he thought was the driest spot in the house to store all his ammunition.

A few years later when the kitchen had a Calor gas oven installed, Barbara had a gas iron. This was much more spectacular, as flames would shoot out at the sides as she moved it up and down. It was however, much cleaner, although she was always in danger of scorching the sheets as well as herself. She eventually took the precaution of putting on a pair of thick gloves before starting the ironing.

Bombo on a visit to Hill Farm one day, offered to do the ironing for her. Barbara passed her the gloves. 'Well you'll need these.'

'Whatever for?'

'You'll soon find out.' replied Barbara grimly.

A little later the Home Guard were given live hand grenades and instructions were given that the men should be trained in their use.

Francis had the men dig a trench and to make a mound in front, propped up with a few sandbags. The idea being that all the men would stand in the trench, and take it in turns to pull out the pin from a live grenade, and to then hurl the grenade out over the top of the sandbags. All went well until one of the more elderly members of the platoon, after carefully pulling out the pin, managed to drop the live grenade in the trench. Yelling to the men to keep down, Francis leapt forward and managed to pick up the grenade that exploded a moment or two later in mid-air as he flung it over the top.

Francis returned home that night with burns up his arm, and despite having saved not only himself but the whole platoon from being blown up, characteristically made light of the whole incident. After all, it did make a good story to tell in the pub later.

Exchanging stories about the Home Guard would naturally be the main topic of conversation between Francis and his brother-in-law Jack, when the two families did find time to meet up. Jack was Platoon

Commander at Preston and would laugh about the time that he had received orders to organise his men to guard a bridge. At least that was what he understood he had to do.

They were given the special task of keeping watch for enemy parachutists and infiltrators. With his band of men being mainly made up from cowmen working at nearby Favor Parkers, Jack had returned to the bridge only to find the post deserted. His men, it turned out, had all gone home, as it was time for milking.

Orders, when they were received, were often obtuse and the subsequent chaos and confusion that might have ensued, had an invasion actually taken place doesn't bear thinking about.

How was a Suffolk farmer supposed to make any sense of the following?

<u>(To) No. 8 Company L.D.V. (From) Headquarters: An Appreciation and Orders</u>

*'I thought an appreciation of the situation might help Platoon Commanders of this company, to realise what is expected of us.*

*There are two distinct plans, yet there is only one plan.*

*The first phase or plan is parachutists, and to cope with these we defend our villages and have our patrols out just before daylight till after daylight, as the days get shorter there comes the difficulty of personnel for patrol work, but this I will deal with later in consultation with you.*

*Reverting back to parachutists; when seen by patrols the patrol leader should send one man back to telephone for the inlying picket at Lavenham first, then inform me and the Platoon Commander. He must inform the inlying picket where to come to as arranged with his patrol leader before he leaves him to telephone, he will then stop at the place arranged till the picket arrives and conduct them to the vicinity where the parachutists have landed. The remainder of the patrol should keep in touch unseen with the parachutists.*

*The Order Block Roads will be given by me, if not already given by the Police, rapidity of informing the picket and the Platoon Commander as well as myself is essential.*

*When non parachutists are in or seen in the vicinity but the Order MAN BLOCKS is given the blocks already used will be manned as arranged, each man knowing to which block he should proceed and battle parties take their position, all being ready for the command BLOCK ROADS. Challenging will of course come into operation on Man Blocks.*

*$2^{ND}$ phase .... This is more complicated and is to be adopted on information of invasion with the exception of Lavenham. All the sections of the Platoons will fall back or advance as the case may be and man the Block Houses on the C Line that is the Railway Line from Bury to the Railway Bridge South of Lavenham inclusive. It will be impossible to man all the Block Houses, so I have arranged for the Field Company R.E. to man certain Block Houses whilst we man certain others. Those to be manned by each platoon will be given separately to each Platoon Commander by me as all are not yet built, I cannot at this time give you fuller instructions but roughly the R.E. will man from Lavenham Station exclusive to Cockfield Station exclusive Cockfield Platoon – Cockfield Station inclusive to Searchlight position inclusive – Stanningfield Platoon Searchlight position exclusive to Welnetham Station exclusive – Welnetham Platoon – Welnetham Station inclusive to Rushbrooke Lodge inclusive R.E. Rushbrooke Lodge exclusive to Bury exclusive.*

*Lavenham being a nodal Point will man the Block House Slough Bridge and the one at the station also certain points round the town to be selected, this particular Nodal Point is under discussion....'*

These incidents were small in themselves; the experiences of two Home Guard platoons in rural Suffolk. But all over Britain similar incidents were happening and tales being related and these would become part of the many fragments of memory of the war, as it was experienced up and down the country, by those left to defend it.

By 1941 being 'at war' had become a way of life. The slogan 'Make Do and Mend' became the rallying call for women across Britain; nothing was to be wasted. Clothes were made or unpicked and re-made into garments for children, and then passed on to others; sheets were patched or turned side to middle; socks were knitted and darned, then darns were re-darned; jumpers were patched and re-patched and then unravelled and the wool re-used.

Precious clothing coupons weren't spent on anything as frivolous as a new dress but were hoarded carefully and used to buy basic necessities like sheets and blankets. And like millions of other women that message would shape Barbara's outlook on life forever.

Life at Hill Farm was certainly primitive in those early years of the war. With her skill at the sewing machine (her wedding present from Francis) and a little distemper, Barbara soon had curtains at the windows and the walls re-painted and, besides, nothing could suppress the joy she felt when she discovered that she was expecting their first child.

With the Blitz of 1940 and the bombing of London, the war had begun to feel very close. Barbara and Francis would often stand at night in the back bedroom that overlooked the yard, looking towards London with the sky illuminated by the effects of the bombing.

At first it had felt remote and they, along with most other people, had thought it would soon be over. Could it actually be going to last as long as The Great War; memories of those four terrible years were still very vivid in many people's minds. Comparisons were inevitable, the future uncertain.

For those living in the countryside the effect of the bombing was more haphazard, particularly in the South and East. Not always a direct or intended target, bombs were often dropped at random by German planes turned back by the R.A.F. and the fields became pitted with bomb craters.

With Hill Farm being so close to the aerodrome, Barbara and Francis did not get allocated any evacuees – their position was considered too vulnerable, for Stradishall was a target and as the war progressed this became only too evident.

Early in the morning often before 6.00 a.m. the sky above them would be thick with planes taking off on bombing raids and later they would see gliders destined for the Normandy invasion. They would watch them being towed along, low behind the barn at the back of the house, and then see with horror many of them crashing to the ground.

The wives of young airmen would sometimes telephone to ask if they could be put up at Hill Farm for a night – having heard that their husbands or boyfriends were being stationed at Stradishall. How often Barbara would make up a spare bed only to find that the young woman never arrived, realising that her young man must be among those who hadn't returned from a bombing raid.

A mine was dropped in Captain's, the field opposite the house that Francis had planted up with apple trees a few years before. The navy were called in to disarm it. It had floated down in the night – a huge bomb on a parachute. The next day everyone turned out to look at it and Bow, curious to see what the bother was, had wandered over and cocked his leg on it, as if to say that's just about what he thought of that.

Barbara was quite far into her pregnancy when she and Francis received an invitation to go to tea at Seabrooks; it was still a private house then. They were all deep in conversation when there was a sound of planes overhead. No one took much notice until suddenly a loud rat-a-tat-tat was heard close by and a hail of missiles and bullets went whistling past the windows. Everyone but Barbara fell flat to the floor.

She had been sitting close to the fire and having been told that the chimney, being built of brick, was the safest spot, she stayed there. Besides, throwing herself down and lying flat on the floor wasn't really an option at this late stage in her pregnancy. Francis came back to find her. 'Aren't you coming down?'

'No', she replied, actually more interested than frightened. 'I'll stay where I am and watch.'

Another slogan of those early war years was, *'Careless talk costs lives, Be like Dad keep Mum.'*

How significant these words would be, no one could have foretold. The idea of actually having a spy in their midst would, at one time, have seemed pretty far-fetched, but that is exactly what they did have, and there wasn't just one.

A young man in his early thirties had moved into the village in the early months of the war. He lived with his English wife and little boy in a house on the Wickhambrook road, not far from the Stradishall crossroads. He was a quiet fellow who didn't mix much and to all outward appearances this would not have aroused any suspicion. Well, none other than the usual village gossip about who they were and what they did or didn't do. But there was something different about this set-up – the young man was German.

And then, quite suddenly, he was arrested and taken away along with some other men who lived in the immediate area. And then the story came out. It seems that before the war a number of young German men working for German intelligence, had come over and married English girls. Becoming quietly established and integrated into British life, some of these had come to live in and around Stradishall. In fact it turned out that the houses they were living in, were actually situated right around the aerodrome.

Francis and Barbara visited his parents at regular intervals, driving over to The Four Swans in Sudbury every few weeks. Francis had by now bought his father the little house in Stour Street and he would later take on the responsibility of managing their money for them. It was on one of these visits that they had broken the news that Fanny and Robert were to be grandparents again.

Fanny was by now well practised in the art of being a grandmother, with Adrian and Marjorie's three and Stephanie and Jack's little boy, Adrian. She was of course pleased to hear their news, provided they understood that she was always to be called 'Fanny' and never 'Granny'. Robert however, was overjoyed. He bent over and kissed Barbara's hand. 'My dear, you have made me a very happy old man. I always wanted to be there to see Francis' children.'

Despite Fanny's kindness to her, Barbara did find some of her ways a little unusual. Being a staunch atheist, Fanny had announced some time ago that she did not 'do' Christmas. Well, Barbara did. And she had made a point of making her parents in law a little present each Christmas. The first of these was a photograph of Hill Farm that she had stuck to a piece of card, together with a small calendar. Always addressing them in those early days of marriage as 'Mr and Mrs Bell', it was a formality she would stick to for several more years.

And Francis actually quite took to Christmas once he got used to it. Always gregarious, he would say he especially liked, 'the crescendo leading up to it.' And being Francis, much of that 'crescending' would take place at 'The Cloak', Wickhambrook. Now a private house, the pub would always be laughingly referred to by the men as, 'The Foreman's Rest' for Ian and Francis would usually go down there for a pint of beer each night after work. Here Francis would meet other farmers too, friends from around the district who would chat over a game of darts or dominoes.

Peter Hanbury Bell arrived on March 4th. And despite Barbara being convinced she would be 'stuck like this for the rest of [her] life' in fact he was two days early.

A friend of Edith's who was a midwife had agreed to come to Hill Farm and help with the birth and then to stay on for a while, intending to stay with Justin and Edith for a few days until the baby arrived. She was met at the station by Francis. One look at his face told her all she needed to know. Her stay at Clopton Hall would have to wait.

The doctor from Wickhambrook was an old man – in fact Peter would be the last baby he would deliver. Coming down stairs he congratulated Francis and told him he had a fine son, but that he really had been too big for a first baby. Francis was puzzled. 'Oh dear,' he replied, 'did we do something wrong?'

Once she was up and about again, Barbara was worried that Bow would be jealous of the new baby. Kneeling down beside the dog and cradling Peter in her arms, she introduced them, telling Bow that this was his baby. Seeming to take on the responsibility of protecting the baby from that moment, the dog never left Peter's side, and would keep a daily vigil, lying down beside his pram in the garden. And it was there that the doctor found them one day.

Leaning over the pram, he was talking to the baby when Barbara, seeing him there, came out and asked if he wished to come in?

'Oh, no thank you my dear,' he replied, 'I'm just saying goodbye to my last baby.'

Justin was particularly delighted with the birth of Francis' baby son. With his own son Charles now 10 years old, he felt that this baby's arrival was further affirmation that the future of the farm was safe.

'Now we both have sons there will be continuity; Charles will look after the arable and you can teach your son all there is to know about fruit and he can take over from you. You take care of the education Francis and I'll do the rest.'

And Francis, looking down at his little son, felt that both their futures were secure.

**Francis in Home Guard uniform with Peter (aged 4 months) in the garden at Hill Farm, July 1941**

Nancy Hardwicke was 17 years old when she started working in the office for Justin Brooke, just before the war. And later, when the business became a company, she was their first company secretary.

She first lived in a cottage known then as Brook Cottage that was situated next to The Plumbers Arms in Wickhambrook, and later in a semi-detached cottage at the top of Edmunds Hill in Stradishall.

She stayed on through the war, working in what was a reserved occupation. She became deeply involved and interested in the daily running of the farm, not leaving until 1954, when she went on to marry Carlton Whitlock.

Inevitably she and Francis developed a close relationship and she would always be there at the Clopton Hall breakfast sessions. When Francis particularly wanted to get Justin to agree to something, he would catch Nancy's eye. She would indicate, by the merest shake of her head, if 'the old man' was in a bad mood, and Francis would know that he would have to bide his time, although he usually got his own way in the end.

Francis used to laugh when Justin wanted to do something himself. 'We are not here to make money – remember that.' And Francis knew that Justin was going to do it anyway.

With the formation of the Local Defence Volunteers, Francis soon found that he was unable to keep up his pencil-written diary and he came to rely solely on the detailed individual field records he had started to write up more fully in 1939. It became the only record of work being undertaken between '39 and '43 - there just wasn't time for more.

In the autumn of 1943 Francis had the idea of writing what at first would be an almost daily account of the ongoing work in the orchards. The setting down of his thoughts and ideas and of course recording the weather. These would amount to something more than a thousand typed foolscap pages, all written in his own time.

Carefully indexed and in the form of a diary, this was almost to the world of fruit growing what Gilbert White's journals recording his work at Selborne had been to natural history. He continued writing these diaries through to the early 1950s when he changed the format to a more formal annual report on each crop.

Alongside this, he had the idea of further enhancing his work by starting to write up a history of each separate field.

October 3rd 1944 ... *'We have now been writing this little account for a year and are considering drafting a book for the costings of each separate field. Separate costings have never been kept of the different fields, and I think this should now be done so that one can look back for several years into the treatment and working of each field separately.'*

A month later he wrote ... *'Our maps and history of the orchards is making progress. It is extraordinarily difficult to recall planting dates etc. if there is no written record available. I think it will prove a blessing to us in years to come ...'*

He hoped that this history, together with his diaries would be a record not only for posterity but also for use as a personal reference - he had realised that with such a rapid programme of planting and expansion, it would be difficult to remember details of diseases and of the various problems encountered. It was also important to see and compare the results both of his spraying programmes and of the various pruning techniques being employed.

Nancy used to come up to Hill Farm two or three times a week after supper, and Francis would dictate the diary for her to type up. And although of course they dealt with the technical side of fruit growing, in their daily recording of events around the farm and the personal comments made by Francis, they also leave us with a valuable piece of social history.

Barbara found it very hard to watch the light-hearted banter that accompanied the dictation. She must have felt, after spending a day with a toddler and their new-born baby who had since arrived, that it was an intrusion into the time that she and Francis should have shared together.

The War Agricultural Executive Committee, commonly referred to throughout the farming fraternity as 'The War Ag', had suspended any further planting of fruit trees during the War and this was a cause of much frustration to both Justin and Francis.

For the most part, as far as the fruit side of things went, they were generally left alone, but when they did receive an order to cut the Hollow Ditch, never very tolerant of 'little men', as he would call anyone he considered to be officious, Francis' reaction was predictable.

May 16th 1944 ... *'The War Executive Committee, whether through stupidity or spite, have ordered us to cut the Hollow Ditch. Actually this suits us, as we were going to do it anyhow. But they may possibly have in mind disturbing my system of dams. I cannot think why this order has been put on* us as it does not help the arable farming one jot, and if they had known we are going to clear it on account of the frost, they would probably have forbidden us to do it, as they are very anti-fruit in any form.'

'The War Ag' was an offshoot of the Ministry of Agriculture and each county had a committee, with local farmers being co-opted on as agricultural advisers. Any surplus land, however small or unsuitable, had to be ploughed up for the growing of arable crops. A constant stream of directives were sent out by 'The War Ag' about what could or could not be grown and they had the power to reclaim land and put out tenant farmers, if they were considered not to be doing well enough.

Another frustration that Francis expressed was the fact that Justin had odd fruit trees planted all over the farm in little corners, and he found this intensely irritating.

1st October 1943 ... *'The greengages in the Pightle have cropped well for the last two years and I wonder if they will continue to do so. I wish all our gages were in one field. Four odd trees in Short Deadmans and the odd cottage garden stuff always cause more of a headache in the fruit season than twenty ton of plums, picked in a straightforward manner.'*

9th October 1943 ... *'J.B. is impatient to plant peaches in every possible odd corner. I only wish we could get permission to plant more acres of these but I expect we shall have to wait until after the war. I cannot bring home to him, the exasperating task of having little bits of things scattered pell-mell all over the place. They never get the individual attention they would have if they were together in one block. They never get hand-hoed as they should be for the first year or two. You drive miles with a sprayer and then always forget some. For picking also, they are a nuisance.*

*We have experienced all this before with the greengages as I have already mentioned... I would much rather wait till we are allowed to plant out and set out in a decent piece rather than have a few trees here and a few trees there on odd headlands which, when they are planted, do not amount to more than an acre altogether.'*

His sentiments over peach trees being planted in odd corners were not however confined to the war years and three years later he was still expressing his frustration.

June 11th 1946... *'I regret to say we have two bushels of Peach stones to set this year. This will mean another little mess in the middle of another big field, and with something quite out of our line too, especially as we are buying several thousand peach seedlings from Holland for budding. We have been through it all before, first with briars, which came to nothing, and for the last three seasons with sweet corn. A row or two to play with in the garden by all means, but three or four acres means one more added worry to those we already have. This kind of work requires a lot of detail, and should not have been thrust into our extensive farming.'*

Francis was always looking for ways of being more cost effective and he felt that too many pickers were being employed full time, with insufficient work being available between crops.

Perhaps Justin, remembering earlier picking seasons when he was able to give employment to so many, loved to see the whole place filled with young people. He would say that it was preferable to have too many rather than too few and run the risk of getting into difficulties with the fruit ripe and not enough labour to pick it. But Francis was not convinced.

26th October 1943... *'Last year's fruit picking season was a nightmare. We actually had 190 people here at one period, so that once the blackcurrants were done we were hard pressed to find work for them. Half of this number were schools who never did a day's work anyway, and quite a number who came to pick fruit spent time cutting down hedges. One does not want to be burdened with hedge cutting in the middle of the fruit season, or with the organization of 100 school children when 20 good women could do the same amount of work, quite apart from the mass feeding and sleeping of such a number. I would far rather be working till nine o'clock at night than have an occurrence like this again. Apple picking is simpler, especially in wartime, and we must certainly try piecework picking with these fruit next year.'*

Arguments about employing such a quantity of full time pickers would rumble on, as well as Justin's desire to plant up more peach trees –

29th December 1943... *'We have passed the Christmas holiday – work is just getting into its stride again ... my suggestion to reduce the acreage of loganberries has been taken up together with a more drastic one of cutting down blocks of currants every year ...the only reason for the cutting down of these is to avoid the picking ... I am glad of this cutting down of soft fruit. It has unbalanced the whole farm for several years now. Perhaps too it will mean an end to the nightmare picking in July, when the whole place becomes like a 'Butlin's Camp.*

*J.B. is also afraid of the Czar plums. I do not consider we have ever been in a muddle over picking these. Last year, with a crop of eighty tons we did our best to make them spin out to find work for the hordes of children. It is true that as long as there is a corn harvest to gather it is unlikely that men can be brought in to pick at this time of year, but plums are a cheap commodity and it would be a frightful tragedy if, in a bumper year, we found ourselves unable to pick them... I consider it a very short-sighted policy to scrap these trees in order to gain a year in the planting of a few peaches. We have never failed to gather these plums yet, and I should want to see them rotting for two years running at least before I considered scrapping them.'*

Francis set out details of how many pickers he felt would be needed the following year, based on his experiences the previous year, in a separate report that he headed *'Picking Problems'* and he gave this to Justin to read.

Justin would have none of it, totally disagreeing over reducing the number of pickers employed full time and counteracting Francis by sending him an equally forceful response.

The pencilled note that Francis scribbled at the bottom of this riposte is an indication of the exasperation that he was beginning to feel.

*'Evades all my points. Not worth a reply. F.de W.B.'*

In fact the problems of coping with the hordes of pickers would continue until after the war. And like most of the discussions between the two of them, Francis would usually have his own way in the end.

31st July 1945 ... *'It is very noticeable how comfortably we have managed our picking this year with roughly 100 people. It is true we were behind with the currants but this was mainly due to the early season. We have managed to get off 90 ton of Czars and 30 ton of Cherry Plums with a day or two to spare, which means that one person per ton of plums is a comfortable formula for this period of the season.'*

But it also has to be said that there was actually less soft fruit to be picked and there had been a general down-turn in the soft fruit market. Francis later wondered about going out of soft fruit altogether but Justin wouldn't agree – saying that one day they could have an over-seeing manager.

In a way it must have been difficult for both men. Francis, as the younger man, with his head full of new ideas and bursting with enthusiasm, must have felt that some of Justin's ideas were getting out of date and were impeding progress. And how difficult for Justin who felt he knew a great deal about fruit growing, to have to stand by and watch this authoritative younger man not only contradict him, but quite often prove to be right.

Alongside the problems of the long picking season, came the marketing for which Francis was also responsible. Eventually fruit would be sent to markets all over the country as far afield as Manchester, London and Bristol as well as to jam and canning factories. The transportation of this wholesale trade was done by the company's own lorries, a method which Justin preferred rather than using hauliers or rail, and Francis remarked on the increased flexibility it gave them.

*'We find our own lorry transport to the markets very useful. One can decide about the destination much later, and switch the plans about far more than when one relies on rail. We are running four lorries now on long distances and expect another quite soon.'*

With such a growth in the wholesale trade, it is interesting to see how far the fruit had expanded since those early days in the 1930s when the roundsmen were selling chip baskets from the back of the Trojans. And to compare just how valued those retail customers were then in contrast to Francis' comments in 1943, though no doubt at the time he was very charming to the lady concerned.

6th November 1943... *'The retailing of fruit today is nothing but a nuisance. Since we gave up delivery vans we have had no organisation whatever for selling retail.*

*Odd people pop in at odd times for odd amounts of fruit. It is nobody's business to see to them and no one can ever find change. Or more vexing still, people ring up on the telephone for an odd pound or two of soft fruit, and when we are busy picking tons for the factory one has suddenly to remember that Mrs. so-and-so wants two pounds to be left at the farm, and though every year rules are made that no orders for fruit are to be taken, exceptions are always made and it has become nothing but a nuisance.*

*I always remember being stopped on the way home one night by a W.A.A.F. who wanted one pound of plums. We had picked ten ton that day. The store had to be unlocked and scale and weights found, and she gave me a pound note for five pence-worth of fruit. I do not object to retailing, but we should be organised for it. A kiosk on the road, open for a few hours every day, or some such arrangement would probably be the most satisfactory.'*

Francis was only too aware that modern fruit-growing had become big business with its use of machinery and science but he was also very aware of the fact that much of what they were doing was experimental. The National Farmers' Union had stopped their Fruit Tours during the war and he missed the opportunities these gave for sharing knowledge.

The spraying programme was constantly under scrutiny and he was continually looking for ways to speed up the work.

7th Dec. 1943 ... *'My head, at present, is full of ideas for making two-wheeled trailers to carry spray out-fits, and I want to get the carpenter to make one of these as soon as possible. I am sure that they would answer our purpose better than the four-wheeled trolley we use at present. The big snag is the wheels available. I only have ordinary car wheels and I think lorry wheels are necessary to take the weight of 300 gallons of water and a spray machine.*

*The balance is important, as, when the spray tank is full, the weight will be at one end, and when it is empty, it will be the other. A very strong draw bar is also of paramount importance. If properly balanced and of really strong construction there will be a number of advantages. The foremost being the low loading level of the whole outfit, and easier traction in mud. I want to construct one with an ordinary pair of car wheels. This might do for a light outfit for the soft fruit, and if it is a success I should be tempted to utilise a lorry chassis which we at present use as a four wheeled trailer.'*

Francis went on and designed this two-wheeled trailer which proved highly successful and sent for more lorry wheels in order to have several of these made up.

He loved machinery and some years after the war went on to design a prototype spraying machine with an aircraft engine and aeroplane propeller and had Carlton Whitlock's Dinkum Digger Company make it up for him. Carlton Whitlock had an engineering firm at Great Yeldham and they designed and manufactured the original Dinkum Digger, which was later sold out to JCB.

Later when Francis put Bill Day in charge of the spraying, Bill remembered this spraying machine, 'With its six cylinders Gypsy Moth engine, it would have taken off if it hadn't been towed by a tractor.' He would also say that he had to go round to all the surrounding houses to tell people to take their washing in before setting off with it. 'If the wind was right the spray would fly some 200 to 300 yards and with the spray being bright yellow, I used to look like a Chinaman.'

This was the sort of blanket coverage that Francis was seeking. 'You want to see it come out of the top of the trees. If you can see it a mile away it's doing its job!' He would also say of his new sprayer, 'It cost as much as a bloomin' Jaguar and couldn't even pull itself along!'

Despite sounding like a jet plane taking off, it did however prove remarkably successful and the design went into general production, becoming the prototype of modern spraying machinery today.

Bill Day would say of Francis, that 'He was always the same. The men loved him. He knew how to talk to you.' And he remembered how, after the war, when Francis was given an old Jeep, he would drive round the farm seeing everyone each day, and how he always had a cheerful word. Perhaps dropping in at dockey time, he would chat with the men and sometimes tell them about the time he was in The Argentine.

**The ex-American army jeep that Francis used after the war – Peter in the back aged 5**

'We used to go off with the gauchos and were on the pampas for days castrating calves. We were days at it, but guess what we had for breakfast? They were delicious. We used to toss them in the pan.'

Later when the jeep had been replaced by a Land Rover, Frances had a metal cycle rack made up at the farm workshop to fix on the back. One of the men lived at Hundon and Francis, wanting to save him a tiring five-mile ride, would often run him home along with his bike.

And it wasn't always work. One year Francis arranged a coach to take Bill Day, Ernie Edgeley and most of the men down to London to the Chelsea Flower Show with a show in the evening. Bill remembered it was a very merry party that eventually found its way back to Wickhambrook. With fish and chips for supper and plenty of other liquid refreshment stops, 'Francis and Ernie became very merry and kept everyone in fits all the way back.'

Francis always used to tease Bill, and tell him it was time he got married, and that when he did, he was going to come back to be his best man. It seems that Bill and Edie Rose had been courting a long while. When they did eventually marry, Bill was fifty and she was forty-nine, but they then went on to have another forty years together.

A particular friend of Francis' at that time was Victor Mapey. Victor worked for Murphy's Sprays and was an extremely kind, deeply respected man.

During World War II, Victor was a Lieutenant Colonel in the Cambridgeshire Regiment. He, along with other members of the 2nd Battalion, was captured and imprisoned in a Japanese Prisoner of War Camp at the fall of Singapore. In June 1942, with what was *'perhaps the first secret radio in Japanese POW camps in Singapore'*, made up with *scavenged parts, and 'concealed in a latrine with the antenna hidden in the attap roof'*, it became possible to hear the B.B.C. World Service news broadcasts each night. These vital news bulletins were given to Victor as CO, *'for him to disseminate at his discretion.'*

*'When the party was ordered to Thailand, the radio was dismantled and concealed in empty food tins under the care of the Quarter Master.'* Later, five or six miniature battery powered radios would be made out of the Battalion's radio parts and built into cigarette tins.

As prisoners of war in Changi Camp, the 2nd Battalion were part of the slave labour used in the building of the Burma Railway, working and living *'under intolerable conditions.'* Keeping the morale of his men up, Victor risked his own life many times to get better food and conditions for them. Getting out into the surrounding jungle, he would forage for anything that looked edible; trying it first to make sure it could actually be eaten.

None who survived would ever forget him, and for his selflessness Victor was awarded an O.B.E.

A former comrade David Langton would later write of him in his account of the 2nd Battalion Cambridgeshire Regiment, cut off as they were from the rest of the world for *'three and a half bitter years.'*

*'It is a tale of disease, degradation, cruelty and death and much of it is best forgotten.*

*However, it also brought forth some things that should never be forgotten: cheerfulness, comradeship, unselfishness and bravery, and such are the qualities that a regiment may be proud to find in its members, whether in victory or in ruin. Though it was not to win laurels on the battlefields of the world, yet perhaps after all we won a victory of our own, for each man overcame selfishness and brought out the good that lay in him for the benefit of his comrades in misfortune. Wherever fate led them, Cambridgeshire men stuck together and the strong did their utmost for the sick and dying. They also learnt a loyalty, which was not limited to their own regiment alone; many took it upon themselves to suffer that others might have better treatment and of these the name of Lt. Col. E.L.V. Mapey, O.B.E., T.D. will be remembered.'*

The award of 'Territorial Decoration' (TD) was only given to Lt. Colonels and above.

It would be Victor's generosity of spirit and selflessness that would later 'rescue' Francis and Barbara in what for them would be their time of dire need.

The men on the farm would always know when Francis was coming by the strong smell of tobacco that accompanied him. In fact it was a give-away and at the first hint of it, someone would usually say, 'Look busy, Francis is coming.'

Tobacco seemed not only to permeate the air, but his clothes and every fibre of him. Always a heavy smoker since his days in The Argentine, he was rarely seen without a cigarette or pipe in his mouth. It became a sort of trademark and something that would always be associated with him.

Tobacco salvage was sent to the farm during the war to be put on the land around the apple trees and it proved to be very effective, but of course the men as well as Francis used to help themselves to it, roll it up and smoke it.

In a similar way they were also sent chocolate waste from bombed-out factories, which was supposed to be fed to the pigs. The pigs of course slapped it up and put on weight, but quite a lot of it found its way into other mouths.

Francis grew his own tobacco in what used to be called the orchard at the bottom of the garden at Hill Farm. In fact all that remained of 'the orchard' were a couple of old walnut trees. Here he grew his tobacco, cutting down the leaves and threading a piece of wire through each in order to hang them up to dry in the old cart lodge situated opposite the house, across the driveway.

Once dry he would roll them into cigars or chop up the dried leaves to make tobacco for his pipe. In fact he tried smoking most things. In later years he paid his children pocket money to go off into the fruit orchards with sacks and a wheelbarrow to pick plantain leaves. Fortunately he realised that they had probably received a lot of spray and did decide on that occasion not to smoke them.

He eventually streamlined his personal tobacco harvest by bringing in a Fergie tractor, and cutting down the whole tobacco plant, loaded them on to a low trailer and hung the whole plants up to dry. When, after the war, the kitchen at Hill farm was renovated and an Aga was installed, he used to try and speed up the drying process by placing the leaves in the oven. Coming home to a kitchen completely filled with smoke and the pungent smell of tobacco, where his leaves had begun to catch light, Barbara did put an end to this by insisting that all future drying should take place outside.

Once dry, Francis put the leaves into a block press he had made and after applying various techniques like sprinkling the block with molasses or water, he turned the block of tobacco out and attempted to chop it up. Finding a bacon-slicer didn't really cut it up finely enough; he eventually bought a guillotine especially for the job.

Whenever Francis walked the orchards it was always with his pruning knife in his pocket and a magnifying glass in his hand – he was always increasing his knowledge.

15th January 1944... *'We have noticed that some of the young wood has a quantity of blister on it and until today I did not know what it was. But I have discovered it in a booklet on fungus diseases. They call it rough scab or branch blister ... they say it is associated with dry seasons and lack of potash...'*

*'...as this* [Risby] *plum suffers from red spider we are considering giving it a petroleum winter wash. As it suffers from none of the pests that tar-oil will kill, we have never sprayed it with this. I have ordered this wash, and if it arrives in time we shall see the result this summer.'*

His term 'winter wash' would cause his brother Adrian much amusement. Francis was visiting the family, when Adrian asked him to have a look at his fruit trees. Looking them over Francis told his brother that they could do with a 'winter wash.' Well, Adrian found this advice very funny, particularly as it was January at the time and rather cold. 'Poor trees,' he said, 'I shouldn't think they would like that much!'

Francis, always the more practical of the two brothers, often used to laugh and say, 'Adrian spends too much time leaning on a gate watching a beautiful sunset when he should be getting on with his ploughing!'

But then as Francis himself would write of the very deep joy he experienced looking out over an orchard of blossom, perhaps he knew exactly how Adrian felt.

In organising his workforce for carrying out the spraying, Francis usually handpicked his gangs, though perhaps his comments on women would be considered somewhat sexist today.

19th November, 1943 ... *'I have used two men and two boys on the spraying over here. I was rather timid about the boys to start with, but this gang has really got on quite well. Boys love a tractor and the joy of this seems to keep them going. Stanley Rutter and Cockle have proved a very good combination too and I consider the work done by this team has been very satisfactory. In spring and summer spraying I feel that skilled and interested men only should be used, but in these autumn and winter washes, provided* the trees get a good cover, it is not so important who actually holds the guns. I do not like using girls or women if it can be avoided. The feminine mind seems unable to concentrate and is too liable to cause diversion!'

Thirty women were normally employed on the farm at this time with an additional twelve land girls and Francis was very aware of how hard it must have been for them to work in such an alien environment.

7th December, 1943... *'The Land Girls are picking up the prunings of the Wellingtons ... this is rather a laborious job. I should very much like to give these girls more varied occupations, but their capabilities are very limited, and a variety of work at this time of year is difficult to find. It is very hard on these girls. Most of them were typists before the War, and now they are shot out into the wet Suffolk mud to do jobs in which they have not the least interest. The more of them there are the more rigid the discipline has to become and the more monotonous the work. I am full of admiration for the way they are sticking it uncomplaining. Disinterested female labour is very difficult to employ full-time anyway. Naturally enough they have no interest whatever in their work, and usually get the dullest of jobs to do. I am sure we should be better off with three or four land girls instead of the dozen we have now. They must all feel that they are still at school. These silly rules of getting them home at ten o'clock at night simply make life more irksome for them.'*

Interestingly in his account, Francis set out the cost of labour in 1943 when detailing the cost of production per acre of Coxes apples. A man earned £3 13s. 4d. a week for a five and a half day week; whilst a woman, working the same hours, earned £2 11s. 4d. a week. For the men this was for an 8-hour day spent outside in all weathers, pruning fruit trees. A tractor driver was paid the same per hour at 1s. 8d. as a man pruning, but could earn more by doing a 10-hour day.

Women were brought in during March and set to work on hedging, ditching and hoeing before the soft fruit was ready and the picking started. Then they were then given the sack in the autumn and re-employed again the following spring. This way they could draw the dole, which at ten shillings a week was good money on top of what they had earned after six months work.

All the women used to go to the village Post Office at Wickhambrook, which was run by Mrs Hurrell, to draw their dole money, and a special arrangement had to be made to ensure there were sufficient funds to pay out. An official over from Bury one day took one look at the queue of ladies waiting and much to their amusement announced,

'Oh it's Brooke's women!'

After the war the basic wage went up to £4 a week and at the Horkey Justin announced a rise of 2s. a week for everyone. And when the annual bonus for the previous year was announced, the six or seven ex-servicemen, who had just rejoined the company after the war, received the same bonus as the rest of the men.

Percy Nunn had got married during the war and, desperate for both a job and a house, had been one of those ex-servicemen who returned to work at Wickhambrook. With the milk business being sold up after the fire, and Justin eager to expand the fruit side of the enterprise, Percy was offered a job tractor-driving and fruit-pruning and later Francis gave him the job of taking the fruit to markets. He was also given a rent-free bungalow down at Wickham House, providing he and his wife would put up two of the fruit pickers each year.

They were offered No. 10 and whilst looking round noticed that the whole bungalow was fitted out with linoleum. Edith, who had put the lino in some years earlier, saw them looking at it. 'Yes, we'll have to have that out.' The young couple, hoping that they could have the lino, offered to buy it, but Edith was reluctant. Justin remonstrated, 'Come on Edith. This is Mrs Nunn's first home.' And so the lino was left but they had to pay 10s. a week for it, until they had paid £5 in all.

Of all the men working on the farm during the war, it was with Jack Loader that Francis would form a particularly close bond. They were both passionate about pruning. Jack had been working on a fruit farm in Kent before coming to work for Justin before the war.

Stan Rutter too could always be relied upon, and he and Jack would go with Francis to look at the orchards and see the effects of their work. It was one of the ways Francis had of making the men feel valued and their jobs more interesting and he was always open-minded and ready to hear their views.

1st October 1943 … *'Yesterday I took Loader and Rutter over the apples. Never was an hour better spent. Year after year these men prune the apples and never see them in full crop. Year after year they have sprayed these apples and never see the results of their work. I am quite sure that in future both these operations will be carried out with a clearer knowledge and understanding than before. I enjoyed discussing the various problems with them and I feel they took a real interest in what they saw.'*

20th November 1943…*'Loader, as usual, had some very sensible suggestions. He is very sound on fruit topics, and always talks good sense.'*

Francis not only sought to motivate the men, but also was also very aware of the necessity to teach them.

3rd December 1943… *'There are six men pruning currants, two of these only have any idea what they are doing. This is not very important on currants, because it is more or less straight forward, but on trees it will be different. It is important to teach men how to prune, and as long as unskilled men ask questions and watch carefully all will go well. Pupils and hangers on are rather a nuisance. Given a pair of secateurs they are inclined to run amuck. There is an urgent fascination to cut something without thinking what they are doing, and having seen one tree pruned, they think they are quite competent to go ahead. Usually they are doing more harm than good.'*

In his diaries Francis drew diagrams detailing how to prune effectively and wrote endlessly on the subject. It fascinated him. He was working on a theory of pruning apple trees, so that they were open in the middle and umbrella shaped for ease of picking, with the branches hanging downwards, though not too near the ground. This method would later become common practice.

One source of advice that was available to Francis was the East Malling Research Station down in Kent. Francis was able to send them samples of diseased twigs and leaves when he needed an analysis done or advice on sprays. After the war he would regularly take one or two of the men with him for a visit there, the men taking it in turns as to who went. One time it would be Jack Loader, another time Bill Day or Stan Rutter and Bill remembered being amazed at how many people Francis used to know personally in the fruit-growing world.

September 8th 1945 ... *'On Wednesday we went to East Malling Members Day, the first for six years, and it was very interesting. Jack Loader came with us and greatly enjoyed the visit. One can always learn something new and interesting on these visits. Much of the ground they covered was commonplace but a visit when the fruit is on the trees ready for picking is particularly interesting. I was most interested to see that [they] had an even finer crop of fat hen than we produce here, and though they cannot rival our docks, their orchards abound in stinging nettles, which must make picking very unpleasant.'*

N.F.U. or East Malling Fruit Tour late 1940s or early 1950s
Centre left, Justin, Francis centre and Nancy Hardwicke to his right.

Peter Wheldon, who owned a fruit farm near Sudbury, was another contact and the two men would talk fruit and exchange ideas over a period of many years.

May 8th 1946 … *'I had an interesting talk with Peter Wheldon last night when he came over to see me. I always find him very interesting and progressive. He is trying our methods of strawing without cultivating and his interest in cover crops is the same as our own, the main drawback being that we never get a big enough sward to cut. He is going to try irrigating to make his cover crop get really lush. I hope to go over to his place soon.'*

Francis had had an article published in *The Grower* the previous year, on the effects of using straw in the orchards, which added to the humus in the soil but which he felt was proving very costly to carry out.

As early as 1943, he had been considering the idea of sowing a permanent cover of grass and clover in some of the established orchards, rather than cultivating around the trees, and despite Justin being adamant that there was no benefit to be gained, in time it would become accepted as common practice on the farm; as would the sight of the gang mowers cutting the grassed orchards.

Francis also wrote in his diary of the constant problem of keeping vermin under control. By vermin he was generally referring to rabbits and hares, but he also had problems with birds. Trees and hedges were being removed and the fields fenced in by wire netting but it was an ongoing battle. With the shortages during the war, they had the terrible job of trying to untangle and pick up used wire netting that had become grown in, and then to repair it before they could re-use it.

April 7th 1944 … *'We have been busy lifting old wire netting from Red House and Stew Field during last week. We shall need all this old wire if we are allowed to carry out our planting programme this next autumn. It will be quite impossible to buy new netting for a year or two, even if the war does come to an end suddenly.'*

It seems alien to us now to think of 'blowing up elm trees', even if there were some left to blow up, but in the march against damage being inflicted on the orchards, it was just part of how things were done and accepted then.

22nd January 1944 ... *'During the week we have blown up the elm trees at the bottom of Captains. The ditch is to be piped and then filled in by the tiller. These trees were a regular perching place for rooks and jackdaws. I have watched them use it as a taking off ground from whence to attack the ripe fruit. The job keeping the rooks off the fruit is going to be a serious one. Last year they did an amazing amount of damage, particularly on the pears. They had over half the crop at Stradishall. There is no doubt we shall have to have at least one man keeping them on the move during the summer, and it would be well worth while doing so from a monetary point of view.* [Vic] *Savage used to do this over here, but the lack of 12-bore cartridges last year made it very difficult. It is not only the fruit that they destroy, but also many branches are broken by them. Last summer being very dry, the damage was probably accentuated, but I think they will always be a menace.'*

A few years later Francis would come to regret the loss of trees and hedges and would question the wisdom of their removal.

18th September 1950 ... *'Seeing this gale damage takes one back to the windbreaks. The little row of cherry plums along Kate's corner has saved the Coopers fields crop, the back plantation on Edmunds Hill would have been of untold value for the protection it gives to the pears up there, and Clicket wood could have sheltered New Ley, Millins and Raisins during the gale last night. However it is no good crying over deeds done – we have this tree uprooting mania to cater with, and it cannot be stopped, but it is misplaced energy.'*

Another major problem for Francis at this time was the lack of suitable machinery. As far as tractors were concerned, there was a continual conflict between the needs of the arable farm and the fruit farm. Added to this, tractors were continually breaking down. It was a great relief to him when, with the purchase of a new David Brown tractor, and a second hand caterpillar crawler tractor in 1945, he could actually feel that they were 'getting fairly well set up for machinery'. And he had also heard from 'The War Ag' ...

October 10th 1944 ... *'some moves have been made in permission for planting. We have applied to ... plant quite an acreage* [fifty]. *We have also obtained permission to plant out six acres if we grub out the six acres on East Field. This is sheer joy to me, as the cherry plums on East Field have not grown since the day we put them in some six years ago...This work will be in full swing before the end of the month.'*

As the war drew to a close Francis promoted Stan to supervise the spraying; with the workload ahead looking formidable he felt that this would take a lot off his shoulders.

Life at Hill Farm meanwhile had not stood still. Nor was it without its dramas.

1943 had not only seen the start of Francis' fruit diaries but also the arrival of another baby. The pregnancy did not get off to an auspicious start. Letters kept from the time reveal Barbara taking Peter back with her for a prolonged stay at her parents' house, leaving Francis at Stradishall. The start of morning sickness, followed by a bout of mumps, were doubtless responsible for her stay in Spalding for more than a month, possibly six weeks. Although it would seem from Francis' comments that Barbara didn't realise when she left that she was actually pregnant.

She was certainly there from the end of September, the whole of October and probably on into the November; Francis missed her and Peter terribly ...

*Hill Farm,*
*5th October 1942*
*'Getting on alright here – it's the nights that feel a bit lonely. Stay until you feel better and have got over the mumps, hope Pee- wee* [Peter] *is well. The bowee dog and quackies wholly miss you and so does your old husband, but then he doesn't really appreciate you enough when you are here. It'll do me good to miss you ... all love darling'*
*14th October 1942*
*... 'I wholly miss you old girl, but would rather you came home feeling better, than only half a tool. The evenings are the worst but then I'm usually*

*Home Guarding or at the local. The girls [land girls] came round for a duck and gin with me last week and enjoyed it, and Nancy was round one evening against orders.*

*You really have got a bun in the oven. I was working out today it should arrive in May – nice month too.*

*Peter will hardly know me when I see him again – everybody round here misses him – Charlie in particular. I do hope you won't get the mumps and perhaps you will soon be over the worst of your sickness – all in a good cause.*

*I miss you my love, but if you feel rotten you are really better at home [in Spalding]... But don't be away too long – because home isn't the same now ... all love darling,*
*Francis'*

Working out on the farm all day with a shortage of men, fulfilling his Home Guard duties at least three nights a week as well as some weekends, returning home to a house shrouded in darkness, which would require blacking out before he could even light a fire, pumping up the water, trimming the oil lamps and getting himself a meal; it is not surprising his poignant letters to Barbara have an air of desperation. Phone calls were difficult too with the phone at Hill Farm often out of order, and he was constantly worried that Peter wouldn't know him when he returned. Six weeks or more away from home, no doubt being thoroughly spoiled by Bombo, Mannie and their friends and relatives, would have been a long time in the life of an eighteen-month old toddler. And Francis fears would prove to be fully justified. Barbara would always later say that Francis, who adored Peter as a small baby, seemed to lose interest in him once he became a toddler. In fact perhaps, it was probably the reverse, when taken from a small child's perspective.

On returning to Stradishall, Peter would no doubt have clung to his mother's skirts and stared up at the tall figure of his father and perhaps hardly have remembered him. With Francis working long hours and with Home Guard duties, their time together previously must have been limited mainly to weekends. He hadn't seen him for such a long time, and he would have almost seemed a stranger, the perspective of time being so different in the life of a young child.

Barbara wanted Francis to come over to see them, but with petrol rationing and travel limited to weekends, the only time that Francis could get off, it would prove impossible. A scribbled timetable on the back of an envelope, shows how Francis had gone to enquire at Clare Station, only to discover there were no trains running from Spalding to Clare on a Sunday and it seems only one to Spalding on a Saturday at 3.17 pm. If he could have caught it, he wouldn't have been able to return the next day. Letters and occasional phone calls would have to suffice…

*19th October 1942*

*'Darling Barbs,*

*I just got back from a day's shooting with Fred Taylor, and very nice too. He gave me a brace of partridges and two pheasants, so the larder is well set up. My meal was left ready by Milly,* [Mildred] *but I had to black out and light the fire, and now feel a bit lonely. Still there is always Bow…*

*You asked if I could come and see you, but it seems so hopeless by train for the weekend. I think I will leave my holiday now till after Xmas and perhaps we can have a fortnight then. I've rather given up the idea of a Home Guard Course; I think I'll just sit and get fat, and we shall avoid the freezing weather here…*

*I had a letter from Hugh* [McCartney] *on Saturday, but there isn't much news in it – he sounds a bit fed up.*

*I bought you two pullets last week to go with the cockerel we have left. We haven't found any guinea fowl yet. The rabbits are nearly fit to kill.*

*I shall have the girls* [land-girls?] *round next week to help me eat a pheasant, and as I got a bottle of 'black market' we ought to be well away. I wish you were here old girl, I miss you and Peter very much; but you are quite right if you feel rotten, after all there's no one here to help you if you feel ill. I do hope it won't last long though – your old mum must be in her second heaven – 'a nice thing' – and a 'good rest' and so forth. Bring her back for a little while when you return, just to help you settle in here again. You shall not feel sick for long now should you?*

*I shall hardly know Pee wee when I see him again, the dogs here miss him almost as much as I do and Milly says it's very dull without him.*

*Well, old girl, don't forget you've got a home of your own will you, and don't forget I do miss you both very much.*
*All love darling, Francis'*

26th October 1942
'Barbie Darling,
*I got your letter this morning. I'm very sorry to hear you are in bed – do hope you won't be there for long. I think it would be a 'nice thing' if your Mum came back with you for a bit when you return – holiday for her. And she could help you across country… it would be much better if she and you came sometime midweek. Anyway I'll leave it up to you; don't be too long before you return…I've no faith in your doc at all… But you are right if you feel rotten, better there than here.*

*I haven't done much lately; plenty of game in the larder and no one to eat it. I've sold the rabbits and am on the trail of some guinea fowl.*

*The chimneys are being swept next Thursday … I am hoping to have our pig killed soon. I should think we can deal with it, if I give Mrs. C. and Milly a bit each. Home Guard still keeps me busy, but that is likely to keep on, whether you are home or not.*

*Glad to hear Pee wee is well in spite of the rest of you; I won't recognise him when I do see him again. Charlie is always asking when he is coming home… Fred and I shot two hares, three partridges and three rabbits just walking round on Saturday. The girls came for a meal last week and I'll get them again this week too. It's lonely at night when I'm in, which isn't often…*

*Well don't be too long away, and see what you can do about getting someone to come home with you. Weekend travel is ghastly and that's the only time I could get off; we are still pretty busy. Heard from Hugh last week, I expect he is fighting by now.*

*Hurry up and get well dear, I'm tired of being alone and miss old Pee wee too. Sally should be due about May, according to Nancy's calculations.*
*All love, F.'*

The assumption that the new arrival would be a girl and was to be called Sally can only be described as prophetic on Nancy's part. Perhaps Barbara had never suffered with morning sickness whilst she was pregnant with Peter. It certainly seems to have taken her by surprise and made her feel rotten. Her prolonged stay with her parents was understandable. It would have been so much easier to be in a comfortable warm house with every amenity, meals cooked and Peter cared for. And perhaps these different symptoms would indicate to everyone, that the new baby she carried would be a little girl, and this would prove to be right. Certainly it would seem that the inclusion of Nancy's comment in Francis' final letter was enough to bring Barbara home.

'Sarah Frances' as Sally would be christened, was born on May 21st and Francis was delighted. Daughters and fathers did seem to have a special relationship of their own.

He had been particularly fascinated with his little niece Anthea, Adrian's daughter, especially as she showed off her prowess at reading fluently at a remarkably early age – something that Barbara had found particularly daunting when she was taken over to meet the family shortly after she and Francis had become engaged. His sister Stephanie and Jack's baby girl Geraldine had also been born a few months after Peter, in the October.

It was not that Frances had much time to be involved in babies, though he had mentioned in passing, that he thought Barbara could now stop sterilising everything that went into Peter's mouth. This was after finding his two-year old son sitting amongst the hens in the mud out in the yard, eating the crusts of bread that had been thrown out for the birds.

Another, more potentially life-threatening incident did occur around this time and this would remain etched upon their memories. There was an absolutely enormous explosion at the front of the house one night. Barbara, convinced she had lost both children, shot out of bed and rushed along to the front bedroom just to the left of the porch. A large piece of shrapnel was embedded into the lid of an old oak chest on the landing. Through the open door she could see Peter sitting up in his cot surrounded by shards of glass. The piece of flying shrapnel must have missed him by inches. He beamed up at her,

'Big bang Mummy.'

Nothing was left of the windows, just twisted metal. And Sally, new born and lying in her Moses basket, was sleeping peacefully.

In fact every window was broken, the roof was damaged and the plaster had been blown off the front of the house. It was a bomb that had so narrowly missed Hill Farmhouse - dropped by a German plane, perhaps mistaking the road for a runway. Next morning revealed the extent of the damage, and a number of strange men could be seen wandering about outside with clipboards in their hands. Glancing up, as Barbara hung a blanket over the gaping hole that had once been a window, one of them called out, 'Anything broken?'

Proximity to the aerodrome certainly made life exciting if somewhat unpredictable.

With the house surrounded by orchards and with food rationing and a general lack of everything, people seemed prepared to take enormous risks. Barbara and Francis' sleep was often broken by the discovery of airmen stealing apples. It was becoming quite a problem.

October 16th 1944 ... *'We caught three men on Dead Hill last week, stealing apples. The fact that there are pylons with lights for the Aerodrome all through the orchards makes this work of stopping stray thieves very difficult. We have written a strong protest to the Air Ministry.'*

Another time Barbara was woken by the sound of boxes being dragged up the road outside Hill Farm. She woke Francis who, armed with a heavy poker, went out in his dressing gown to investigate. There he discovered quite a number of men at work. Luckily Barbara had borrowed his dressing gown a few days earlier, and finding a pencil and paper in one of the pockets he took down the names and details of all the men.

It turned out that one of the airmen had a brother in London who sold fruit and that this was a well-organised crime.

September 18th 1945 ... *'The rooks are a bit of a menace and do quite a lot of damage, as do the airmen. I caught three carloads of these last week stealing Coxes and am hoping to convict them.'*

About a year after Sally was born, Barbara was bathing her one morning, when she realised that Peter didn't seem to be about. Thinking that he was playing in the yard outside, she finished doing the baby and went to check up on him. To her horror he wasn't anywhere to be found. Checking about the yard she found that Bow was missing too. She rushed indoors to telephone the farm office to let Francis know. She was particularly worried, as she had seen masses of soldiers milling up and down the road. Later she realised they were assembling for the D-Day landings. Francis organised search parties and the men started combing the farm for him. Francis and some of the men went through the orchard behind Hill Farm and eventually they found him in Clicket Wood near to the Aerodrome. It was coming on to rain and Peter was sitting on the ground crying, with one shoe lost and the other off, and the faithful Bow beside him. But however had he walked so far on his own?

Barbara and Francis realised that they had often taken him and Bow for a walk through the apple orchards in the early evenings, whilst Francis carried his gun, hoping to bag a rabbit for the pot. And when Peter told them that he was looking for 'bunny rabbits', there was no doubt that he had thought that he would bag one for the pot too.

It was towards the end of the war that Barbara's sleep was once more interrupted; this time by the urgent sound of knocking. Francis was deeply asleep and, going downstairs, Barbara found Charlie's wife at the back door, looking rather distraught.

'Whatever has happened?' Barbara asked.

'Oh, Mrs Bell, could Mr Bell come at once? A plane has come down in the field at the back and I can't let Charlie go in case it's a German one and I don't want Charlie to get shot.'

Well, Barbara wasn't too keen on Francis getting shot either, but of course she woke him and armed with his 12-bore shotgun, he went out to investigate.

The crashed plane in fact turned out to be British.

April 17th 1945 … *'A tragedy happened last week when a bomber crashed on New Ley. We had just planted potatoes there, in between the young trees. The bomber itself has not done much damage, but no doubt the R.A.F. will make a beastly mess taking it away.'*

Crashing as it did on top of the fruit trees had no doubt cushioned the plane's landing. There were no casualties – just a number of rather dazed young men. Francis invited them into the kitchen while they waited to be picked up by the R.A.F.

Charlie and his wife lived in one half of a pair of semi-detached thatched cottages just down the lane from Hill Farm. In fact they were Francis and Barbara's most immediate neighbours. Charlie and his wife were childless, but with children up at Hill Farm, Charlie would take every opportunity to visit them. Of course back in the days when the pigs were kept there, he had come up to feed them every day, but now with the excuse that the chickens needed feeding, he couldn't keep away. And being Charlie, he would always come out with exactly what he thought.

'That boy needs his hair cut, Missus,' he told Barbara one day, looking at her small son's rather long, very blonde hair. 'He looks like a girl.'

Despite any problems he might have had with Peter's gender however, Charlie took great pleasure in wheeling the little boy about the yard in his wheelbarrow. And later, when the family had grown to three, his special treat would be to push the children on a makeshift swing that had been fixed to a beam in the cart lodge.

Francis had had the swing made up at the farm workshop. It had thick jute ropes along with a good solid wooden seat. And it was amidst shrieks of terror and delight, that Charlie would push the children to dizzying heights till their feet touched the beams in the roof.

Always known to Barbara as Mrs Cutts, when Charlie's wife was diagnosed with cancer and finally had to go into hospital, Barbara offered to drive them in. As they started from the cottage, it seemed that everyone in the village had turned out to wave. Royalty could not have had a better send off. And somehow, everyone knew it would be her last journey.

Another close neighbour was Susan. Her real name was Susannah Cook but she was always known as Susan. She lived in the cottage next to Charlie's. Like most of the cottages it had few amenities, but unlike most of the other residents, Francis discovered that she was getting her drinking water from the land drain on the other side of the road. Realising that this was draining directly off Captains, Francis thought that he had better stop spraying the trees with arsenate of lead. Not that it seemed to have any dire effects on her as she did live well into old age.

Susan had a huge old greengage tree in her garden and one year, when there was a glut of fruit, Justin being very keen on greengages, wanted the fruit picked and marketed. Francis was sent round to Susan's garden to pick it but try as he might, he could not get the fruit from the top branches.

'Don't worry Mr Bell,' Susan called up the tree. 'I'll send up the boy Frank.' Well, the boy Frank was her lodger and couldn't have been a day under 70.

Francis had always kept an eye on Susan and, before the days of the National Health Service, had helped her by paying for visits by the doctor. Years later the village policeman, who had taken to checking up on her daily, had called as usual and got no reply. Cycling up to Hill Farm he asked if Peter, who was home from school and a teenager by then, could climb through the small window at the front of the cottage and unlock the door. The window had been left ajar and the policeman being very rotund was unable to climb through.

The sight of poverty that met Peter's eyes was shocking. A filthy table with several layers of grubby newspaper on it and a single chipped cup, engrained with grime. A rickety old broken chair and a broken saucer on the floor where Susan must have been feeding her cat. A room absolutely bare apart from these few items and a heap of long forgotten dead ash in the grate. The smell was appalling. Old age and poverty had long rendered any pretence at housekeeping quite useless.

Peter, wrestling with the large chain across the inside of the door was ashen and gasping as he stumbled out into the light. The policeman found poor old Susan upstairs in bed, still alive but very unwell. Admission to Bury Hospital followed shortly after, where she died within a week. Some would say, perhaps not too kindly but probably true, that this was a result of the bath they gave her on arrival.

Such things made up life in a small rural community in an age when every village had a policeman and everyone knew one another.

The winter of 1945 had been a hard one. In fact Francis recorded the weather over Christmas as being *'the severest we have had for many years with 14 degrees of frost.'* and by January 5th it had snowed. All the work with the spraying and pruning had been held up as *'the weather continued cold – snow storms, hard frosts and cold winds.'* And just when it had turned a little milder and pruning had recommenced, he writes *'A 90 mile an hour gale last night* [January 18th] *has brought with it snow and the return of winter.'* By the time he takes up his diary again on February 9th, the weather has continued to deteriorate. *'Since last we made an entry, the weather has been most violent. Intense frost (the worst in 50 years) with snow and gales, followed by a period of rain brought the work almost to a standstill.'*

It was a bitterly cold world that Barbara Judith made her entry into on January 27th, for Francis had become a father once again and Peter and Sally had a new baby sister.

Judy was just a few weeks old when her grandfather Robert told them he wanted to come over to Hill Farm to talk over something with Francis. He had told them he would only stay a day or two, but

Barbara found herself still coping with an extra mouth to feed a fortnight later. With Robert's very delicate stomach, finding light easily digestible meals in wartime was not easy, and to make matters worse, Robert had come without his ration book.

Another problem was he would wander off. Francis, arriving back at Hill Farm, with only half an hour to spare, would miss his lunch, spending the time combing the surrounding countryside for his father. Luckily he did stick to the roads, and was sometimes found as far afield as Seabrooks. As an old man now, perhaps Robert had felt the need to revisit for the last time, the places that had been so influential in shaping his family's destiny.

Back at Hill Farm, however, it was the new baby that really fascinated Robert. Was it with his life in journalism and newspaper deadlines to be met, that he had missed so much of his own children's childhood? He would stand for hours gazing down at Judy asleep in her pram. 'What a remarkable child – she'll do great things.'

They never did find out what he needed to speak to Francis about and began to think, that perhaps he had just felt the need for a little quiet and reflection. Despite having the tiny house in Stour Street to retreat to, his acute deafness was a considerable handicap, and having to be sociable whilst resident at The Four Swans, though never a problem to Fanny, must have been especially hard for him.

Barbara and Francis didn't lack for distinguished neighbours. Geoffrey, the younger brother of the well-known economist Maynard Keynes, also a long-term friend of Justin's, came to live at Home Farm for part of the war, and another immediate neighbour during that time was the Reverend Kenneth Riches who had first come as a student plum-picker. His elderly mother had lived in one half of the semi-detached cottages at the top of Edmunds Hill for a while at the beginning of the war, and when she died, he had returned there himself. Like most of the other residents in Stradishall, he accommodated students during the plum picking.

Bryan Matthews, later to become Sir Bryan Matthews, moved into the cottage when he left. Educated at King's College, Cambridge where he took a first class honours in physiology in 1927, Bryan became a Fellow in 1929. He was a colourful and exuberant young don, astounding the world with a series of radio broadcasts, when he converted the electrical currents of his own body into sound through an amplifier and a bell.

As head of the RAF Institute of Aviation Medicine and consultant to the RAF in Applied Physiology, he did much to improve the safety of pilots and paved the way for high altitude flight. He would be remembered for his huge contribution to the War effort, through his work at Farnborough, where he and a colleague had invented the aeroplane ejector seat. After the war he returned to Cambridge where he was Professor of Physiology.

Bryan was a friend of the Brookes and had attended Justin and Edith's wedding, signing the register as a witness. When his first marriage failed, he moved to Stradishall with Constance. She was remembered as a 'huge load of fun' and as 'being in theatricals'. She was also a potter and loved boats. As Bryan was also a very keen sailor, they would spend the summer sailing.

They had a dog called Aggie who had a great personality, but because she was seasick, went to spend the summer with the Brookes. They entered Aggie in the Wickhambrook Show one year, in the 'Ugliest Dog' class, and poor old Aggie won.

Bryan owned a beautiful 70ft ketch called *Lucretia* which he had on occasions sailed as far as South Africa, taking students from Cambridge with him to crew. With the arrival of Bryan and Constance, Barbara experienced, for the first time, what it was to have a neighbour popping in and out for tea and coffee. Being rather shy, she always felt she was on the periphery of Francis' reflected glory - so much so, that when Francis invited some fellow fruit growers whom he had taken on a tour of the orchards, back for a cup of coffee at Hill Farm, they were amazed to find he was actually married.

But now she and Constance struck up a friendship and she actually found herself returning her visits. It certainly made life a little more fun.

## *Lucretia*

Another major event in the history of Hill Farm at this time was the modernisation of the kitchen. The whole of the old kitchen was gutted, walls were knocked down and a passageway incorporated, producing a larger and lighter effect. The old brick floor was dug out and a suspended wooden floor and joists put in. When told that this modernisation would include some new shelves, Barbara asked if the shelves could have doors on them and Justin agreed. She would have cupboards at last.

The installation of a solid fuel Aga for cooking, and another smaller solid fuel boiler providing a constant supply of hot water, were perhaps the greatest innovations. And with a kitchen that was always warm, life with three young children was made considerably easier.

Alongside the renovation of the kitchen, a new downstairs bathroom was also installed where the old coal shed had been. The dairy, however, at the back of the house, was still kept. With its flight of stairs that led to nowhere and its steep sloping roof, it would remain for many more years. Late in the nineteen fifties, with the building of a new gable end, the knocking down of the wall between the dining room and the playroom, the installation of electricity and an upstairs bathroom, the layout of the old house would change yet again.

**The new gable end being built on at Hill Farm**

Help at Hill Farm, after Rosy had left, was by way of Mildred. Mildred had a large parrot and lived on the road to Denston, just off the Haverhill road. Leaving eventually to marry a policeman who presumably liked parrots, Barbara and Francis would always remember 'Milly' as being the best help they ever had and certainly the longest lasting.

Milk was collected from Home Farm; dipped out of a churn which had various sized measures hung around the rim. Mrs Roly Smith, as she was always known, now lived there; her husband Roland was a tractor driver on the farm. Mrs Roly used to baby-sit for Francis and Barbara and being a lady whose figure rather suited her name, Francis would make great play of getting his shoulder behind her to heave her up into the Land Rover when he took her home. The children would also take wicked delight in getting her down onto the floor to play musical cushions, knowing full well that she'd have the greatest difficulty in getting up again.

Her husband Roland would always insist on driving the largest of the tractors regardless of the job to be done. He would often make the men laugh, arriving at an orchard to mow the grass, looking totally incongruous with a great big tractor and the smallest of cutters behind.

The war was coming to an end. On May 8th 1945 V.E. Day, (Victory in Europe) was celebrated on the farm with two days' holiday. Francis acknowledged this briefly, though he seemed more concerned that the holiday had put the work behind. The R.A.F. had now removed the crashed bomber behind the house and the damage was not as bad as he had feared with ... *'only about 30 trees destroyed.'*

There were still a few land girls working on the farm along with some German and Italian prisoners of war. The latter were housed at Stoke by Clare and brought over daily. Francis was actually very short of labour at that time and grateful for any extra help, setting them to work ... *'to do a bit of hedging for us.'* Two or three ex-service men had also come as trainees but, like the prisoners of war, they were unskilled.

For some time Francis had found the way in which the strawberries had been planted to be very unsatisfactory and time-consuming.

December 5th 1944 ... *'They are all planted on old pasture, but have been put in, in such a way, that they have all to be hand worked, which is going to make the job twice as expensive as it should be and there is no system to it. I am not forgetting that the W.A.E.C. (The War Ag.) is responsible for some of this, as they have made us inter-crop some of the fields. But I feel I could have laid out the fields much more systematically.'*

March 16th 1945 ... *'We have employed some of the women forking over the strawberry rows on the Green ... they have made quite a good job of it* [but] *the strawberries are going to be very troublesome this year...'*

They would continue to be a source of great irritation, taking up too much labour that he felt could be used elsewhere. He felt they had been planted far too wide apart and mixed in as they were with young plum and apricot trees along with a mass of winter weed *'there* [was] *barely room for a Fordson* [tractor] *to pass between the rows.'*

It was perhaps due to this problem with the strawberries and the lack of skilled people to work or at least oversee the work being done, that more specialist help was brought in.

November 13th 1945 ... Francis had *'just returned from* [his] *holiday and* [was] *a little out of touch with the work. ... tomorrow we expect a new man – Burton – who has had ten years' experience with Chivers.'*

Bringing someone in who could take on the responsibility of the soft fruit, was all part of getting the work of the various departments of the farm delegated, taking some of the workload off Francis' shoulders and leaving him as General Manager and overseer. In a similar way Ron Ellse started working for Brookes in 1946 and again Francis' diary recorded his arrival.

April 11th 1946 ... *'A man, Ellse, arrived this week. He is a potential pig-man and seems a nice fellow, and I am hoping one day to hand over the herd to him.'*

Ron Ellse fulfilled Francis' expectations and, with the expansion of the herd, did eventually take over its management, becoming a dedicated and hard-working man that Francis could depend upon. With the installation of modern pipeline feeding, Ron would often stay up all night in winter thawing out frozen pipes.

The arrival of Harold Burton however, did not go so smoothly. Francis, always so conscious of the economics of production, now found the situation worse rather than better. Instead of speeding up the work by mechanisation, Francis felt that Harold seemed determined to compound the situation.

December 11th 1945 ... *'We have made a start digging over the strawberry beds. This work is quite fantastic. There will be no profit in strawberries if we work this way. The whole thing can be done with a horse hoe.'*

And it didn't seem to get any better.

January 5th 1946 ... *'The girls - there are only three now - are digging over the strawberry beds. I shall send the trainees there on Monday to try and get the job finished as soon as possible. I think it quite impossible to make strawberries pay using so much labour on them.'*

March 19th 1946 ... *'Our strawberry growing is at present on a very uneconomic basis, no mechanical tool being used at all. This is absolutely killing. We cannot hand dig the rows at £3 10s. a week, wages per man.'*

Francis found *'the amount of work to be done on* [the strawberries] *very depressing'* and the fact that *'unskilled labour is all we have available for them.'*

In the 1950s Francis invented, and got made up, a device for speeding up the strawberry hoeing and making it a less boring job. It was a rather wonderful idea and very simple. It consisted of a wide plank set across the back of a Ferguson tractor on the hydraulics. Here four men could sit, resting their feet on shaped footrests in front of them; they were then lowered close to the ground by the hydraulics. At this more restful angle and with specially adapted short-handled hoes, it was an easy job to lean forward and hoe between their legs, as the tractor slowly drove forward. The job was made more interesting by each of the men taking a turn driving the tractor.

Harold was quite convinced it wouldn't work, but in fact it did, perfectly. Everyone knew of the relationship between Francis and Harold and Percy remembered someone drawing a cartoon of the hoeing device in action, with the figure of Harold in the background jumping up and down fuming. It hung in the farm office for ages.

Reading through his diaries, which were, after-all, intended as a personal reference and dealt with the technical side of his job, elements of Francis' character are also revealed. Always seeing the best in people, he would put a name to someone he found particularly easy to get on with and who was willing to work and learn, commenting on them in a positive and encouraging manner. Yet when he found someone he personally disliked or found difficult, he rarely named him, but rather commented on the effect of that person's work on the smooth running of the farm. For him that was the important factor rather than anything personal.

As early as 1944 Francis had been looking into the possibility of building a large store and pack-house for the fruit.

He drew up a design for one that would also hopefully include an automatic weighing machine and a grader. He had read about such a system and envisaged such a packing shed being built into the side of a hill, centrally situated to be accessible from all points of the farm, and with one end partly underground. Here he thought, fruit could be stored during glut periods, whilst other activities like grading and packing were being carried out in another part of the building. These stores would be cooled by electric fans run from a small electrical plant on site.

However it would not be until the 1950s that his idea would come to fruition and in the meantime he had a problem.

15th October 1946 ... *'Next season we look like having to do some grading to apples as prices are beginning to slip. We are at a great disadvantage in having no place to house a grader. As it is at present we have to sort over all the Bramleys out of doors. This is a longish job and the apples are roughly handled. If we could only get Hill Farm barn repaired temporarily we would be able to carry on with that for a year or two. But one of the walls may collapse at any minute and there seems little likelihood of getting any repairs done. At present I have 800 boxes of Coxes housed in this barn.'*

Interestingly at this time, Francis' cousin Carlos, (his Aunt Kate's younger son) came over to visit them at Hill Farm. Francis must have taken Carlos out to have a look at the state of the barn, for recorded in Carlos' diary for July 20th 1946 is the following entry: *'At Hill Farm in the afternoon. Behind the yard there is a barn with a name and date carved on one of the beams: 'J. Davy 1835'. Another barn on the same site burned down at about this date. Marks of scorching* [are] *still visible on the foundation bricks of the present building. The man responsible for setting fire to the old barn was hanged at Chelmsford after a reward of £100 had been offered for evidence. The man's wife married twice and both husbands were hanged, one for arson, the other for sheep stealing. In those days a farm labourer's lunch was often no more than a turnip pulled from the field.'*

Was this a case of a personal grudge against the farmer or part of the general rural unrest of the 1830s that resulted in the destruction of threshing machines and rick burning? A protest which had its roots deep within the hunger and oppression of the agricultural labourer and which would result in 9 hangings and 500 transportations?

Francis, however, was able to get the go-ahead to start repairing Hill Farm barn a month later so that this building could then be used as a temporary measure.

6th November, 1946 ... *'We have taken the tiles off the barn at Hill Farm, Stradishall, as this was near to collapse. We hope to be able to make use of this for a year or two as a packing shed. We are in great need of a building in which to sort apples.'*

In fact the work on the barn at Hill Farm was held up. This was undoubtedly due to the weather and to the fact that in the end, most of it had to be pulled down and rebuilt. It had been found to be in a dangerous condition and would not be completed until the following July.

With the ordering *'at last'* of some gravity conveyor belts to help with the packing of the next year's crop of plums, Francis felt that he was finally progressing towards the sort of automation he envisaged. It was all to do with making the various jobs easier, saving *'a lot of back-ache'*, bringing the farm up to date and eventually making it highly competitive economically.

31st December 1946 ... *'The time has come when we must be very much more careful of the condition of the fruit. The war years have been bad for us in that respect, as anything dumped in a box would sell. There is no doubt that next year we shall have to do a certain amount of sorting and grading. Here again we are at a disadvantage with no grader and no shed to put it into. Some improvisation will be necessary for the next year or two... we got in a muddle with our peach crop this year through lack of facilities for packing.'*

Francis would continue over the next few years to be very aware of the need for care over grading and packing. He could foresee a time when fruit would have to be placed in much smaller boxes and trays with presentation being of the utmost importance. Fruit he felt should be packed by equal size rather than weight, with the greatest of care being taken in its presentation and wrapping and each piece being handled as delicately as an egg.

He was delighted, when he was able to find and train up a team of local women to do this, all with an eye to the future when the pack-house would be up and running and he needed trained people to pack the fruit as it came off the grading machines.

18th September 1950 ... *'There has been one bright spot – we have collected about a dozen Stradishall women to help wrap the apples, this will be most helpful in the future when we have the packing shed and we have a crop.'*

The grading machines available at this time were a great source of frustration to him – he knew what he wanted but there just didn't seem to be the right machine to do the job and breakdowns were a constant worry.

October 7th 1949 ... *'The only disappointment is the grader, this machine just doesn't work. They are coming to have a go at it next week, but I don't think it will be much good, and in our own minds we have more or less written it off. It means that our grading has to be done by eye, and it is difficult to get a true grade like that. We should be very much better off with a belt to pick off.'*

Eventually he would have the system he envisaged: a means of automated grading whereby, through a system of rollers and belts, apples would gently run down into graded individual sections, to be wrapped and packed, all of a uniform size per box. The girls were shown how to make the fruit look its most attractive, with alternate rows of wrapped and unwrapped fruit.

All of this was years ahead of its time, long before the demands of supermarkets and the E.U. would call for any such uniformity in presentation, size and colour. And meanwhile there was still the question of the new packing shed.

Estimated costs for the building of the pack-house would be in the region of £30,000. It was a huge investment. Francis felt it was essential. He had seen two built on similar lines in Kent and he was convinced that it was the modern way forward. Shortages of concrete and steel after the war would hold up its completion. Once it was finished with its packing, grading and storage, staff facilities and offices, Francis felt that it took the farm to the forefront of commercial fruit production in the country at that time.

There would be teething problems it was true, like the use of moss as a coolant in the fruit stores. Justin was very keen on the moss storage idea, with its theory of water dripping through banks of moss to keep the apples fresher and in better condition. But the trouble was it never really worked; major alterations had to be made and Francis summed the whole thing up by saying he thought, *'the designer of it had fled the country.'*

**The Fruit Pack house**

The weather, which plays such a vital part in everything connected with farming, featured constantly in Francis' diaries; he monitored it minutely. He had small weather stations strategically situated about the farm. He inspected and recorded their readings every day. A late frost would wreak havoc and destroy acres of budding fruit overnight.

May 12th 1944 ... *'As I forecast, the cold winds of last week ended in disastrous frosts. I do not think it too much to say that the sharpest frost of Sunday night did us £10,000-worth of damage... I am waiting to see the accounts of the frosts in the trade papers and find out how it has affected* other districts. I think it has been very widespread and we shall not be the only sufferers. However it is very disappointing to see the fruits of one's labour struck down in a night.'

Despite reports of such weather, it would be the truly terrible winter of 1947 which brought the direst problems to those working on the land and, like the rest of Britain, Suffolk was brought to a standstill.

Despite being able to help themselves to firewood, it was bitterly cold in the bungalows down at Wickham House. *'A large number of men [were] laid up with 'flu' and to make matters worse there was a national coal crisis.'* The appalling weather seemed unrelenting...

5th February 1947 ... *'Great deterioration in the weather during the past fortnight – unprecedented snow showers. The lowest temperature we recorded was 21 degrees (Fahrenheit) below. It then started to thaw, but the blizzards have now returned and we are under snow again... all the usual work has been stopped...'*

14th February 1947... *'Cold weather continues unabated – ice, snow and cold winds make organising the work very difficult...the frost has got right into the land...Forecast still promises cold weather for several days.'*

But there would in fact be no respite for several months.

21st February 1947 ... *'Weather continues cold with snow and ice, freezing every night...This weather has been with us for a month or more and we are beginning to despair of it changing; it is just possible to plough but we break too many machines so we have had to give up.'*

5th March 1947 ... *'Continuation of bitter weather, but we have had an odd day or two when work was possible. It is snowing hard at the moment... We have had to turn the men onto hedging to keep themselves warm... They keep talking of a thaw but it never comes.'*

12th March 1947 ... *'Very cold weather continues – the worst blizzard within living memory – just as we thought we were having a thaw. Most of the farm spent three or four days clearing roads. It has been practically impossible to do any constructive work, though we have tried out our new sprayer, but even that had to be postponed, as it was impossible to pull it through the snow… We are slowly spreading straw on the front field – even this is difficult owing to the bales being frozen.'*

All over Britain farmers were struggling to feed their livestock. Not only was there a general shortage of animal feed, but also the task of keeping drinking troughs free of ice during the terrible weather. It was a constant battle. Francis had by this time cut down by half the number of pigs that were being kept on the farm and this was making life a little easier. His decision was due to the shortages of animal feed after the war and his need to have someone to take over the pigs. When in time the herd was built up again, this would be Ron Ellse.

The thaw when it came brought torrential rain and floods and although *'the land was in a shocking state'* the temperatures were at last rising and the snow had gone.

20th March 1947 … *'It is indeed a change to hear the birds begin to sing in the morning after the bitter weather we have experienced during the past six weeks. All we need now is a little sun and in a week the land would be fit for anything.'*

Francis' elation, however, was short-lived. With rain and gales, the weather once again deteriorated

3rd April 1947 … *'The weather is now unspeakable. Instead of those drying winds and sun for which we had hoped, all we get is wet, and last night there was a snowstorm. We are forecast more snow for tomorrow – Good Friday.'*

In fact it wouldn't be until almost a week after Easter that the worst weather in living memory actually began to improve and the terrible winter of 1947 drew to a close. And although the wind and rain would continue often at gale force, right into May, the snow did not return.

Not everyone found the snow depressing. In fact for six-year old Peter, setting off on a Monday morning along the road to Newmarket, towering banks of snow piled higher than the roof of the car, made it feel the like an adventure.

He'd started school at Fairlawn, a small pre-prep school run by one of Nancy's relations. She had recommended it to Barbara and Francis, and Peter had started there the previous year. He had felt somewhat phased when at five years old he had been left on the school doorstep that first Monday morning by Barbara, who had cheerily told him, 'Now be a good boy Darling, I'll see you on Friday.'

'Friday?' Even to his untutored five-year old mind he knew that today was Monday, and that 'Friday' was at some long distant time ahead. What did she mean by 'See you on Friday?' Tears coursed down his cheeks as he watched her drive out of sight. Thankfully kindly hands appeared at that moment to gather him up, but somehow no one had explained to him that going to school would mean being a weekly boarder and staying away all week.

Francis meanwhile, had rather taken things into his own hands regarding three-year old Sally's education. Much to Barbara's amazement, he announced one day that he had made arrangements with a retired teacher in the village to give Sally reading lessons.

When he could be torn away from the farm, Francis was actually rather enjoying fatherhood now the children were no longer babies. He was always whistling and like Fanny, had a repertoire of funny little songs and ditties that he was always coming out with. Fanny's most remembered one being:

>'Down went Maginty to the bottom of the sea,
>He must be very wet 'cause they haven't found him yet,
>And he's dressed in his best Sunday clothes.'

He devised magical games for them whereby he would toss a ball up into the air that would disappear and not come down. Amidst screams of delight, the children would search his pockets and pat him all over finding nothing – only to be amazed when it appeared again as if by magic in his hand.

He would spend the evenings, when not dictating his journal, making and whittling toys for them. Always innovative, his mind forever full of ideas, he made a wooden clown that rode on a one-wheeled bicycle. With a string strung across the dining room, the clown could be induced to pedal back and forth along the string when one or other end was raised.

The Italian prisoners of war, brought over to cut the hedges around the garden or to work in the buildings, would often stand and watch the children playing. No doubt they were a poignant reminder of their own families back home.

One of them fashioned a toy for Peter, which he shyly gave him. It was like a ping-pong bat. On it were six little wooden chickens. Strings were attached to each of their necks and fastened through to a wooden ball beneath the bat. By pulling the ball the chickens all bent their heads and pecked. Francis was quite intrigued by this and copied the 'pecking hens' idea and made more of the same. He had also got hold of a book on toy-making and soon had clowns and monkeys turning somersaults up poles, a wooden train with trucks, two dolls cots and a magnificent sailing boat with sails that could actually be raised and lowered for sailing on the pond. All these would be Christmas or birthday presents for the children.

Christmas at Hill Farm was always fun. There was a large tree with real lighted candles clipped onto its branches and figures that Francis had made out of pipe cleaners. Sometimes Christmas was spent alone, but more usually with one or two friends and family joining them.

Christmas morning started with the ritual of going up to the Hall for drinks and 'the bran tub'. Barbara stayed at home to cook the lunch, but Francis took the children up to Clopton, where he would have a drink and a chat with Justin, whilst Edith organised the children. Small hands would be guided towards an appropriate little present, but it always seemed that quite by chance the lucky dip into the bran tub brought out just the right gift.

On occasions Bryan and Constance would come down or Jo Hitchcock, a fruit-farming friend. Barbara's brother Newy too would come and stay with his newly-wed wife Margaret.

Francis would usually get out his accordion or strum a few chords on the piano, and accompany the singing from a battered copy of *The*

*Oxford Song Book.* All usually in a fairly merry state from the effects of his home-made wine, which he made from almost anything he could get hold of.

One year, he had the idea of making pure alcohol by placing some elderflower wine to freeze in the snow outside, on the assumption that he would be left with the liquid alcohol that wouldn't freeze. The resulting fire-water turned out to be extremely lethal but sadly without much flavour. Crème de menthe was added to help with this, but the end result was a complete failure.

Another time, feeling that jars and demijohns were rather on the small side, he seconded a used carboy from the farm and set a huge quantity of wine to ferment in it. Unfortunately, giving it a stir one day with a pole, Francis was a bit too enthusiastic and the carboy broke, sending wine and shattered glass cascading all over the kitchen floor. Barbara was horrified at the mess and Francis at the loss of his wine. The place smelled like a brewery for weeks.

In those days before refrigeration, Barbara would spend the summer salting down runner beans from the garden to eat the following the winter. Kilner jars were used to bottle fruit, tomatoes, in fact almost anything. Once filled, with their rubber seals and glass tops held in place by a metal screwed band, they were sealed by being placed in a pan of boiling water.

Another form of preservation was water-glass. Before the days of the battery hen and birds bred to lay throughout the year, eggs were preserved for use in winter. During the laying period and ideally between March and June, whenever there was a glut of eggs, the surplus was placed in a large glazed pottery egg crock that stood on the floor of the pantry. Each layer was then covered with water-glass. This was a mixture of soluble silicates of potash and soda that was bought at the chemist.

It first had to be dissolved in hot water, previously well boiled to kill any bacteria that might be present; a small tin and a gallon of water would usually preserve about fifty eggs. The water-glass then simply closed the pores of the eggshell and excluded the air, thus preventing deterioration. Making sure the top layer was well covered eggs could continue to be added each day. They were by no means perfect when they came out but they could be tested for freshness by seeing if they sank in water – bad eggs always floated. And Barbara would always take the precaution of breaking each one into a cup before using it, just to make doubly sure.

A pig too would be killed and butchered. After the joints had been thoroughly soaked in brine, Francis would smoke them by hanging them up in the wide old chimney down at Home Farm. Removing them later, he wrapped the joints in muslin before hanging them from a beam in the cart lodge.

Scalded cream was made by placing a large jug of milk in a pan of water, and bringing it up to boil. After twenty minutes or so, the jug was removed and left to cool overnight, creating a layer of delicious crusty cream by morning. Fresh meat was stored in a wooden meat-safe that was hung in the pantry on the north side. With its fine mesh door to keep out the flies, it had a wet sack hung over it to keep it cool in summer.

Holidays were always difficult. And of course during the war and with petrol rationing it was difficult to go anywhere. But with such an intense spraying programme throughout the spring, the picking season starting so early with the soft fruit, and then the plums and continuing right through to the autumn with the apples, Francis could never take a family holiday, when the children were home from school.

His journals record that once he was married, at least up until 1949, he always took two weeks off in the middle of November and some of this time would be spent visiting Barbara's parents in Spalding. Despite what would often be a poor time of year weather-wise, it should have given Francis the opportunity to relax, but it seemed that Francis found it very difficult not to be thinking about fruit farming. It totally absorbed him and he couldn't resist taking the opportunity to slip off and visit one or other fruit farmer he knew of in the Spalding district.

26th November 1946 … *'The last fortnight has been the worst weather we have experienced for twelve months. Continual rain and winds. All the land is completely waterlogged, and floods are out in many places. Having been on holiday, I have missed most of this. I had an interesting walk round Selby's place while I was away. They are experiencing difficulty with eating apples in the Wisbech area owing to canker. His orchards are eight or nine years old, and show excessive growth in spite of being grassed down.'*

Not long after the war, Barbara drove the children up to Hunstanton for a seaside holiday. Bombo and Mannie had rented a house called 'Bee Farm' in Old Hunstanton - situated between the church and the beach.

Barbara's sister-in-law Christine, her brother Peter's wife, joined her there later with her three girls and it was a family holiday format that would be repeated for several years.

Barbara had had the forethought to bring Mildred along with her; with Judy still in nappies, she proved to be an invaluable addition to the party that set off from Hill Farm. The journey, as all journeys seemed to be in those days, was quite an undertaking and such outings were always considered to be an expedition.

There was a shortage of good tyres after the war and with most of the tyres on the car threadbare and in places, worn through to the canvas, punctures were a regular occurrence on most journeys. Very often a lorry driver would stop and help Barbara change a wheel.

Once when driving over to Spalding with all three children, who were not very old at the time, Barbara got a puncture about a mile outside of King's Lynn. The journey hadn't started well, as she had found that the catches on the back doors wouldn't hold. Before setting off, she had sat all three children on the back seat and secured the doors on either side, by putting a rope right across in front of the children, and tying the ends through each door handle. The road that day seemed particularly deserted, and now with a puncture, she waited hopefully for someone to stop and help her. No one did.

Locking up the car as best she could, and with strict instructions to the children to stay where they were, which wasn't difficult with a rope stretched across in front of them, Barbara set off to walk to the nearest garage. An anxious eternity seemed to pass before she reappeared with a man from the garage – and in the meantime not one of the children had moved.

But now, with her carload of children, buckets and spades, luggage and Mildred, it was just so good to be having a real holiday after the monotony and uncertainty of the war years. Along with Bee Farm, Bombo and Mannie also hired a large beach hut right on the sands and it was a well-laden cavalcade that trooped down there each day. Carrying an assortment of games, buckets, spades, sandwiches, drinks and clothing for every eventuality, along with Mannie's First World War yellow rubber dinghy, they would spend each day bathing, sitting in deckchairs chatting and watching the children playing.

A strong swimmer himself, Mannie had taught all three of his own children to swim and had once been awarded a medal for saving the life of a woman at Skegness. She had become trapped in the quicksand there, and was rapidly sinking, when Mannie, realising her plight, managed to find some planks and spades, which he placed down on the sand. By lying along this makeshift support, he was able to pull her to safety.

Mannie was really rather splendid on the beach. He absolutely loved it and always entered into the spirit of the occasion. Arming himself with a full-sized spade and galvanised bucket and dressed in

**Old Hunstanton – the Kingston cousins on holiday**
Left to right; Peter (with Judy hidden behind) Sally and Jane Kingston
in Mannie's World War I rubber dinghy

what must have been an Edwardian all-in-one black bathing costume, he would supervise and undertake the building of extensive fortifications in the sand. Wonderful castles with moats that filled with seawater - pinnacles and turrets soared on every corner and of course the sun shone each day.

It was two weeks of sheer heaven. And for Mildred, with only the lightest of duties during the day, and the added attraction of evenings off, and visits to the local cinema with a rather attractive young soldier, that first holiday in Hunstanton was a great success.

Sally had initially joined Peter at Fairlawn as a weekly boarder, but when she was six, she was sent to Moreton Hall near Bury St Edmunds, and this time Judy joined her. Later they would go as boarders to Runton Hall, near Cromer.

Both initially at Moreton Hall as weekly boarders before later becoming termly, it was a difficult transition for Judy as a little girl of four years old. Being sent away from home at such a young age was something she would always find hard to come to terms with. Both girls would say that they felt that they never had a home life. Barbara felt it was lonely for Judy at Hill Farm, once the other two were away

**Francis with Sally and Judy going back to school**

at school. The reality behind that decision was more likely to have been that sending Judy off to boarding school, along with the other two, would give Barbara freedom during term time. With the children all away to school, Barbara was invited to join Bryan and Constance on *Lucretia* for a sailing holiday. She absolutely loved it. She had been before on shorter trips, with Judy staying once with Justin and Edith, but now, with Judy at school, she joined them for a longer trip down the French coast.

*Lucretia* was a big boat and Bryan would usually have extra crew, mainly students, dropping some off at a port to return home, and then picking up others. They provided a useful carrier service too it seems. Francis wrote to her, his *'by hand'* letter reaching her undoubtedly via the Cambridge students or friends who were joining the boat at a later stage. It was written at the time when the dining room and playroom at Hill Farm were being made into one.

'My Darling,

We've heard all about you – I am missing you very much....

Many thanks for your notes. Pete's never came, so all is well. The plasterers have started, but have gone on holiday – they will be out before the [school] holidays. Been very busy lately and not much time. I go to Helen's quite often; they don't seem to mind me. Thanks for the brandy – see if you can get another.

All love darling – longing to be able to love you again.

Your old man, F.'

Francis was never actually that keen on sailing. Sometime later, he was invited to go for a sail with them, but after one such expedition he refused to go again. He really couldn't bear to be away from the farm for more than a day or two. And as he would say, 'Why is it that you get a perfectly nice chap on land, get him on a boat and he starts shouting at everyone?'

**Barbara, Constance and Bryan on a sailing trip about 1950**

By the time Peter had started at The Glebe, a prep school in Hunstanton, another summer holiday with cousins was planned. This time Francis would be involved, but only for a weekend at either end. He just couldn't leave the farm.

Barbara had decided that they should hire a small caravan for a week, and Adrian had agreed that it could be put in the orchard at Redisham. From this base, Barbara reasoned, she could drive the children over to the beach at Southwold.

Their cousins, Martin and his twin sister Sylvia, being only a year or two older than Peter, were becoming regular visitors to Hill Farm.

With their father Adrian suffering from totally debilitating migraines, and the need for quiet in the house whilst he wrote, the relaxed regime at Stradishall was always welcome, and their Uncle Francis was always such fun.

Sylvia in later years would remember him with deep affection. 'I was in love with him at the age of fourteen ... Francis was all the bright and breezy things our part of the family wasn't.' She remembered one particular visit when, after supper in the big family kitchen at Hill Farm, 'Francis brought in an accordion and played and sang to us across the table in the lamplight'... playing by ear without the need to read music, a talent she would really envy.

**The caravan holiday at Redisham – Sylvia at the window Judy, Peter and Sally on the step – and Francis with his accordion**

It was arranged that Francis would tow the caravan behind the Land Rover to his brother's, with Peter accompanying him, whilst Barbara drove over in the car with the two girls and the luggage. Although the journey seemed to take ages, with Francis having to drive very slowly, the caravan was actually tiny. It had bunk beds for the children, which Sally promptly fell out of, and not much more. On closer inspection, Francis flatly refused to sleep in it and took up Marjorie's offer of a bed in the house for the night.

It was during this holiday that their Uncle Adrian, seeking to amuse the children, produced an archery set. It was full size, very real and quite magnificent. Where it had come from they couldn't imagine.

Adrian set up the target at one end of the orchard and after brief instruction to the gathered archers, retired to his study to continue writing, for what he no doubt hoped would be a peaceful hour. All went well with everyone taking turns and older children helping younger ones, until the two boys felt it had become a rather tame affair. 'How about seeing how far we can shoot the arrows?' one of them suggested and the idea was quickly taken up.

Soon arrows were flying through the air in all directions, high over the hedge; across an adjoining field; up into the trees beyond the target; it was all very realistic and quite satisfyingly like the 'Battle of Agincourt'.

It wasn't until Adrian, looking up briefly from his work, seeing arrows whizzing past his window, realised that things were rapidly getting out of hand; the bow and arrows were tactfully removed and another, safer game suggested.

It would be years later before the origin of the bow and arrows was discovered, and this through one of Adrian's books. There, in *Music in the Morning,* he described how he had been invited to join a local archery club soon after Anthea had been born. In his inimitable style, he wrote of the gathering of *'The Oatcott Archers'* with all the humour and delight that he so readily found in the simplest of things.

His nephew and nieces found him enthralling. He had a way of telling them a story that would have them spellbound. Being an author meant nothing to them – writing was just what Uncle Adrian did and he knew that was where his strength lay. But he had longed to be able to farm again.

In 1943 he had been able to buy up a small farm about a mile from Redisham. His latest book, *Apple Acre,* published in 1942, had sold 30,000 copies within a year. *Corduroy* was being reprinted too and it seemed that with his intimate nostalgic vignettes of English life, he captured the hearts and imaginations of service men far from home in a Europe torn and ravaged by war. He could now afford to buy Brick Kiln Farm at Weston, a forced sale under the War Ag. at ten pounds an acre and fulfil his dream of returning to farming.

For all the children, it was the pond at Hill Farm which featured most highly during school holidays, whether it was its frozen delights in winter, or its murky depths in summer.

**The pond at Hill Farm**

Protected on one side by the backyard wall, its shallow expanse of water was bordered on the far side by weeping willows. Although it wasn't very deep, it was extremely muddy and was naturally quite irresistible to children. The problem was they would keep falling in.

Sailing the boat that Francis had made was fairly straightforward. Home-made boats out of logs were also fine, if a little less satisfactory. But it was when it came to the raft that Peter and Martin constructed out of planks, that the real problems started. Crowding everyone on caused the raft to submerge, but with the aid of a pole, it could still be punted along albeit under water. Progress was somewhat slow, with muddy water lapping up to within an inch or two of the top of their Wellington boots.

Experience usually enabled Peter to remain upright, but Martin or sometimes his twin Sylvia, being unable to see the sides of the raft, would with unerring regularity, step over the edge and fall in. Covered in black slimy mud, they would emerge dripping, and squelching their way back to the house, greet Barbara politely at the back door. 'I'm awfully sorry Aunt Barbara, but I've fallen in the pond again.' And Barbara, showing a great deal of restraint, would once again, scrape off the worst of the mud before sluicing one or other down and issuing yet another set of clean clothes.

Yard cricket was also a great favourite, and yet again the pond would feature. If the ball was hit into it, the batsman immediately scored six and out, but a combined effort was then involved to retrieve the ball and someone usually fell in.

The children were all back at school when news reached them that Grandpa Bell had died on 2nd December. The year was 1949. He had become very much a shadowy figure of late and since he and Fanny had moved to a genteel nursing home in Sudbury, he seemed to be more withdrawn than ever.

When they had first taken up residency at Ballingdon Grove, the sight of the grand piano in the large entrance hall had cheered him. He would spend hours playing to the other residents, particularly when Fanny wasn't around. Francis and Barbara made a point of coming over every other weekend, and bringing the children with them when they were home from school. How ironic that the son Fanny had almost forgotten she had would at the end, be the closest to her. Once when they arrived they had found Robert playing alone and Peter, standing beside the piano transfixed. He had never heard music like this before. And the old man, seeing the look of rapture on his grandson's face, continued to play. The tableau was shattered in a moment by the arrival of Fanny. Sweeping in, she slammed the lid of the piano down with a theatrical flourish, narrowly missing amputating her husband's fingers. 'Oh do stop Robert. The boy doesn't want to hear that noise.' Actually the boy did.

Then, as Francis quietly took his father off to sit in the garden, Fanny proceeded to hold court herself, handing round chocolates, and telling the children anecdotes which she interspersed with little snatches of song. She really was an extraordinary grandmother.

Once, on a whim, she had made a little tube of farthings and sent it to Peter at school. It had arrived unheralded; it wasn't his birthday and she never wrote to him again, but something had prompted the gesture, had stirred a maternal chord momentarily.

But now Robert had died. His book of poems *After Thoughts* had been published in 1929 by Methuen & Co. and remains a memorial to him. For here, amongst its pages, is the essence of a man, whom acute deafness had all but eclipsed in later years. A glimpse is caught of the perception and humour, still fresh today, that along with Fanny, had fashioned the men their sons would later become. There was no pretension with Robert, no illusions of grandeur; he slipped as quietly out of life as he had spent his final years. His poem, 'The Pool' perhaps sums up his philosophy on life and death, particularly his own.

> '*A moment since, I stepped ashore,*
> *And all is placid as before:*
> *Not any trace*
> *Of my impetuous embrace:*
> *Not even the remembrance of an eddy:*
> *Is that a ripple? No – it's gone already.*
> *And when at the appointed time,*
> *Out of the pool of life I climb,*
> *I'll look behind*
> *To see the gap I've left, and find*
> *The waters unperturbèd and serene,*
> *No sign at all that I have ever been.*'

After Robert's death, the little house in Stour Street was sold and Barbara and Stephanie went over to sort out his things. Within two days of his father's death, Francis was back at his diary.

There was little respite in the work to allow time for mourning, though mourn him he did, for there had always been a special relationship between father and son. But for Francis it was a quiet personal thing that didn't spill over into work. It was the way he wanted it to be. And for all of Francis' extrovert behaviour and head for business, he was a deeply sensitive man. It was this sensitivity that made him so aware of the needs of the men on the farm, and they loved him for it.

In later years Arthur Gibbs, who worked on the corn drier and also on the mixer for the pig food, came to Francis and told him about a Scottish chap they had working there. He had caught him stealing corn. Francis had no alternative but to sack the man, but he was very upset having to do so.

In the September prior to his father's death, the twenty-first anniversary of the farm had been celebrated with a very successful Harvest Horkey, followed by a firework display. It was a huge affair and just the sort of occasion that Justin loved. It had even received a write-up in the local press.

By this time it could be said that Francis was reaching the pinnacle of his career. The new pack-house was *'now in the hands of a Norwich firm of builders'* and was going to be built on the site of an old sandpit in Stradishall, adjacent to the Hollow Ditch. Although it wouldn't now be finished until 1951, once in operation, it would streamline the handling, storage and packing of fruit and take the farm to the forefront of the industry. The farm was now well equipped with both men and machinery and with the delegation of the various departments to foremen and women was running as smoothly as Justin had once envisaged, when he spoke to Adrian in the 1930s.

Francis' diaries, even by the previous year of 1948, record the *'Present Organisation of Clopton Hall'* and it's interesting to see the strata of management and distribution of responsibilities. Christian names, where known, have been added.

*'The Managers' Meeting deals with all questions of policy and planning.*

*Bookkeeping is in the hands of Jimmie James*
*Office and Statistics – Nancy Hardwicke;*
*Correspondence & Secretarial Work – L. Mitchell;*

*Fruit and General Supervision including Pigs – Francis Bell (A)*
*Farming – George Charnock (B) and Mrs. Brooke (C)*
*Under (A)*
*Nursery    - Bob Metcalfe*
*Soft Fruit- Harold Burton*
*Peaches – Lew Brennan*
*Pigs – Ron Ellse*
*Spraying – Stan Rutter*
*Pruning – Jack Loader*
*Engineer, pumping, electric light and cars – Jack Bishop*
*Tractor repairs – Bill Blewitt*
*Carpenter – Jack Finch*
*Under (B)*
*Hedge and wood clearing – Arthur Gibbs*
*Under (C)*
*Catering – Elizabeth Brooke*
*Canteen Cook – Rosy Nunn*
*House Cook – B. Edgeley*
*Billeting & assistant cook – J. Bishop*
*Hostels – Mrs. Roly Smith and Mrs. Hickey'*

The farm was gaining a reputation in the agricultural world as an industrialised fruit and arable unit and people wanting to know about fruit would seek out Francis' opinion and also send apples for identification.

His expertise was beginning to be recognised by people from all over the country and he would often receive phone calls in the evenings, asking for his advice over a particular problem and spend an hour discussing it. He was a regular recipient of *The American Fruit Grower* as well as its English counterpart, and he was in frequent correspondence with American fruit farmers through its pages. It was all the more creditable that his technical knowledge had been acquired whilst working at his job. He was constantly reading up and learning about latest developments, particularly in the use of sprays, and his scientific knowledge was becoming extensive.

In the 1930s people had congregated around Justin, but after the war and into the 1950s Francis began to be the centre of attention as his knowledge and authority grew. Justin on the other hand, must have felt that he had taught him all he knew, which of course at first, he had done. It must have been hard for him to acknowledge that Francis was held in such high esteem in the fruit growing world and to see now people coming up to Francis for advice and discussion. It was something that Francis was acutely aware of, and he would always make a point of referring people to Justin, when the two of them were together. A lot of people were visiting the farm now. Justin had published a book called *Peach Orchards in England* in 1947 and this had attracted an additional number of visitors that year and they would continue to come.

Charles Brooke would be described by his step-sister Elizabeth as 'a charming little boy'. He had remained the only child of Edith and Justin's marriage; she had been very ill after his birth. And loving children as she did, Edith 'doted on him.'

Charles never attended a day school and, with no other children to play with, was sent to Bedales in Petersfield, Hampshire. Justin's obituary in 1963 would indicate that he was also educated at Bedales before going to Cambridge, which undoubtedly influenced their decision to send Charles.

Bedales School was founded in 1893 and was co-educational from its outset. It was non-denominational and with its liberal ethos, emphasis on drama and the arts, was in complete contrast to conventional Victorian schooling. With its air of informality and freedom of expression, emphasis on lack of *'petty rules … no school uniform … staff and pupils call*[ing] *each other by their first names …'* it was an obvious choice for Justin and Edith - and how much it must have helped to shape the man that he became. It fitted in with their philosophy at the time and was quite unlike any other traditional boys' private school that they might otherwise have chosen for Charles.

During term-time, when he was about eight years old, Charles suffered a double mastoid – a very severe, deep infection of the ear, or in Charles' case, both ears. This type of infection was the dread of all parents and usually resulted in hospitalisation and an operation. In those days, before the use of penicillin, there was little else that could be done and the pain was agonizing.

It was a terrible shock for a child to endure such pain, especially being away from home, and Charles would never again be the 'merry little boy he used to be'. He changed completely, becoming over-anxious and very dependent upon Edith.

When the time came for Charles to start getting involved with the farm, Justin placed him under Francis' tutelage. 'Anything you need to know about the farm or the fruit, ask Francis' he said, and that is just what Charles did.

Francis taught him a lot, giving him a good grounding. He took Charles out with him and started teaching him how to prune. At first the other men were a bit wary of Charles, but after a while they realised that he was totally inoffensive and in the end they hardly noticed he was there at all and treated him pretty much as one of their own.

Charles used to sometimes laugh about his father – saying to a man he saw picking and eating an apple, 'don't let my father catch you. We don't get apples like that up at the house – we eat all the rough ones!'

Percy Nunn remembered Charles as never really getting on well with Justin – they were so totally unalike. Francis felt very sorry for Charles and helped him as much as he could – taking him around the farm in the Land Rover and explaining what was going on.

Once when Charles was still in his early twenties, he was heard driving through the village one morning hooting his horn and shouting that his father had had a stroke. The story spread like wildfire. Francis, returning from his breakfast meeting, also told Barbara that he thought Justin had perhaps had a minor stroke as one side of his face had dropped. Although he did seem to recover, Francis felt from that moment Justin seemed to change.

1953 would be a momentous year for various reasons, not least in being the year that saw the Coronation of Queen Elizabeth, Mount Everest conquered by Hillary and Sherpa Tenzing and the end of sweet-rationing. Yet it had not had a particularly auspicious start.

At the end of January, violent north-easterly gales swept down the East coast of England and across to Holland and Belgium, with surging high tides causing massive flooding and loss of life. It was all the more disastrous as there had been no warning. Such sea defences as there were proved totally inadequate and were swept away like balsa wood by the oncoming deluge.

In Hunstanton, the headmaster at The Glebe at this time was a Mr Coghill, and he took Peter and some of the more senior boys out during the early evening to witness the storm. Perched as the school was, high above the sea, though thankfully far back from any cliff edge, the view was spectacular. Standing in the lee of the building and huddled in their raincoats, the boys watched as the wind bent great trees almost to the ground. Who could have foreseen what the rest of the night would bring, as houses, roads, bridges and people were swept away?

For the boys, it made a welcome diversion. The novelty of turning on the taps the next morning and finding only salt water coming out soon palled. They quickly found out how unpleasant it was to clean their teeth in seawater, and how much more thirsty they became when they realised there was actually no water to drink; the local reservoir they later learned, had been flooded with salt water.

With communications down and no immediate danger to life, it would be a day or so before relief came to the school – the first being a consignment of oranges which were doled out at a rate of one per boy. Then a few days later, amidst tumultuous cheers, the arrival of a water bowser full of drinking water, strictly rationed of course.

What a sight of devastation met the boys when they were at last taken out for a walk. The scene now calm looked surreal. Gone were the well-known landmarks; huge boulders of concrete that had once formed the promenade were broken and tossed about like pebbles thrown by a giant hand; bungalows that had once been holiday homes were now submerged with only their roof tops showing, as a sea of water lapped against them.

Naturally the boys couldn't take in the full extent of the disaster, but they all knew they were witnessing something momentous.

The weather on June 2nd was also wet, but it had been declared a national holiday. Once again amidst great pageantry, another monarch was going to be crowned and there was even talk that this could be the dawning of another great Elizabethan age.

The new decade had already been heralded in with the *Festival of Britain* in May 1951. It was held on the south bank of the Thames, to mark the centenary of Prince Albert's *Great Exhibition* in the Crystal Palace in 1851. As Britain came out of the austere post-war years, it was felt that the time was appropriate to celebrate national achievements in architecture, design and inventions. It would not only boost morale at home, but also attract custom from abroad. Despite Francis thinking the whole idea was crazy, Barbara felt the children ought to be taken to see it.

Her brother Newy and sister-in-law Margaret had bought a house north of London, and she made plans to drive the children down as far as her brother's. Here they would stay the night and travel into London on the Underground, the following day.

Joining an enormous queue on what would prove to be the hottest day of the year, with record crowd attendances, Barbara began to think that perhaps Francis had been right. Arriving exhausted back at Newy and Margaret's late that evening, her brother greeted her at the door. 'Sit down – here's a large whisky - we'll put the children to bed.'

'And what?' the children were asked the next morning, 'did you enjoy the best? The Skylon, the Dome of Discovery?'

'No,' they replied, upon reflection. 'The best things were the moving staircase, the underground train and the picnic.' The expedition would remain Barbara's sole attempt to broaden her children's horizons or her own.

There was now to be another great event taking place in London, and this time there would be no question of joining the crowds that lined the streets to watch the royal procession. Every town and village throughout the land would hold their own festivities to celebrate the coronation of Queen Elizabeth II.

Her father, the late King George VI, had died the previous year at Sandringham in Norfolk, less than a year after attending *The Festival of Britain* Dedication Service in St Paul's.

It had been a poignant moment for Peter. Along with the other boys from 'The Glebe', which was situated only a few miles from Sandringham, he had stood cap in hand, on a cold, dreary February day, watching the slow cavalcade of soldiers bearing the late King's coffin. Standing under the dripping trees that bordered the narrow lane leading down to Wolferton Station, amidst much marching and shouting, the boys stood silently watching as the coffin passed, on what would be the King's final journey back to London.

Elizabeth's Coronation was to be a lavish and spectacular affair. And it would be all the more vivid and immediate because it was going to be televised. This meant that 'on the day, over 20 million people watched the event.' People could actually see events as they happened and for most of the population this would be the first time they had ever watched television. At this time 'a mere two million' people owned television sets and in the few homes that had one, friends and neighbours crowded round the tiny fuzzy screens set in a large wooden box, to watch the coach as it made its way to Westminster Abbey.

Francis, Barbara and the children watched it at the Bryants. Their house was situated on the main road towards Wickhambrook and had the benefit of mains electricity – a luxury, along with running water, that wouldn't reach Hill Farm until the late 1950s.

The room was crowded and the children were soon bored with it. Francis, peering at the grainy picture, privately declared himself unimpressed and showed his preference by chatting to all and sundry, refilling glasses and toasting the new Queen. He had decided that his outfit for the village fancy dress parade, that had been arranged to celebrate the coronation, would be a nightshirt complete with nightcap and chamber pot. It wasn't hard to assemble, being his usual nightly attire, but at least being Francis he felt he had entered into the spirit of the occasion. He took his place amongst a motley collection of cowboys, Indians, pantomime dames, nursery rhyme characters, bicycles, prams, bandsmen, Union Jack flags and bunting and his own children – Peter dressed as a pirate, Sally as a Chinese coolie and Judy as Little Bo Peep.

**Queen Elizabeth' Coronation Day, June 2nd 1953,
Fancy Dress Parade at Stradishall Place**
Left to Right: Lew Brennan, Fred Cutts, Claude Palfrey, Albert Hurst, Frank Watson, Joe Brown, Francis in his nightshirt kneeling, Alan Cutts, Terence Hurst, Alan Unsworth (at back), Ron Ellse, Alby Cutts, Jim Missen, Colin Wyatt, Roy Cutts, Arthur King, Michael Palfrey, Raymond Whitehead, Jimmy Kemp, Maurice Cutts.

Games and races were held at Stradishall Place and Francis hurt his back when he fell, trying to keep his balance on a greasy pole, whilst having a pillow fight with another competitor. Edith handed out

'Coronation Crowns' to all the children; these were coins in presentation packs especially minted for the occasion. Justin arranged for a meal and dance to be held in the pack-house and no celebration was ever concluded at Clopton, without a huge firework display.

It had always been assumed that Peter would follow Adrian and Francis and go to Uppingham; in fact his name had been down for the school since he was born. But now the time was approaching for him to sit the Common Entrance exam and with two more children to privately educate, the decision was made for him to go to Framlingham.

Although Barbara was rather horrified at how Spartan it seemed, she was reassured and no doubt influenced by the fact that her own father had been a pupil there, and it did seem to be the popular choice for local farmers' sons. Many of them, like Peter, whose name was down for 'Writtle', were destined to go on to Agricultural College after a year of practical farming experience when they left at sixteen.

Peter had really done rather well during his time at The Glebe. Being tall for his age, (Francis often got away with taking him with him to The Cloak at Wickhambrook aged twelve or thirteen) he had the advantage over smaller boys in athletics and coming up to his final year, had also become head boy. Passing his Common Entrance exam would prove to be a short-lived accolade academically, once the competition widened, but he had been happy there. Barbara and Francis marked his leaving with a gift for the Headmaster, of a signed copy of Robert's book of poems.

Fanny had been showing signs of a gradual decline for some time. Despite this deterioration she had always remained attractive; always taking such trouble to be well turned out - now cancer would destroy what nature had preserved so well. Bed-ridden in her final days, her breathing terribly laboured, Stephanie and Francis were often at her bedside. For Adrian, the all-enveloping possessive love with which she had tried to hold him would keep him from her to the last.

Her death on January 26th 1954 was not unexpected but left Francis with a deep sense of loss. It was hard for him to come to terms with - that indomitable spirit so full of life and laughter now quenched for ever. He had been to see her the day before she died and been deeply touched when she told him, 'We've always been good pals, haven't we?' They were the first and last real words of endearment she had ever said to him.

And now with her death came an unexpected testimony that Fanny did perhaps, after all, feel that she had something to make up to Francis for – was she trying to make amends for the start in life her second son never really had, or was it to repay him for all he had done for both of his parents for so many years? She left her entire estate to Francis – it amounted to some £6,000. This was a considerable sum in those days and one that would have been quite sufficient to set him up with a house and a few acres of land to plant up as an orchard.

But of course, being Francis, he didn't feel that was being particularly fair to Adrian and Stephanie, and there was his own job and Justin to consider. He immediately wrote out two cheques for £2,000 each, which he sent to them. Stephanie tore hers up immediately, telling Francis that they didn't need the money, but for Adrian it was an absolute godsend. With school fees to pay and an uncertain income with which to find them, he never forgot Francis' generosity.

Nine years later, after Francis' own untimely death, and Barbara having very little money at the time, Adrian sent it back to her, saying how much it had helped him and that now it was only right that it should help her.

After Fanny's death, Francis did look at several possible smallholdings in the district and, being Francis, got very enthusiastic. There was a particular cottage with land at Cowlinge that really took his eye. His idea was that he could have something set up whilst still working for Justin – had an orchard planted and have something of his own for later on.

Despite living as well as they did at Hill Farm, they had no house of their own and he had no pension. Even £4,000 would have set him up quite nicely, but Barbara was very dubious. She was mainly concerned about upsetting Justin, if Francis was seen to have an outside interest. Rational or irrational, it was an opportunity that was allowed to slip away and one that would significantly change the outcome of their lives.

Of course the money was extremely useful and it certainly helped with the considerable drain of three sets of boarding school fees. Although at the time he was extremely well paid, those fees must have been taking half of Francis' salary annually. He would later say that he always regretted having spent money on school fees, when perhaps it would have been better to have bought somewhere, and to have set them all up in business.

In 1952 David Lee had come to the farm straight from 'Writtle', along with three other students. They had come as farm assistants and initially the boys lived in the house with Justin and Edith. Francis, who would often arrive early to speak to the pig men, would see them rushing out of the house and take great delight in pulling their legs, 'Hmm. Late again boys.' Of this particular bunch of lads, David would be the only one to stay on. In fact Francis recommended him to Justin.

David would describe Francis in those days as the 'top dog' on the farm and of his being so loved by all the men. The 'second prime man', second only to Justin. And he would speak of the two men seeming so close. He remembered Francis always having a Land Rover for the job and a handed down Daimler or Rover for his personal use; and the breakfasts spent together each morning, when the decisions of the day would be made and any problems aired. Both men were so passionate about the fruit and it would always be Justin's main interest on the farm.

Edith was also remembered as always being concerned about the welfare of the men and their families. Once, when she sat making lace with bobbins, and Justin was playing patience, he mumbled to Edith

'I've sacked Willy Wade today.' After a silence Edith said, 'Do you think you've been right sacking Willy Wade? He's the only breadwinner in a large family'. Another silence and then Justin went off. When he returned he gruffly said, 'I've told Willy Wade he can start again on Monday.'

Despite this, Justin would at other times sack people at a moment's notice. He was the employer and as such it was within his remit to be both hirer and firer. He told David one day about a book he had read about a method on how to fire someone, by making them want to leave. It was done by gradually taking away their responsibilities; as a consequence, the person feels redundant.

Ironically, a few years later, David would see this method being put into practice.

Percy was tying up a set of gang mowers one day when Francis came over to him for a chat. Percy was not in a good mood, 'What is the matter Percy?'

'Oh well, the usual thing – if there's ever a better job you always import someone.'

'Oh? What are you capable of?'

'Well,' said Percy, 'I'm married, I've got all my marbles and I could do something better.'

Two months later, Francis came back to him with the offer of a position in the farm office. Changes had been made with the rapid expansion of the farm and Robert Nightingale had by then been brought in as an accountant, to look at ways of saving the farm money. Nancy was due to leave early in 1954 and Frank Bishop, who also worked there, had been called up for National Service.

Well it wasn't quite what Percy had in mind, but then he thought about it. One thing was that he did have the added responsibility of two children to consider. 'What was the money going to be like?' There was good overtime to be earned on the fruit.

Robert Nightingale came to see Percy and to talk about the wages offered. 'What we've done, we've looked at last year's wages and we'll pay you the same, £8 a week.' Well Percy didn't think that sounded too bad and decided to take the job. He would eventually become manager of the main office and the eyes and ears of much that went on.

Francis would always say that Barbara could rustle up a meal out of anything and usually at a moment's notice. Fruit tours and Open Days were organised and Barbara would often find herself preparing a last minute supper, for anything upwards of twenty people. All this came from Francis' own pocket – always so hospitable and always so well looked after whenever he went anywhere, he couldn't bear the thought of people going away supper-less and, besides, the evening gave the opportunity for continuing discussion and the exchange of ideas.

On one such occasion, Barbara was surprised to get a call from Robert Nightingale. 'Could he join them for supper?' He'd never been before and as he lived locally, Barbara was slightly surprised. She said that she was struggling to find enough as it was, and had hardly enough cutlery and plates to go round.

However Robert persisted, said he wouldn't need feeding and that he would just be interested to sit in a corner and watch. Francis was incensed. He felt that he was going to go running back to Justin saying how well they were living, despite all of this being out of his own salary.

From around this time Robert also began checking up on the petrol consumption every time Barbara went up to Clopton to fill up. It had never been an issue before. Personal petrol for their car was always recorded in the office and Francis paid for it each year out of his bonus. Petrol for the Land Rover was a different matter and had always been part of the job.

Barbara seldom went anywhere other than to take the children back to school or the occasional trip to Bury or back to Spalding, and she found this checking up intensely irritating. Francis too found Robert peering in to check the mileage on the Land Rover.

Francis was only too aware of the need to make the farm pay and from as early as 1946 it was his constant concern.

31st December 1946 ... *'It must also be remembered that we have been through a period of luxury finance when we could afford to spend money like water to keep it from the Government. But things have changed now, and we must prepare to produce more, better and cheaper.'*

Of course Robert felt that part of the reason he had been employed, was to look into ways of possible savings and unnecessary expenditure. At the time Francis never took it really seriously, although he was very annoyed, putting it down to 'officiousness.'

Despite the pressures of work, weekends were always fun.

Bob Berry had remained a close friend. Although it was generally thought he would remain a confirmed bachelor, he had married Vera Bedford (known as Weedy), on the advice of Francis, as they owned the farm next door to Wadgells. Unfortunately for Bob, by the time they got married, the farm had been sold.

**Bob Berry with 'Weedy' (Vera Bedford)**

Bob had had a bad fall whilst riding at a Point to Point and had hurt his back. It was a serious injury and Bob had rather taken to the bottle ever since, by way of anaesthetizing the pain. He would often end up staying at Hill Farm to sleep it off. As these bouts became more prolonged and more frequent, Francis felt that he would probably end up having to look after Bob. Poignantly, Francis himself would die prematurely and Bob would go on to live well into his 90s.

Bob's younger brother Mike would sometimes visit them at Hill Farm, and when the children were young, could usually be persuaded to baby-sit, though it's doubtful whether he ever actually heard them cry out. Coming home one evening, Francis and Barbara found him fast asleep in the sitting room, with a bantam cockerel roosting on the back of the chair. Mike eventually went into the church and Francis would say that he regretted not having gone into the church too. With his atheist mother and upbringing, it was not that he felt that he had any great religious vocation, but that he always thought he would look rather good in gaiters.

Church-going for the Bell family was not a regular occurrence and certainly not at Stradishall. Once, when Francis had an invitation from Harvey Leeder of Denston Hall to bring the family round to the hall after a shoot for drinks after church, Francis felt it would look better, if they actually went to church at Denston first. All spruced up and arriving at the church far too early, they drove around for a while and then of course found themselves late and the service started.

With Barbara and the family occupying a whole pew, Francis had to sit across the aisle on his own. All went well until the sermon, when a sudden loud snoring reverberated around the church. Francis was fast asleep and no one was close enough to give him a discreet prod.

Saturday lunchtimes with the children away at school were usually spent at the White Hart at Yeldham. It was here that Francis had first met his fellow farming friend Joe Hitchcock. Joe's wife Betty, like Carole McCartney, also had a good job working for *Good Housekeeping*, in the cookery department. On the odd occasion during the school holidays, when the children did accompany them, it was not quite so relaxing. The gardener spent the entire time warning them in no uncertain terms, not to go on the beds, which they thought was hilarious.

Betty Hitchcock would often come over and keep Barbara company when Francis in later years, ran the bar at The Country Club at Long Melford on Saturday nights.

The Country Club was run by an ex-army officer, Colonel Collins, and his young wife Joan, who was an excellent cook. Francis and Barbara were often there on a Saturday evening and when Colonel

Collins was taken ill, Francis offered to help out by doing the bar. He was absolutely in his element and enjoyed himself hugely.

When the Colonel later died, Francis offered to carry on. Such was his success as a barman that people used to ring up to book their parties or their evening out, and arrange the date around when Francis would be there. The name Country Club was rather an overstatement, but it did provide a successful means of restricting membership to people they actually wanted to be there.

Other social events would involve the whole family. Visits would be made to Jack and Stephanie's farm at Preston, where there would be dancing to records, playing croquet or joining them for a Christmas party.

Private fancy dress parties and dances were popular then and once at the end of one of his visits to Hill Farm, Martin announced that he needed a costume for just such an event. It didn't take him long to decide. Propped up in the cart lodge was an absolutely dreadful old scarecrow. Full of fleas, filthy dirty and covered in several years of bird droppings, Martin felt it was quite perfect.

**The Bell cousins at Hill Farm**
**Left to right: Sylvia, Peter, Sally, Martin and Judy**

American-style square dances were held at a pub in Haverhill and these were huge fun. With a live band and caller and everyone dressed up in check shirts and neckerchiefs; all the local farming families would be there. On one occasion Adrian and Margery joined them. There was much hilarity as the two families met and went in. Adrian was in the car park when he noticed an enormous muck-heap right near the entrance to the pub. Of course the incongruity of its positioning tickled him enormously, dressed up as they all were, and he made much of walking right around it prodding it with his stick and commenting on the 'good healthy farm smell' which he felt added much to the authenticity of the evening. Twirling round and round with Barbara later, who was not only taller, but who also had a decidedly more substantial frame than his own, he couldn't stop laughing. 'Barbara, I'd have flown out the window if I hadn't been dancing with you!'

David Lee went with them once and remembered Francis as 'such a fun man', his exuberance spilling over and infecting everyone there. Of him charging down the hall with his partner, in a gallop that ended up in the Ladies Cloakroom, every time.

By the time Peter went onto the farm in 1957, first on the arable side and then on the fruit, Francis and Justin had not been seeing eye to eye for some time. For years they had worked so well together. Justin was very good at business and Francis was very good with the fruit, its production and its marketing. And not only that - they shared socialist ideals and had always had a good rapport.

Although the family denied that Justin had had a small stroke, he did eventually have emphysema and hardening of the arteries. Francis felt that from that time, Justin had lost some of his clearness of vision and judgement. Did his medical condition distort how he saw things and give him a sense of being persecuted? Exasperation on Francis' part would lead to disillusionment and a gradual loss of mutual respect.

There were storm clouds gathering and they came from two unexpected sources.

Justin's son, Charles, was frustrated. He felt he should have been more involved in the running of the farm and given some responsibility. Yet here he was, the boss's son and still working as one of the men. He felt he should be beginning to step into his father's shoes. His tutoring under Francis continued and so did his friendship, and Francis began to feel that this wasn't going down too well with Justin. Charles was constantly falling out with his father; there were enormous rows and Francis would often find himself acting as mediator between them.

Charles had married in 1955. He had first met his wife Joyce, a north country girl, when she came fruit picking and after the wedding they lived at Home Farm. He felt that his parents never thought she was the right choice of bride for him.

Elizabeth would say 'there was a marriage settlement, that 'Charles was given company shares and eventually, the understanding was, that he would take over the running of the farm from his father.'

The problem for Charles was this wasn't happening soon enough. With their first baby on the way he would often speak to Francis about what changes he would make, once his father had gone. And Francis too must have had a proprietorial air as they discussed the future. He had no reason to think otherwise. He felt secure in the knowledge that he had helped to make the whole set-up known nationally in the fruit-growing world.

Francis had no sense of self-preservation. He had a sense of fairness – you worked hard and you were rewarded. He would have 'sold himself down the line' for anyone. He never boasted of his achievements and was never knowingly dishonest, though it would have been quite easy to be so. Barbara remembered once when a huge case of wine was delivered to Hill Farm and Francis refusing to take it. It was a bribe from a company he was thinking of buying machinery from.

Francis and Barbara both felt great sympathy for Charles. He had got into the habit of coming to have lunch with them most days up at Hill Farm, and when Joyce was having their first child, this arrangement continued. It would not have gone unnoticed.

Percy remembered that at the time 'there was a good deal of tittle-tattle going on in the office.' Percy would describe it as 'back-stabbing' and of 'running back to Justin.' That 'others could see a way of bettering themselves.' Francis' authority was beginning to be undermined. Things were being arranged without telling him.

Jack Loader was very upset one day. As Francis' foreman, he and Francis had always made decisions together, and one day he found that the boxes had all been put out in the orchards far too early, for the fruit picking. It was quite an operation and was always left to Francis and himself to decide on the timing.

Trees might require further spraying or grass cutting need doing in the orchards. It turned out that Harold Burton had authorised it.

Francis was never interested in company politics. He could never have believed that these people would be taken seriously. There would be a gradual loss of mutual respect between himself and Justin, and a sense of resentment building up, but they were old sparring partners, they knew each other so well. Francis would have felt that his knowledge and expertise were too valuable for there to have ever been any personal threat; that his position within the company was unassailable.

There was a huge row. It was not between Justin and Francis, but between Charles and his father. All the men knew about it and knew that Charles was finally going. It was described as 'a big bust up' and with 'Charles being cut off with a nice sum.'

Charles had decided that he'd had enough. He wanted to farm on his own and was going to move to Dedham Vale to start his own fruit farm. The problem for Francis was that someone had gone back to Justin and told him that Francis had been seen helping Charles to find a small farm. He would go on to help Charles further by advising him and helping him to get started. This too would find its way back to Justin.

For Francis it was the most natural thing in the world – he would have helped anyone in a similar way. For Justin, who was very angry with Charles for going was no doubt feeling deeply hurt. Francis was seen as having been very disloyal to him for helping Charles. For Edith too, the terrible rift would mean that she would lose contact with her only son. She must have been devastated.

Elizabeth remembered her father telling her the news, 'Charles has left and the whole place is a lot happier.'

Francis and Barbara remained in friendly contact with Charles and his young family, giving advice when it was asked for, and Charles would always look upon Francis as his mentor.

David Lee would say later that 'everyone knew that Justin didn't like Francis helping Charles', but Francis took no notice of any of it. He did what he felt was right at the time. With Charles about to move out of Home Farm, Justin offered it to David and his wife Hazel. Such was the relationship between Charles and his father, that when he heard that Justin had told David he could move in, Charles virtually demolished the interior of the house, taking absolutely everything he could. Even the tiles on the floor were ripped up. He made sure that it would cost Justin a considerable amount, both in time and money, to be put right again.

Many years later, in 1977, Edith had a phone call from Joyce. Charles was in hospital and was extremely ill; he had gone in with very high blood pressure. He had become 'very stout' by this time and the prognosis wasn't good. He had sold the farm at Dedham and bought one on the Isle of Man. Elizabeth felt that he must have known that his health wasn't good; there were no death duties on the Isle of Man and that must have influenced his decision to move.

Charles died shortly after. He was 46 years old.

Peter's name meanwhile was still down for 'Writtle Agricultural College'. Francis told him that he could probably teach him more than the college could about fruit growing, but that it would be better to have a proper paper qualification; it would stand him in better stead in the future.

After Charles left, things began to change quite drastically. Francis found that more and more of his responsibilities were being eroded. Decisions he made were over-ridden. The men on the farm saw what was happening and were very upset about it, Jack Loader in particular.

When the day came that Francis had his Land Rover taken away and replaced with a Morris Minor van, he knew that the future was looking very uncertain. He couldn't even do his job properly. It would be impossible to drive round the orchards in such an unsuitable vehicle – a thing that he had done on a daily basis for the best part of 20 years.

With his son's future so linked to his own and to the farm, Francis was beginning to worry about Peter. How could they afford to send him to 'Writtle' themselves and would there be a job for him even, when he came back? One opportunity did present itself at this time and it was an idea that appealed immensely to both Peter and his father. Among the many people he met at The Country Club, Francis had become acquainted with a tea planter. With a country house near Colchester and a tea plantation in Assam, he was the director of one of the country's well-known tea companies. After talking the situation through with him, Francis and Peter received an invitation to join the family for dinner at their Colchester home.

Walking around the beautiful gardens before dinner; hearing of the training programme being offered; of the ex-patriot life that was available with its own bungalow and staff; the fact that the company was in need of trainee plantation managers; it seemed to be a marvellous opportunity. And hadn't Francis himself gone out to South America at a similar age? It was not surprising that he was, as Barbara would later say, 'madly keen on the idea.' Peter too was very excited. He felt that the whole evening had gone really well and it was a very animated pair that returned to Hill Farm that night.

Assam? Barbara wasn't really sure where it was, but it sounded a very long way away and, she argued with Francis, Peter was far too young. Besides, he was a very good-looking young man and very friendly and he was sure to get involved with some native girl. The arguments went on. But Barbara was adamant. He wasn't to go.

Never hearing anything about it again, Peter would always feel that he had failed to make a good impression. That the interview had gone wrong in some way. In those days in the late 1950s, parents weren't to be questioned. Well brought up children simply did what their parents told them. But it was a decision that would affect Peter for the rest of his life. The truth was that he had indeed been offered the job; he would only discover this from Barbara, when she was over 90 and he was past retiring age.

Another chance did present itself a little later and Francis tried again.

This time a friend, Geoffery Turner, the owner of a company that made accessories for the car industry, offered to put up the money to start Peter in a thatching business. With so many thatched houses in Suffolk, Jeffery, as a businessman, could see the potential. Thatchers were in great demand and few in number.

Once again Barbara was adamant. It was not in the least bit suitable for Peter. Climbing about on roofs and kneeling on damp straw in all weathers, would give him rheumatism in his knees. And that was that. Only too aware of how difficult things were becoming on the farm, it was with some considerable relief, that an acceptable solution did present itself by way of a phone call from Barbara's brother Newy.

He was working for Levertons, the Caterpillar Tractor dealers in Spalding. He had heard that they were looking for young management trainees and wondered if Peter would be interested? As a family friend of Barbara's owned the company, and Peter could lodge with her parents who lived in Spalding, it seemed to be the answer.

His place at 'Writtle' was cancelled and he started work at Levertons shortly after.

The end, when it came, was quite sudden and totally unexpected. It was March, 1960. Francis had gone up as usual to Clopton Hall to have breakfast.

Never usually coming in until lunchtime, Barbara was surprised to see that Francis had come home and it wasn't even ten o'clock in the morning. He looked absolutely devastated.

'I've been given the sack.'

There had been an awful row. Francis would always say that Justin had had some sort of brainstorm. He had no idea what he was supposed to have done. Despite all the undermining of Francis' authority, he never suspected that this would be the outcome. It was a total shock.

Justin had told him that morning that he must bring back the car (a Daimler) that he had for private use. Francis said that he wouldn't. 'I destroyed enough of my own cars for you, driving round the fields early on; I shall keep it.'

As he left Clopton Hall that morning, he turned back and said to Justin, 'I'm sorry for you. You have lost your own son and his family, and now you have destroyed my life and that of my son.'

The men on the farm were devastated too. Nesta Loader remembered the day and how upset Jack was. 'He thought the world of Francis and had been deeply upset at what had been happening to him over the past few years.' He and Stan Rutter had been taught all they knew by him and when he left, would say, 'For many of the men it was like the heart going out of the farm.'

The news went round the farm like wildfire and later that same day a deputation of men came to Hill Farm. They told Francis that they were going on strike. Francis told them not to, that they too would lose their jobs and he urged them to go back to work which they reluctantly agreed to do.

Another visitor that day was Victor Mapey. He had driven over to see them, unaware of their own terrible news. Francis found Victor sitting in his car in the yard, deeply upset. He had come to tell them that his wife Margaret had just been diagnosed with terminal cancer and that she was dying.

Victor and Margaret had come over to have lunch with them after

Christmas, and Barbara would remember how ill she was then and how she had spent most of the day upstairs lying on their bed, too ill to join in.

There were two areas of huge concern for Francis and Barbara. Firstly Francis' salary was stopped immediately, so they had no income and secondly they had nowhere to live. Hill Farm was of course a tied house; it went with the job.

Nowadays employees are protected through various Employment Acts; three months paid notice would have had to be given and a redundancy payment made. But this was 1960 and at that time there was no such legal provision. There was however some protection for them in law that they didn't realise, and that was over the house.

They had a phone call from 'young Justin' (Justin's son by his first marriage). He rang Francis and said how upset he was by the news. He knew and appreciated what Francis had done, the way that he had worked and built up the farm. He told them that by law, they could stay at Hill Farm for six months, which was a huge relief.

He later came over to see them and to ask if there was anything he could do to help. He worked on the Stock Exchange and told them if they had any spare money he would help them invest it to make a bit of income. The problem was that at that time they had very little.

There would be many months of uncertainty before Francis did receive some money from the farm, by which time he and Barbara were on the point of moving out of Hill Farm; meanwhile Francis had had the ignominy of going to Bury St Edmunds to claim the dole.

Being Francis, he tried to make a funny story out of his trip. It was a journey, which, perhaps for economy, he rather surprisingly made by bus. Possibly, not having ridden on a bus since he was a boy in Streatham, it was a novel experience for him. He must have looked a somewhat incongruous figure as he sat amongst the housewives, in his corduroys and trilby hat, his pipe clenched between his teeth, stick planted firmly on the floor in front of him. He beamed at the conductress who was making her rather desultory rounds, 'Now, my dear, I want to go to Bury - how much money would you like?'

Arriving at the Labour Exchange in Bury must have been a moment of deep mortification. He could never have dreamt that he would have ended up there asking for help. He would tell the family afterwards of the day and of how going in he had greeted the staff with, 'I have worked for Justin Brooke for 25 years and he's just given me the sack. What can you do for me?'

They were dark days and the initial pall of what had happened, hung over them both. Barbara would remember finding Francis one day with his head in his hands, sitting at the kitchen table at Hill Farm so utterly unlike himself saying, 'I feel such a failure.' She watched him looking out over Captains that Spring, at the apple blossom that he loved so much, remembering how he had measured and set out the field in readiness for the men to plant out the young trees, so many years earlier.

£3,000, the equivalent of one and a half year's salary, would eventually be paid to him; a sum that Francis would have felt was derisory for a lifetime's work and of course there was no provision for a pension or a house. He was 54 years old.

'Young Justin' did invest it for him and although it would have bought a small house for them, Francis was more concerned with finding a way to use it to earn a living.

Sally was in her final year at school, about to take her A levels, and Judy had another year to go until she was 16. Barbara and Francis worked out that they could just manage the school fees out of what was left of Fanny's money, if Judy didn't stay on after 16. Peter of course had by now left, and coming home the following weekend was the first of the three to hear the news.

Returning home on his motorbike on what was a glorious spring morning, he was totally unprepared for the state of shock his father was in. Telling Peter that, 'the old man has given me the sack', Francis went on to say, 'I've done nothing wrong.'

Always so scrupulous in all his dealings, it would be one of the things that would haunt him. The men on the farm all knew what had happened, but perhaps no one else would realise the truth. It was during this time that he wrote to the Rt Reverend Kenneth Riches, who was now Bishop of Lincoln.

Asking him for a character reference that he could use in the future, Francis wrote explaining what had happened, and received a glowing testimonial in reply. In fact the two of them kept up a correspondence all through this time; after all they had known each other since the 1930s. They had been their next-door neighbours, when Kenneth moved into the cottage up the hill from Hill Farm during the war, and he and his wife were often invited to supper.

Easter Sunday in 1960 fell on April 17th, and the two girls didn't hear the news until they came home for the Easter holidays. Sally found her father deeply immersed at his desk in the dining room, updating a *Handbook on Fruit* for the Boots Company. Surprised to see him at home during the day, the girls were told the news.

Sally would always remember it as being so hard to grasp, and that they seemed to still be in the house for such a long while afterwards.

Aphra Wilson had joined 'Boots' in 1936 and in her *Times* obituary in 1976 would be recorded as *'one of the first women to be appointed a director.'* Having made *'a special study of pests and diseases'* after graduating from Imperial College, London in 1921, she had gained a *'national reputation as one of the country's leading plant pathologists.'*

She had initially come on one of the fruit tours around the farm, which Francis had organised. She had quickly recognised the extent of his vast knowledge and practical experience: not only his expertise and understanding of all aspects of fruit farming, but particularly his scientific knowledge in the use of sprays for crop protection against disease.

As the only woman present on that particular tour, she had returned in the evening along with the others, to have supper at Hill

Farm and to 'talk fruit.' Finding Barbara washing up alone in the kitchen, she had come through to chat.

Barbara remembered her as being so kind and thoughtful. Taking Aphra to look around the old house with its many beams and ancient latticed windows, the evening was made memorable for Barbara by being included, and by Aphra expressing an interest in what she knew were Barbara's interests.

As a young woman Aphra Wilson had been awarded an M.B.E. for her work as a despatch-rider during the 1914-18 war. The daughter of a doctor in North Wales, she had returned after her war service, to continue her studies at Imperial College, London. She worked on *'the development and application of colloidal fungicides, a great step forward towards the modern fungicides which would protect the food crops of the world from the ravages of disease'*.

After joining Boots in 1936, *'she contributed so much to the establishment of the Lenton Research Station in Nottingham – now world famous for its successes and her successes, in the field of agricultural and horticultural crop protection'*.

Her obituary referred glowingly to her long career and the great contribution her work had made in advancing scientific knowledge, but they also wrote of her personal qualities.

*'Although Miss Wilson was fully occupied with, and dedicated to, her work, her interest in people and their well-being was paramount. Whenever a need arose she was there to give comfort and practical help – a Christian at heart in fact with never an unkind word whatever the situation.'*

It was due to just these qualities that Francis received a call from her shortly after being given the sack. She had heard the news and was very upset, as well as being deeply sympathetic. Understanding their financial predicament, she quickly found some paid work for Francis to do at home. The project was a detailed account of the farm's spraying programme and its effects; the second, the updating of *Boots Handbook on Fruit Growing*. Here Francis would revise the details of the many apple varieties available at the time, giving their merits and regional suitability, as well as advice on their management.

The work kept him occupied for a time and went a little towards raising his spirits and self-esteem. Aphra Wilson's kindness, recognition and practical help would never be forgotten.

In the meantime there was still the immediate problem of where to go. The discussions seemed to endlessly go around and arrive back at the same conundrum. In a few months they would be homeless. Barbara dreaded having to move into a council house but it did seem as though that would be the only option. She couldn't think how she would be able to tell which one was theirs.

An ancient derelict old mill in the middle of a field on the road to Clare took Barbara's eye. The mill wasn't even for sale and if it had been, they couldn't have afforded to buy it. But at least, as she sketched out her ideas on the back of an envelope of how the mill could be converted, it gave her a sense of doing something.

Another idea she had was that Francis could run the bar at Long Melford full-time, and she could run a hairdressing business from a caravan parked in the car park. This would also double up as a home as well. Quite how they would have fared in winter remains to be seen.

Francis took Peter to look at a field in Clare with a broken down old shed in the middle and wondered if it could be planted up? The small piece of overgrown south-facing land was actually for sale but it was hopeless really – planting up an orchard was a long-term investment. It would be years before any return or income could be realised and it didn't solve the immediate problem of where to live.

Time was pressing on and with summer upon them, their six-month stay at Hill Farm would soon be over.

At the eleventh hour it was Victor Mapey who came to their rescue. Despite all the personal distress he was going through, with his wife Margaret now close to dying, he had found a way that he could help them.

His first wife had died during the war and Victor had returned home to daughter Jill and no wife. He remarried and his second wife

[Norah] Margaret owned a little farm at Stradbroke called 'Everett's Farm'.

Here, behind the small thatched farmhouse, they kept turkeys with a couple of part-time chaps, Percy and George, looking after them. Victor and Margaret had moved into a newly built bungalow next door and Victor had the idea that with the cottage now empty, Francis and Barbara could come and live there and he and Francis could expand the turkey business.

There would also be the opportunity for Francis to go round delivering sprays for Victor, which would get him out amongst the farmers and growers, which he knew Francis would love to do. The cottage would come rent-free, a van was provided and Victor would also pay Francis £10 per week. Later this was increased to £12 and that extra £2 a week would make all the difference. It wasn't a fortune but with a roof over their heads and a little money coming in Barbara would later say that this was the happiest time of her married life.

Margaret Mapey died on the 22nd August and it was shortly after this, in the September, that Francis and Barbara moved to 'Everett's' to what would prove to be their final home. The move was predictably a deeply poignant one.

He described it later in an article 'An Enjoyable Move' which was one of a series of articles he wrote for the *Eastern Daily Press* which was published in February 1961. Francis, despite always making the best of things, wrote of the *'upheaval'* of having *'to pull up my roots after twenty-five years and of leaving all the familiar things behind.'* A prospect he found quite *'frightening'*. Of leaving behind *'the familiar beams upon which one used to bump one's head, for someone else to become used to avoiding, while* [he] *must accustom* [himself] *to fresh obstacles in the new home that* [would] *take months to grow used to.'* Of the *'lovable old shabby furniture'* that in time he would be glad to have around him, finding comfort in its familiarity in unfamiliar surroundings.

But it was for Barbara that he most felt. She had to leave the only home apart from her mother's that she had known; a house where she had lived and borne her children and Francis knew how hard it must have been for her to *'pull up her roots and go… the rummaging through half-forgotten treasures every one with a little memory of its own'*; the enormous upheaval of packing up; *'the phenomenal amount of junk'*; the difficulty in deciding what to take.

In the end it was the children who decided for them. Had they not had a family Francis felt they should have probably sold up everything and started again, but it was the children who thought otherwise.

The move took place over three different days and, despite dreading the move itself, in his article to the *Eastern Daily Press*, Francis would say as moves go, it became *'a very personal and quite enjoyable experience'*. It was the men who made it so.

It had been decided to use Bryants, the local haulier Francis had known and used about the farm over many years. The idea of an impersonal specialist firm of removers, however efficient, somehow seemed daunting to them both. When the cattle lorry turned up complete with its covering of straw on the floor and three cheerful men, all known personally to Francis, they knew they had made the right decision.

*'An old tarpaulin* [was] *laid on the floor to cover up the traces of the journeys to the market'* and *'the whole operation took on a social air … much discussion and loving care went into the loading of articles which were valueless apart from sentiment.'*

Knowing the circumstances and their reluctance to go, the men did their best to ease the move. Willing hands helped place pieces of furniture and much advice and encouragement was received as to what would look well where. And when at last all was eventually finished, their removers promised Francis and Barbara that they would come over during the following summer to see how they were getting on.

All that remained now was for Francis to take the key for Hill Farm back to Justin. How poignant to turn the key in the door of that beloved old house, now standing empty. To lock the door that in all those years had hardly ever been locked and about whose threshold his own family had played and tumbled, and countless others had stepped over to enjoy the warmth and hospitality of their home.

Turning to look back one last time, Francis asked Barbara if she'd taken a cutting from the Albertine rose that grew over the front door. She hadn't and, taking the small pruning knife that he always carried in his pocket, Francis went back and took one.

The Albertine, that lovely old fashioned rambling rose with its soft pale pink fragrant flowers, had originally come from a cutting taken from the garden at Barbara's family home in Spalding, and she loved it. Its progeny would still be found fifty years later growing in the various gardens of their children and Barbara never moved again without 'taking a piece of it' with her.

The flowering cherry tree that Francis had planted in front of the house, when they got engaged twenty-five years earlier was still there. It was now huge but would remain there for many years, a feature of the garden.

Barbara and Francis went back to look at the house a few months after they had moved and Francis wrote of how they felt.

*'Our old house stands bleak and empty now: we saw it the other day. It was a happy house and I hope its next occupants will feel something of this when they come to live there. A little of us died when we left, but we live again in another which to us now is home.'*

In fact 'Hill Farm' would remain empty for some considerable time before eventually being converted into a pair of semi-detached houses, which sat awkwardly beside each other within that ancient old timber frame. The stairs were moved, the pond filled in, the hollow ditch had been piped, and it was as though all memories of their being there were erased. It would not live again until sympathetic purchasers, Robert and Joan Clinton bought it in its entirety; loving the old house and understanding its need to be one again, they knocked through the dividing wall the first night after moving in.

A meeting of the three Directors of Justin Brooke Ltd. had been held on 8th August 1960. Its date remains significant in Francis' story.

Edith was in the chair, with Justin and Elizabeth both present. The minutes would state that there were to be
*'Changes in Administration* [and] *Staff Redundancy.'*

*'Mr Brooke referred to the reorganisation of the administration and the position of Mr. Bell who would thereby become redundant. The Directors decided with regret that in the interest of the company it would be necessary to terminate Mr. Bell's employment and it was resolved that this should be determined with effect from 24$^{th}$ August 1960.'*

Every indication was that this decision had just been reached, rather than that Francis had been 'sacked' before the Easter of that year. This was not referred to, or that he had received no salary since then, over a period of about five months. The Bell family would always maintain that this was what had actually happened.

The Directors went on *'to put on record their warm appreciation of Mr. Bell's long and loyal service with the Company and after some discussion it was decided that it was in the best interest of the Company to recognise such service and to encourage it on the part of others by the payment of a gratuity on termination in addition to such money as would be payable to him under the existing bonus scheme. It was therefore resolved that as soon as conveniently may be after the date of termination of Mr. Bell's employment the sum of £3,000 should be paid to him in addition to and not by way of substitution for his entitlement under the existing bonus scheme.'*

In fact it seems that no payment other than this £3,000 was ever made. Justin had already written to Francis on 23rd July, before the meeting, which indicates that of course he was previously well aware of the situation. In this letter he stated that *'You can count on me carrying out my statement with regard to the money'* and in a further letter dated 29th August, a cheque for £3,000 was enclosed *'as a parting gift. Please acknowledge.'* And this Francis did, as formally and abruptly as Justin's own letters. Writing from Hill Farm just before they moved and dated September 1st 1960...

*'Dear Sir, I am in receipt of your letter dated 29$^{th}$ Aug 1960 with cheque enclosed for which I thank you. Yours truly, F. de W. Bell.'*

He would never see a copy of the Minutes showing appreciation of his work and loyalty. Other than through his own writing and responding to Justin through the pages of *The Commercial Grower* he would never speak or have contact with Justin again. It was a tragic end. He would feel that the money was derisory for a lifetime's work and for all he had done to establish the farm and bring it into public recognition as one of the leading fruit producers of the country.

Francis gave the money to the younger Justin Brooke, who in his position as a stockbroker fulfilled his earlier promise of help, by investing it for them until Francis could re-establish himself.

Francis' family were surprised many years later, to learn that Elizabeth was totally unaware of all the circumstances around his leaving the employment of her father and was totally puzzled as to what had caused such a permanent and sad rift between the two families. All the Bell family knew what had happened, and thought that everyone else did too.

Despite what Justin might have said at the time, realistically he and Edith must have been heartbroken at losing Charles and his family. Did the fact that Francis helped Charles to find somewhere to farm and to advise him on how to set up in fruit growing, cause Francis to become the unwitting scapegoat? He and Barbara thought that perhaps this was so. They could think of no other explanation.

Justin's own health with emphysema and hardening of the arteries could also not have helped him to see things clearly either, and it would seem that Edith was already taking over responsibility in her role as one of the directors. And there were others who couldn't wait to step into Francis' shoes and who furthered their own causes through tittle-tattle back to Justin, undermining Francis' authority on the farm, which had previously been so absolute.

Would it have helped if Barbara had been more involved with his work and with the Brooke family? If she could have developed a relationship with Edith and Justin right at the beginning perhaps things might never have deteriorated to the extent that they did. Her natural shyness must have played a part, as well as her lack of understanding of the ethos behind the setting up of the farm, particularly in the early days.

There can be no denying that Justin and Edith brought so much to the district: the philanthropy behind their providing employment and homes for so many during the bleak years of the depression stand as a lasting testament to their vision. Justin and Edith were worlds apart from the solid traditional world and people that Barbara knew and understood.

It is strange how facts become distorted over the years. Peter would hear many years later, that some people thought that his father had left of his own accord to set up his own fruit farm. Perhaps it made people feel more comfortable to believe it.

One person on the farm who knew what had happened and who continued to be deeply upset, was Jack Loader. He felt that he had been taught all that he knew by Francis and 'thought the world of him.' His wife Nesta would say that 'watching Francis' authority being taken away, Jack thought it was terrible.' She would remember how 'after Francis had gone Jack felt dreadful, and he felt that he couldn't work properly without [him].'

Nesta was Jack's second wife. After his first wife Alice had died, he had married Nesta a few years after the war in the early 1950s. Barbara and Francis had both gone to the wedding.

Nesta's war interestingly had been spent at Bletchley Park, where she had worked at decoding messages. She was a local girl, the youngest child of Alfred Bailey, who along with his son Eric had established a builders business at Wickhambrook. They had built the bungalows at Wickham House for Justin back in the 1930s.

And now for Jack, with Francis gone, 'life didn't seem the same. He stayed on for just over a year, but he didn't like Harold Burton and didn't like going round the fruit with Mrs Brooke.' Somehow, with Francis going, the heart and joy had gone out of the job for him and, despite having spent all of his working life in fruit, he decided that, because of all that had happened to Francis, he would leave too. It was a huge decision and one that would infuriate Edith, but Jack was adamant.

He and Nesta lived in a tied house that went with his job; in fact it was half of the old Rectory in Stradishall, next to the church and opposite the pack-house. They had Jack's two boys from his first marriage living with them, and by now their own young son Graham had been born. Jack was a quiet man, warm-hearted with strong principals; to give up such security was momentous and a great testimony to the esteem in which he held Francis.

Turning his back on all of his knowledge and experience of fruit growing, Jack moved his family to Lidgate. Here he and Nesta took over a local newsagent's shop, which they ran successfully for many years until Jack's retirement.

# Part Six
# Stradbroke

Like all the Bell family, Francis had always been able to express himself in writing. Despite his huge loss of self-esteem Francis would never wallow in self-pity. It was just not in his character.

He now found that he was able to supplement their income by writing and was beginning to get articles published in the *Eastern Daily Press* under their title 'The Country Scene.' He had half a dozen such articles published.

Adrian had been writing weekly articles for them under 'A Countryman's Notebook' since the 1950s and would continue until his death in 1980. And with his son Martin now working as a correspondent for the B.B.C., how ironic the foreboding words of Fanny's father would seem.

Francis' first article was published on December 3rd 1960 and was titled 'Airbase into Sanctuary.' He wrote of how *'nature [was] gaining control of East Anglia's abandoned aerodromes, now derelict and overgrown, and [how] many of the buildings and hutments are becoming sanctuaries for the wildlife of the countryside.'* Of looking into a deserted building and having an owl blink at him before it flew out.

*'How odd the bomb shelters appear today. They are far better camouflaged now than they were in wartime. Nature has performed with time what man's ingenuity tried so hard to copy when they were erected.'* Looking at them reminded Francis of *'the kind of dwellings the natives in South America built for themselves. They were just a hole in the ground with a rough thatch over them, looking for all the world like some animal's cave, especially when half a dozen naked children would bolt from them upon one's arrival. Curious indeed how modern man still has to go to ground when danger is near.'*

How hard it must have been for him watching as spring approached, and the apple blossom started appearing on the trees. Victor had given him the job of going around to the farmers and growers in Norfolk and Suffolk, with his spray deliveries for

'Murphy's'. He must have understood how important it was for someone as gregarious and knowledgeable as Francis, to have the opportunity of chatting and advising people and Francis had a great deal of knowledge and expertise that people were only too willing to pursue.

Although Francis would never have seen it that way, how poignant in the light of his own story does now appear his article, 'Fruit Growing as a Hobby', that was published in the E.D.P. the following April?

He wrote of how *'twenty acres of fruit well cared for can bring in a reasonable living, and marketing can be left to the co-operative packing houses … many retired people have taken to fruit growing as a means of augmenting their pension, buying up land already planted … or buying a house and plot and starting from scratch. If one had sufficient capital this is indeed … not so much a business more a way of life. If one can be quit of financial worry apple growing in particular can be a really pleasant and rewarding pursuit … the seasons can be watched the year round with pruning and spraying, thinning and picking … there were various systems of growing … from the closely planted orchards with as little as four or five feet between the trees to the looser, wider spacing of sixteen or twenty feet apart.'* He wrote of his fascination *'with orchards grown by retired military men who prune their trees in tight rows, each tree an exact replica of the next, just as though they were guardsmen on parade.'* This way of planting and pruning would in time of course become normal modern practice.

Writing in 1961, he wondered what the future held for the small fruit grower with the decline in profitability, when *'the urge to expand'* would perhaps be seen as the only way forward; when the fun had disappeared and it was looked upon entirely from a business angle. He wrote of *'some of the finest Coxes Orange Pippins being grown in East Anglia at the present time, their qualities comparing with that of any district in England'…*

Although he wondered about the future for the small fruit grower, he could never have envisaged what eventually would happen to the apple-growing industry in the country.

What would he have thought now of the site of those thousand acres of fruit? Trees that he had planted, tended and anguished over, every weather forecast anxiously listened to? Trees, which in spring were thick with blossom, that had filled the air and senses as far as the eye could see, and which by the early1990s had all been grubbed out and gone, making way for more profitable arable farming and the British love affair at the time with the French Golden Delicious.

He wrote of it now being the season of spraying *'when the smell of sprays drift through the countryside';* of there being the necessity at that time for *'eight to ten sprays to be used in an apple orchard in order to produce saleable unblemished fruit to which the public has become accustomed';* and of how *'modern spraying machinery had progressed with its precision and accuracy';* all a far cry from the *'days of the Victorian orchard attached to the Manor house.''*

How much he was drawing on his own experiences as he wrote also of it *'now being the season when the fruit grower would listen eagerly to the weather forecasts, of how a night's frost could ruin a low-lying orchard and how, even a well sited one, could lose much of its crop through a capricious wind frost. Of how frost and hail were two of the fruit man's biggest hazards, quite apart from the usual economics of the everyday world.'*

And yet, he concluded, *'in spite of these drawbacks, I still covet one of these little orchards which one runs upon suddenly round the narrow lanes of Norfolk and Suffolk. Pretty little out of the way places; surely here one thinks there must be peace.'*

It would be a quest to which he was constantly drawn.

Sometimes taking Peter with him when he came back for a weekend, driving around the lanes together, they would take a look at this little piece of ground or that, Francis noting the aspect and suitability of it for planting up as an orchard.

Somehow nowhere seemed quite right and it was a friend Tommy Thompson who eventually came up with a proposition for Francis that really appealed. He had met Tommy at the Hoxne Swan.

Tommy, a retired spitfire pilot, had bought a house nearby with a lovely little piece of sheltered south-facing land. It was about four to five acres and would have been absolutely ideal as a small orchard. Knowing very little about fruit growing, he had proposed to Francis, that if he provided the land and some finance, Francis could supply the knowledge and expertise - they could go into partnership and take an equal share in the eventual profits.

Francis loved the idea. There was even a small building on the field that would serve as a little store and pack-house. It was a delightful and generous proposition and one that would give Francis that essential ingredient in his life that he lacked, something to plan and look forward to. He took Peter with him and they spent a weekend getting the field squared up with pegs in readiness for planting.

Sally had left school in the July after Francis had been sacked, after taking her A levels. Any plans for her to go on to university had been abandoned or perhaps never mooted. It was only a week after her arrival home, without any real idea of her future, that a phone call was received from Barbara's Uncle Peter Grain.

Still working in the family firm of Grain and Chalk in Cambridge, he had rung to ask if Sally could help him out.

His secretary, a wartime German Jewish refugee by the name of Schultz, had gone into hospital unexpectedly and Uncle Peter was urgently needing someone to help out whilst Schultz was away. It was suggested that Sally should come weekly to Cambridge by train and lodge with Uncle Peter and Aunt Cis at their home in Shelford during the week, returning home each weekend.

Aunt Cis had always been a favourite aunt of Barbara's; in fact she would say that she had always had a far better relationship with Aunt Cis than with her own mother Bombo. Both sisters were great fun, but perhaps Bombo had tried to rectify some of Mannie's spoiling of his only daughter, by trying to impose a little more discipline than Barbara was inclined to accept as a teenager. Whatever the reason, it would always be to her Aunt Cis that Barbara would feel the closest.

The two sisters, apart from sharing a tremendous sense of humour, were totally unalike. Both were short, but there the likeness ended. Bombo always wore a navy dress with white spots – which she replaced each year from Penningtons in Spalding. It seldom varied, perhaps one year the spots would be a little larger or smaller, but somehow despite her annual announcement that she was off to buy a new dress, she always seemed to come back with an almost identical garment. Bombo's plump figure was the exact opposite to that of Aunt Cis, whose tiny figure more resembled a candlestick.

Aunt Cis would always be remembered for her famous 'bus pudding'. Quite what she was doing on a bus to have overheard the recipe remains a mystery. She was always taken shopping in the family car, driven by their gardener/handyman who was called 'Whiskers' despite being a clean-shaven young man in his 20s. But ride on a bus at some point she did and it was for her 'bus pudding', a sort of upside-down pineapple affair, that she would be immortalised.

Starting work at Grain and Chalk early in the August, Sally would remember coming home by train to Clare station for two weekend visits to Stradishall before the family moved to Stradbroke. She remained working at Grain and Chalk for a couple of years - poor Mr Shultz died in hospital and nothing was ever said about his replacement. She was never asked; it was just assumed that she would stay on.

**Francis asleep at Hill Farm, drawn by Judy, aged about 14**

The school fees for Judy's final year had been allowed for, but there was nothing left to pay for her to stay on to take A levels or perhaps to have developed her considerable artistic ability. Leaving a year later at 16 years old, she went to Norwich to take a domestic science course at City College.

Between October 1960 and May 1963, Francis continued his writing and was free from the restraints that his employment had imposed. He now became a prolific and regular contributor to *The Commercial Grower,* both with his paid articles and through his letters to The Editor, as well as a regular correspondent with *The American Fruit Grower.* His opinion was widely respected and sought. The publication of his many articles indicates how much they were valued

He would continue to write on a wide variety of subjects connected with the technicalities of fruit growing and had a lifetime of experience to draw upon.

Everett's with its thatched roof and attractive position, back from the road on the edge of Stradbroke, proved to be a snug home, easy to run after a draughty old rambling farmhouse. Barbara felt more secure than she had for years. She had Francis to herself too and although things were very difficult they muddled along. 'Making do' always brought out the best in her and she would later say that the three years they spent there were the happiest of her marriage.

**Barbara and Francis in front of Everett's, Stradbroke, summer 1962**

Having cooked for years on the solid fuel Aga at Hill Farm, the Rayburn in the cottage kitchen was no challenge. The kitchen would once again become her domestic domain and the centre of their life there. A small sitting room could be reached from a passage running along the rear of the cottage, along with a little room that Francis used as an office and from where he could write. Upstairs there were three bedrooms. It would all have fitted into about a third of Hill Farmhouse, but it was enough. They had a roof over their heads.

Her relationship with Bryan Matthews continued and he rang and wrote to her regularly, often from exotic parts whilst sailing on *Lucretia*, arranging to meet whenever he could. A small pile of love letters remain, evidence of a love affair and a friendship that seem to have gone on for many years.

Did Francis know of it? It seems that he did. He spoke about it to Judy when she was home from College in Norwich for the weekend. Barbara had gone off sailing with Bryan and he told Judy then, saying that he was hoping that she would come back. Francis told her he had found out about Barbara and Bryan at Hill Farm years earlier and that he had spoken to them then. He told them that he hadn't been 'lily-white himself' and that he 'would turn a blind eye'. It was a relationship that would continue until Sir Bryan's death in 1986.

After Francis' own untimely death in 1963, her own family crises would always come between Barbara and Bryan. Trips abroad would be planned and scuppered at the last moment. He waited a long time for her and must at last have felt the way was clear; must have assumed that she would marry him and was deeply saddened when she seems to have turned him down.

Well, not turned him down exactly, but some other crisis at home would always crop up and have to take precedence. She could have left Francis many years earlier and gone away with Bryan then, but the children were still young and another man's children were not included in Bryan's equations, and Barbara would never have left them. Perhaps she thought he would always be there, a lover in waiting? Their relationship would continue in much the same way, but Bryan needed a wife as well and would eventually find another.

Peter had been working as an apprentice trainee at 'Levertons Caterpillar Tractor Dealers' for a couple of years. Still in the workshop, he was now 19 years old and had discovered that he was not actually enjoying being a mechanic. With his love of the outdoors and having lived his entire life amongst the apple orchards, he couldn't envisage a future for himself in agricultural engineering. An office job would eventually have followed and promotion no doubt to management, but he wasn't happy.

He was never destined to be happy tinkering with engines. Perhaps the only knowledge he gainfully acquired and applied at this time was the building of a 'special'; a car that he and his friend Bruce Potter had made out of an old Ford 10 van. He had met Bruce in The Pied Calf in Spalding, shortly after he had moved there.

Bruce had been on his way back from Choir Practice at St John's Church. He would always say that having hitherto been a devout Christian, a member of both church and choir, it was that meeting that would ensure he was not to set foot in a church for another 50 years. And this was despite the flamboyant remonstrations of its renowned vicar Canon Lancelot Smith.

The Potter family lived on the far side of Spalding. Bruce's father, William Charles Potter, known of course affectionately by all his men as 'W.C.' had run a very successful road haulage company and Bruce, as the only son, was heir apparent. A clever deal a few years earlier had been achieved with British Road Services, when the whole transport system of the country was nationalised in 1948.

The British Road Services transport company was formed by the nationalisation of Britain's road haulage industry, as a result of the Transport Act of 1947 – all part of the wave of post-war nationalisation policies brought in by Labour when they were swept to power in 1945. His father, astutely realising that the takeover and compulsory purchase were inevitable, unlike his competitors who couldn't contain their anger at the nationalisation programme, went out of his way to get the very best price possible. All had to go; absolutely everything bought under the company name.

So he made sure that every vehicle gleamed and stood to attention, every nut and bolt, every hammer, every tool, every spare part was polished and neatly laid out in graded rows; the books were all in impeccable order, the assessors were wined and dined at the house in fine style and consequently he got a very good price for his business.

With a good-sized yard and empty buildings, he then took in a partner and set up a business selling supplies of engineering parts and also invested in a tarmac business for Bruce to manage. With plenty of money floating around and a steady supply of expensive cars that were regularly wrecked, it was the classic story of the profligate son. Of course Bruce wasn't doing what he wanted or was destined to do, which was to become later a highly regarded primary head teacher and life-time friend of the Bell family. But all that was in the future.

It took little persuasion for him, with Peter and a group of similar minded young men, to be spending a lot of time together and having a great deal of fun about the town.

Having Peter live with them in Spalding must have tested Bombo and Mannie's love for their grandson on many occasions. They appear to have been remarkably tolerant until a court case made the local papers. A beer barrel, in the form of a small table had been taken from a pub in Northamptonshire by one of the group. The police had been called and things, Mannie felt, had got somewhat out of hand.

Appearing before the Magistrate, the chastened four tried their best to look suitably contrite. Peter wore his old school tie from Framlingham, as he felt it added a bit of class to the proceedings, although he afterwards reflected that it would have probably let the school down instead.

After appropriate words like 'Boys like you should know better', etc. they all received a Conditional Discharge and had to report to the Probation Officer in Spalding. The Magistrate put it all down as 'exuberance of youth', which of course it was, but it must have added to the concern Francis was feeling about Peter's future.

It was actually Francis, who was first approached by Devora Peake during the spring of 1962; she was in need of a fruit farm manager at their farm at Boxford and wondered if he would be interested.

He wasn't personally, but knowing that Peter was not enjoying working at Leverton's, he suggested to the Peakes that his son was keen to get back into fruit farming and that he would mention it to him. Devora Peake was the daughter of Russian parents and had been brought up in Tel Aviv. Inspired by her father's orange and almond groves in Israel, she moved to Suffolk in the 1930s, where she and her first husband developed a 120-acre fruit farm at Boxford. She would later marry her second husband Bill Peake, a neighbouring farmer.

It would be more than 30 years before they bought their first fruit press and began producing freshly pressed undiluted apple juice that would, in 1996, win Devora Peake an M.B.E. in recognition of her contribution to fruit growing and juicing. That apple juice, the very first of its kind not to be made with concentrate was called 'Copella'.

All this would come later; in the meantime Devora was in need of a manager or at least a trainee manager. Bill had developed tuberculosis and, although still able to work at times, was sometimes confined to his bed. His bedroom was rather innovative for Suffolk and much in keeping with the idea of tubercular patients needing fresh air. His bed had been brought down into the sitting room overlooking the orchards and the entire outside wall of the room had been quite roughly knocked out. The open space had then been covered in chicken netting and here Bill lived and slept, rain or shine, winter and summer.

In Switzerland, with its blue skies and clear crisp mountain air, the sanatoriums achieved great success with their open-air treatments; here in Suffolk with its damp mists and autumn fogs, the success of the treatment was a little more difficult to imagine.

Peter certainly was interested in getting back into fruit farming and by June 1962 had started working for the Peakes. Half a house went with the job and Peter moved into one side of 'Honey Tye Farm' at Leavenheath immediately. Working under Bill and Devora, Peter was soon amongst the apple orchards, organising and carrying out the work as the season progressed. Francis did call occasionally – how could he have kept away – but it was always with a word of encouragement or a helpful suggestion.

Judy meanwhile had finished her year's course in domestic science at Norwich City College, boarding in Norwich during the week and travelling back to Stradbroke at weekends. Now 17 years old, she moved to Cambridge and got a job at the University Library.

With Sally still working at Grain & Chalk, it was an obvious move for the two sisters to share a room together in Cambridge. Ironically both girls would meet their future husbands at this time.

It was just such a meeting, and the fact that the young man in question was engaged to another, that lay behind the decision that Sally made, to contact a Nanny Agency in London and enquire about vacancies. She went to London for an interview and was accepted for a job. A wealthy American family living in Pasadena, California was looking for an English nanny or mother's help for their four children.

The Agency would make all the travel arrangements and Sally, together with several other girls flying out to the States with her, would fly first by Air Lingus to Ireland. From there they would fly on to New York and be put up in a hotel while awaiting flights to their final destinations. In Sally's case, that would be Los Angeles. At 19 years old she didn't realise that she would also need to get her parents' permission. The job was to last a year.

Barbara drove over to Cambridge to collect her, and Sally and Judy said their goodbyes there and then. It was November 1962 and the world beckoned.

It was a poignant little family group that saw her off on the London train from Diss. Even in 1962, America seemed a long way from home. Francis turning back to Barbara as he waved, said, 'That is the last I shall ever see of that dear girl.' How could he have known?

The Williamsons were certainly a wealthy family with even wealthier connections. Mrs Williamson's father had owned a ranch on what had now become Wilshire Boulevard in Los Angeles. Mr Williamson was a stockbroker and his mother was Lady Crocker, who had married an Englishman of 'Betty Crocker Cake Mix' fame.

Meeting Sally at the airport, the Williamson family introduced her to their children. There were three little girls, aged 6, 4 and 2 and a baby boy called Henry aged 6 months. Stepping forward Sally asked if she might hold the baby for a moment and watching her, Mrs Williamson seemed to breathe a sigh of relief. It was as if Sally's confidence had given her confidence too. Perhaps with a new nanny arriving each year, she hadn't always had such a positive experience.

Francis wrote to her regularly. Going down with yet another bout of his annual bronchitis he spoke of the winter that year seeming endless and of how he longed for the spring and warmer days. The bronchitis hung around well into the spring and Francis continued to struggle to get back to a reasonable state of health.

Bombo and Mannie came over for Christmas that year and all the family missed having Sally with them. A constant stream of letters kept her up to date with news. Events and change in the Bell family seemed to follow one another in rapid succession. In February 1963 Peter who was not quite 22 years old was marrying Carola Vaizey, the daughter of a retired Brigadier living in Halstead. His cousin Martin was to be best man and sister Judy a bridesmaid.

Francis, writing to Sally, confided in her his fears for Peter's hastily arranged marriage and for his future. He was worried by Peter's lack of a profession and about his ability to support a wife and family. It was just the sort of haphazard outcome that he had feared for him. Two little boys would be born in quick succession but it was a marriage that would only survive a little over three years and Francis would never live to see his first grandchild.

Francis wrote of the possibility of putting in an offer to buy a 20-acre plot of land nearby with his friend Tommy Thompson, with the idea of planting it up as an orchard. It could perhaps have been something for Peter, in the future.

Between his writing and delivering sprays, Francis had lately put a little money into Victor's turkey business. They had become joint partners and Francis was full of ideas as to how they could expand. The turkey sheds were situated in a field at the back of Everett's. Although they were purpose built for raising turkeys, they weren't used all the year and Francis had another idea. He was going to try forcing rhubarb.

Discussions were soon under way with a neighbouring farmer Francis had become very friendly with, who agreed to grow the rhubarb. The idea was that the young rhubarb crowns would be transferred to the turkey sheds when they weren't occupied. Francis would then continue to grow the rhubarb, forcing it on in the half dark sheds to produce an early saleable crop in time to clear the sheds for the next intake of turkey poults. It was a little business venture that appealed to him immensely and he was eagerly anticipating starting it.

Returning to Stradbroke one weekend in late spring, Peter was shocked to see how ill his father was looking. In fact he looked terrible. Struggling to move some tins of spray to a new shed that he would formerly have lifted with one hand, Peter rushed to help him. Francis was looking ashen and grey and seemed to have no energy or strength. Speaking to his mother, it seemed that Francis and Barbara hadn't registered with a doctor's practice since moving to Stradbroke. On the Monday, Victor arranged for an appointment with the doctor at Hoxne, who saw Francis later that day and arranged for him to be X-rayed at Ipswich General Hospital.

Driving him in, Barbara waited in the X-ray department and was told that they wanted to keep Francis in for some more tests; that she should return tomorrow. The next day she was told that Francis had perhaps three months to live. He had the worst cancerous mass in his lungs that they had ever seen in 20 years. A lifetime of smoking had wrought its havoc.

Ironically, only the autumn before, there had been the first reports suggesting that there was a possible link between smoking and lung cancer. Hearing of this somewhat scornfully, Francis had puffed his chest out and said, 'Never done me any harm.'

Barbara was told that he would have to stay in hospital and she said that she was told that Francis must not know how seriously ill he was, it would distress him too much - no one was to tell him that he was dying.

It is incomprehensible now to think of someone not knowing; of not having the opportunity to prepare themselves and to put their affairs in order. The family were rung and close friends told, but the first news of it that Sally had was when she received a letter from Barbara. How hard that must have been for her, to have been told not to come back to see him, in case he wondered why she had returned and guessed something was seriously wrong.

It is difficult to believe that Barbara got this right; that this was the medical advice of the day in the best interest of the patient; but it seems that this was so. The Williamson family offered to pay for Sally's flight home to see Francis, but Barbara was adamant that she shouldn't come, and could have had no idea of the effect that decision would have on Sally. She and Francis had such a close relationship.

Through his letters, it is evident she had become his confidante, despite her tender years; a sign of her own maturity and of the love and respect they had for each other. It must have been a heavy burden for a 20 year old and a great sadness and frustration. Just when she felt her father needed her, she was more than five thousand miles away and could do nothing.

Among the hospital visitors that Francis did have, was his old friend Jack Loader. Jack was deeply shocked to see how ill Francis looked. Francis as always was so pleased to see him and told Jack, 'You've been wonderful to me Jack; I've enjoyed your company.'

Jack was very upset and later said to Nesta, 'I never thought I would see poor old Francis like that.' Jack would always maintain that it was the shock of losing his job that killed him.

Another visitor was Elizabeth Brooke. She came to tell them that Justin had just died, and when his funeral would be. She thought perhaps that Barbara would want to go. Barbara declined, saying that Francis was dying, and that she felt her place was at his bedside.

Justin had been unwell for some time. Having decided against going onto Warfarin (used for thinning the blood), he had said that he preferred to go quickly but to have quality of life for the time left to him. When Elizabeth and her four children had come over to Wickhambrook that Easter of 1963, Justin had fallen asleep at the table during the meal and she knew something was wrong. The children knew their Granddad was ill because he had only told them two stories.

No one envisaged how short a time was left for Francis. His brother Adrian and Marjorie came to visit; Peter came each evening after work and Judy at weekends. All were shocked to see how weak he was rapidly becoming.

Barbara would drive over each day, eating her sandwiches in the car before spending the afternoon at his bedside. He was reading a new book that had just been published a year earlier and had taken America by storm, it was Rachel Carson's *Silent Spring*. For a man who had spent the major part of his working life in the study and application of pesticides used on a massive scale in the fruit orchards since the introduction of D.D.T. in 1945, it made devastating reading.

*Silent Spring* exposed the hazards of D.D.T., citing it as the most powerful pesticide the world had ever known. Through years of meticulous research she detailed how it had entered the food chain with devastating cumulative effects. How over 200 toxins had been found in a bee's body, and of the effects that accumulation had on the fatty tissues of all animals, including human beings. Alongside medical researchers, she was able to provide overwhelming evidence to support the pesticide/cancer link.

Today we know that D.D.T. exposure causes neurological problems like Parkinson's, along with asthma and a wide range of cancers, but in 1962, when her book was published, it was groundbreaking science. It would initially create aggressive criticism and denial by the chemical industry.

Rachel Carson was an American marine biologist who turned her attention to conservation and the environmental problems caused by the use of synthetic pesticides. She wrote of her conviction that for a wide range of animals and most noticeably for certain birds, D.D.T. was actually toxic and could be held responsible for their decline, including that of songbirds. Farmers would often exceed the dose indiscriminately by blanket spraying by air, showering both inhabited and agricultural areas. Across America, Rachel Carson's book raised public awareness to the dangers of the use of pesticides and environmental poisons and would lead to the banning of D.D.T., a reversal in the national pesticide policy and the birth of Environmentalism.

Always so ahead of his time, always so interested in scientific research particularly in relation to fruit growing, Francis was aghast. He would undoubtedly have been following the response and interest in the book in *The American Fruit Grower*. He had already been studying the idea of controlling pests with predatory insects before he left Brooke's, although he would at that time, have had no idea of the toxic effect of D.D.T.

Thinking of all those years of chemical spraying he was deeply shocked. 'What have I done?' he asked Barbara. Barbara replied with sagacity that perhaps she wasn't feeling at the time, 'you have fed a lot of people, and made fruit available to people who might not have been able to afford to eat it.'

The final call, when it came, was early. The hospital rang Barbara at 6.00a.m. to tell her that Francis was dying and would she come. She rang Stephanie to ask her if she would telephone Bombo and Mannie.

Yes she would, and could she come with Barbara? But no, Barbara wanted to be alone. Sitting holding Francis' hand, she could tell that his breathing had become much heavier, that his condition had changed. And then in her words, 'The breathing just stopped.' He had suffered no pain, had had no drugs.

Francis died on the morning of the 11th June 1963. He was 57 years old. He had been in hospital scarcely two weeks.

No writing about Francis should ever end on such a sad note. He would have hated it. He was a man who loved life and was full of fun and eternal optimism, a man of deep personal charm and concern for others.

Throughout my research into his life, the many hours talking to his family and to a great many people who knew or worked with him, hardly anyone had a bad word to say about him. And despite the passing of nearly 50 years, no one who knew him ever seems to have forgotten him either, always remembering Francis with the greatest of affection.

# Bibliography

Bell, Adrian, *My Own Master*, Faber and Faber 1961: *By-Road*, Cobden Sanderson, London 1937.
Bell, Robert, Book of Poems, *Afterthoughts* 1929.
Berry, Robert, letter to Barbara 1938.
Brooke, Justin and Edith *Suffolk Prospect*, Faber & Faber 1963.
Carson, Rachel, *Silent Spring*. Hamish Hamilton 1963.
Gander, Ann *Adrian Bell: Voice of the Countryside* Published by Holm Oak Publishing, 2001.
Gibson, T.M. & Harrison, M.H *Into Thin Air. A History of Aviation Medicine in the RAF* with details of Sir Bryan Matthews' Work at Farnborough. Published by Hale Books 1984.
Hanbury, Ada and Blanche *Vere Foster's Drawing Books – Advanced Studies of Flower Painting in Water Colours*, published 1885 by London, Blackie & Son, Glasgow, Edinburgh and Dublin.
*History of Justin Brooke Ltd. 1928 – 1978.* Company booklet.
Horridge, Glenn, *The Growth and Development of a Family Firm, Chivers of Histon 1873–1939*. Published c. 1982.
Locke, A. Audrey, *The Hanbury Family*, Published by Arthur L. Humphrays, London 1916.
Moore, Judy, *The Bloomsbury Trail in Sussex*. S.B. Publications 1995.

## Online sources

ADC Theatre – *A Potted History*, www.adctheatre.com/15/09/2011
B.B.C. History, *Queen Elizabeth's Coronation*
Bedales School
Cambridge University Marlowe Dramatic Society – Chronology of Productions and 'About The Marlowe'.
Coppella Fruit Juices – History of Coppella
David Langton COFEPOW – The Armed Forces, 2nd Battalion, Cambs. Regiment.
Patrick Macdonald, *The History of The Cambridgeshire Regiment*.
Graham McCann, *The Home Guard and Dad's Army*.
The Ruskin School of Drawing and Fine Art.
Spartacus Educational, Biography of David Garnett.
Wikipedia – Cambridge Apostles; Rachel Carson; Climate of Argentina; John Ruskin.

## Other Sources

*The Commercial Grower,* Published Articles and Letters by Francis Bell, October 1960 – May 1963.

*Eastern Daily Press,* Published Articles by Francis Bell under the title 'The Country Scene' - 3.12.60, 25.2.61, 29.4.61, 31.3.62., 2.6.62, 29.9.62.

*?East Anglian Times,* Obituary of Justin Brooke, 1963

*The Independent,* Obituary of The Right Rev. Kenneth Riches, 19th May 1999

*The Times,* Obituary of Sir Bryan Matthews, 23.7.86; article on Aphra Wilson, 17.1.76

## Unpublished sources

Francis Bell, Manuscripts of Ingeniero Foster: Work Diaries 1936–1939: handwritten letters to Barbara 1938-1949: Spray and Field Records 1939-1943: Fruit Diaries 1943–1950.

Letters, cards and postcards from Sir Bryan Matthews to Barbara Bell, between July 24th 1952 and February 16th 1986, in the possession of Peter Bell.

And other letters mentioned in the Acknowledgements at the beginning of this book.

# INDEX

Alonso, the storekeeper, 40, 50,57, 58, 85
Arthur, 'the Boy', 168-169
Avis Brothers, 142
Bailey, Alfred, 278
Bamford, Tommy, 158
Bell, Adrian, 5, 6, 8, 9, 10, 13, 16, 17, 19, 20, 27-28, 31, 94, 107, 110, 120, 121,122, 123, 124, 130, 131, 137, 138, 144, 152, 153, 161, 201, 240, 241-242, 253, 254, 261, 280, 294
Bell, Alexander, 111, 112
Bell, Anthea, 20,124, 164, 212, 241
Bell, Barbara (née Kingston), 6, 121, 188, 190, 219-220, 231, 233-234, 235-239, 240, 243, 244, 250, 251, 253, 254, 257, 258, 259, 261, 262, 264, 265, 268, 269, 271, 272, 273-275, 277-278, 283-284, 285, 286, 290, 292, 293-296.
  marriage:155-172
  early married life:174-177, 180-181, 184, 185
  first child: 187
  second child: 208-216
Bell, Fanny (née Hanbury) 5, 8, 9, 15, 16, 18, 24, 26, 27, 29, 48, 109, 112, 114, 115-116, 119, 130, 155, 161, 164, 186, 187, 218, 231, 243-244, 253, 254
Bell, Frances de Witt,
  death: 6, 8, 292-296
  departure for Argentina: 5, 9,
  education: 19, 20-21, 28, 104
  Home Guard: 177, 178-180, 181-183, 209, 210, 211
  in Punta Arenas: 28
  in Ingeniro Foster: 32-106
  leaves Hill Farm, 272-275
  relations with mother: 17,18,243, 265-266
  sacked: 267-268, 275-276
  smoking:199-200
  wedding: 163-171
  **et passim**
Bell, George and Mabel, 27, 31

Bell, Judy, 6,218 235, 237, 238, 240, 252, 260, 269, 284, 286, 290, 291, 294
Bell, Marjorie, 110, 120, 124, 130, 153, 241, 261, 294
Bell, Martin, 153, 240, 242, 243, 260, 280, 291
Bell, Peter Hanbury, 6,187, 188, 197, 208, 209, 210, 211, 212, 213, 214, 215, 216-217, 231, 232, 236-237, 239, 240, 242, 243, 249, 251, 252, 253, 261, 264, 265-266, 269, 272, 278, 283, 287, 288, 289, 291, 292, 294
Bell, Robert, 5, 15, 16, 17, 18, 20, 21, 27, 29, 48, 94, 107, 111, 114, 120-121, 130, 155, 161, 164, 186-187, 218, 243,244
Bell, Roy, 21, 48, 110-112
Bell, Sally, 6, 212, 214, 231, 237, 240, 252, 260, 269, 270, 283, 284, 290-291, 293
Bell, Stephanie, (later Thorpe), 6, 18, 19, 28, 48, 107, 110-112, 113, 114, 153, 163-4, 212,244, 254, 260, 295
Bell, Sylvia, 20, 153, 240, 243, 260
Bell, Vanessa, 128
Berry, Bob,116-17, 155, 157, 158, 159, 160, 162, 163, 164, 174, 177, 258
Berry, Mike, 117, 258-259
Berry, Vera 'Weedy' (née Bedford) 258
Bishop, Frank, 256
Bishop, Jack, 246
Blewitt, Bill, 246
Brennan, Lew, 246, 252
Brooke, Arthur, 133
Brooke, Charles, 138, 188, 247-248, 262-263, 264, 277
Brooke, Edith, 125, 128, 130, 135, 147, 148, 152, 163, 167, 172, 203, 219, 232, 238, 246, 247, 252,255, 264, 276, 277, 278
Brooke, Elizabeth,125, 138, 146, 246, 262, 264, 276, 294

Brooke, Jennifer, 138
Brooke, Joyce, 262, 264
Brooke, Justin, 6, 124, 125, 128, 129, 130, 131, 132, 133, 134, 135, 136, 137, 138, 139, 140, 144, 146, 147, 148, 149, 150, 152, 153, 163, 167, 175, 188, 189, 190, 191, 192, 193, 194, 203, 205,206, 216 , 219, 220, 228, 232, 238, 247, 248-249, 252-253, 254, 255, 257, 261, 262, 263, 264, 267, 269, 276-277, 278, 294; Justin Jnr, 138, 268, 269
Brooke, Pleasance, 138
Brooke, Rupert, 126, 127
Burton, Harold, 223, 224, 246, 263, 278
Cadbury, George, 126
Cameron, Alec, 24, 25, 26, 30, 31 32, 33, 35, 36, 37, 38
Cameron, Amy and Heather, 30, 31
Carson, Rachel, 294-295
Chalk, Tom, 162
Charnock, Ian,' George', 139, 140, 144, 147, 155-156, 167, 170, 172, 176, 177, 187, 246
Churchill, Winston, 176
Clinton, Joan and Robert, 275
Cockle, 201-202
Coghill, Mr, 249
Collins, Colonel, 259, 260: Joan, 259
Cook, Susannah, 216-217
Crocker, Lady, 291
Crueslain, Jorge,34, 35, 36, 37, 39, 40, 41, 42, 43, 44, 47, 48, 50, 51, 54, 55, 57, 58 59, 60, 61, 65, 66, 69, 71, 72, 73, 77, 78, 79, 81, 84, 86, 94, 97, 98, 101, 110
Cutts, Charlie, 175, 211, 215, 216, 252
Cutts, Mrs, 215
Day, Bill, 133, 134, 196, 205
Earle, Michael, 160
Eden, Anthony, 176
Edgeley, Ernie, 197-198, 246
Ellse, Ron, 223, 230, 246
Emerson, Mr, 168
Finch, Jack, 246
Ford, Betty, 118
Gander, Ann, 10, 11, 12, 28, 107, 111, 130

Garnett, David, 128
Gibbs, Arthur, 245, 246
Graham, the Boss, 32, 34, 35, 45, 52, 53, 54, 55, 66, 80, 81, 84, 85, 86, 87, 89, 96, 98, 99, 100, 105
Grain, Cis (née Kingston), 283-284
Grain, Olave, 156
Grain, Peter, 161-162, 283
Grant, Duncan, 128
Grimwood, Nellie, 155
Guaraglia, the mechanic, 81, 86, 101-103
Hanbury, Aunt Ada, 9, 10 ,11, 12, 14, 25
Hanbury, Blanche (later Rowe) 9, 10, 14, 15, 19, 20
Hanbury, Charles de Witt, 16
Hanbury family, 11-15
Hanbury, Fred de Witt, 16-17
Hanbury, Gertrude, 10, 12-13, 14
Hanbury, Katie, 21-22, 23-24, 25-26, 28, 225
Hardwicke, Nancy, (laterWhitlock), 188-189, 190, 205, 211, 212, 246, 256
Hempstead, George, 28
Hickey, Mrs., 246
Hitchcock, Joe, 233, 259
Hitchcock, Betty, 259
Hurrell, Mrs, 203
Ince, Mr, 168
James, Jimmie, 246
Jorge, see Crueslain
Keynes, Geoffrey, 218
Keynes, John Maynard, 127, 128
Kingston, Christine, 235
Kingston, Emeline Barbara, 'Bombo' (née Chalk), 156, 157-158, 162, 163, 164 , 165, 170-171, 173, 181, 209, 235, 236, 283-284, 288, 291
Kingston, Harold, 'Mannie', 156, 162, 163, 164, 165, 170-171, 173, 209, 235, 236-237, 283, 288, 291
Kingston, Newy, 163, 164, 173,178, 233, 250, 266
Kingston, Peter, 163, 164, 177-178, 235
Krebs, Carl, 'Don Carlos', 86-92, 93, 95, 96, 97, 98, 99, 100, 103, 105, 142

Langton, David, 199
Lee, David, 141, 255, 256, 261, 264
Lee, Hazel, 264
Leeder, Harvey, 259
Lesniff, the Russian, 34, 44, 48, 49-50, 58, 59, 62, 72, 76, 77, 75, 76, 82, 90, 91, 94, 96
Lesniff, Madame, 49-50, 62, 72, 76, 77, 81, 84
Loader, Jack, 203-204, 205, 246, 263, 265, 267, 278-279, 293-294
Loader, Nesta, 267, 278, 279, 294
Long, Carl, 117.118-19, 162
Lufkin, 168
Lunnis, Will and Annie, 107, 139
Macchi, the chemist, 85, 86
Mapey, Victor, 198-199, 267, 272-273, 280, 292
Mapey, Margaret, 267-268, 273
Matthews, Constance, 219, 220, 223, 238, 239
Matthews, Sir Bryan, 219, 233, 238, 239, 286-287
McCartney, Carole, 172, 259
McCartney, Hugh, 129, 140, 167, 172, 175-176, 210, 211
Metcalfe, Bob, 246
Mildred, (Milly), 210, 211, 221, 235, 236, 237
Mitchell, L., 246
Morris, William, 126
'Mussolini', 56, 57, 67, 74-5, 79, 83
Nicholas, Canon, 163
Nightingale, Robert, 256-258
Nunn, Bob, 155
Nunn, Fred, 129, 211
Nunn, Percy, 134-135, 203, 224, 248, 256, 263
Nunn, Rosy, 155, 161, 163, 172-173, 221, 246
Pascual, 77, 78
Peacock, Carlos, 22, 24, 25, 28, 225: Tom, 28
Peacock, Dr William Ernest, 22, 23, 24, 25
Peake, Bill and Devora, 289-290
Pereyra, the horse-keeper, 38, 53, 54
Piludski, Mr, 70-71
Potter, Bruce, 287, 288
Potter, William Charles, 287-288

Riches, Kenneth, (later Bp of Lincoln) 136, 218-219, 270
Rose, Edie, 198
Rowe, Revd Theophilus, 19: Benedicta, 19; Dorothy, 19-20
Ruskin, John, 10, 25, 31,
Rutter, Stan, 201-202, 204, 205, 208, 246, 267
Savage, Vic and Martha, 27, 28, 105, 107, 108-109, 113, 114, 115, 119, 122-123, 131, 164, 207
Schultz, 283, 284
Scofter, 73, 74,
Scott, George and Isobel, 153
Scott, Gerry, 112
Smith, Mrs Roly, 221, 246
Smith, Nan, 157, 158, 160
Smith, Roland, 221-222
Swann, Arthur, 108, 164: Florrie, 108, 119, 122-123, 124: Margaret, 108, 109, 119, 120, 164: Winnie, 108, 122-123, 124
Taylor, Fred, 210
Taylor, Jimmy and Olive, 119-120
Thompson, Tommy, 282, 292
Thorpe, Adrian, 153
Thorpe, Geraldine, 212
Thorpe, Jack, 112, 113, 163-164, 182, 260
Turner, Jeffrey, 26
Vaizey, Carola, 291
Wade, Willy, 255
Wheldon, Peter, 206
Whitlock, Carlton, 189, 196
Wilby, Mrs, 118
Williamson family, 291, 293
Wilson, Aphra, 270-272
Wormell, Miss, 119